Critical Reflections on Information Systems: A Systemic Approach

Jeimy J. Cano
Newport University—Colombia Branch, Colombia

IDEA GROUP PUBLISHING
Hershey • London • Melbourne • Singapore • Beijing

303.4833
C93c

Acquisition Editor:	Mehdi Khosrowpour
Managing Editor:	Jan Travers
Development Editor:	Michele Rossi
Copy Editor:	Lori Eby
Typesetter:	LeAnn Whitcomb
Cover Design:	Integrated Book Technology
Printed at:	Integrated Book Technology

Cau

Published in the United States of America by
    Idea Group Publishing (an imprint of Idea Group Inc.)
    701 E. Chocolate Avenue
    Hershey PA 17033-1240
    Tel: 717-533-8845
    Fax: 717-533-8661
    E-mail: cust@idea-group.com
    Web site: http://www.idea-group.com

and in the United Kingdom by
    Idea Group Publishing (an imprint of Idea Group Inc.)
    3 Henrietta Street
    Covent Garden
    London WC2E 8LU
    Tel: 44 20 7240 0856
    Fax: 44 20 7379 3313
    Web site: http://www.eurospan.co.uk

Library of Congress Cataloging-in-Publication Data

Cano, Jeimy J., 1973-
    Critical reflections on information systems : a systemic approach / Jeimy J. Cano.
       p. cm.
    Includes bibliographical references and index.
     ISBN 1-59140-040-6
     1. Information technology. I. Title.

    T58.5 .C36 2003
    303.48'33--dc21

                                                                        2002068781

eISBN 1-59140-069-4

British Cataloguing in Publication Data
A Cataloguing in Publication record for this book is available from the British Library.

NEW from Idea Group Publishing

- **Digital Bridges: Developing Countries in the Knowledge Economy**, John Senyo Afele/ ISBN:1-59140-039-2; eISBN 1-59140-067-8, © 2003
- **Integrative Document & Content Management: Strategies for Exploiting Enterprise Knowledge**, Len Asprey and Michael Middleton/ ISBN: 1-59140-055-4; eISBN 1-59140-068-6, © 2003
- **Critical Reflections on Information Systems: A Systemic Approach**, Jeimy Cano/ ISBN: 1-59140-040-6; eISBN 1-59140-069-4, © 2003
- **Web-Enabled Systems Integration: Practices and Challenges**, Ajantha Dahanayake and Waltraud Gerhardt ISBN: 1-59140-041-4; eISBN 1-59140-070-8, © 2003
- **Public Information Technology: Policy and Management Issues**, G. David Garson/ ISBN: 1-59140-060-0; eISBN 1-59140-071-6, © 2003
- **Knowledge and Information Technology Management: Human and Social Perspectives**, Angappa Gunasekaran, Omar Khalil and Syed Mahbubur Rahman/ ISBN: 1-59140-032-5; eISBN 1-59140-072-4, © 2003
- **Building Knowledge Economies: Opportunities and Challenges**, Liaquat Hossain and Virginia Gibson/ ISBN: 1-59140-059-7; eISBN 1-59140-073-2, © 2003
- **Knowledge and Business Process Management**, Vlatka Hlupic/ISBN: 1-59140-036-8; eISBN 1-59140-074-0, © 2003
- **IT-Based Management: Challenges and Solutions**, Luiz Antonio Joia/ISBN: 1-59140-033-3; eISBN 1-59140-075-9, © 2003
- **Geographic Information Systems and Health Applications**, Omar Khan/ ISBN: 1-59140-042-2; eISBN 1-59140-076-7, © 2003
- **The Economic and Social Impacts of E-Commerce**, Sam Lubbe/ ISBN: 1-59140-043-0; eISBN 1-59140-077-5, © 2003
- **Computational Intelligence in Control,** Masoud Mohammadian, Ruhul Amin Sarker and Xin Yao/ISBN: 1-59140-037-6; eISBN 1-59140-079-1, © 2003
- **Decision-Making Support Systems: Achievements and Challenges for the New Decade**, M.C. Manuel Mora and Guisseppi Forgionne/ISBN: 1-59140-045-7; eISBN 1-59140-080-5, © 2003
- **Architectural Issues of Web-Enabled Electronic Business**, Nansi Shi and V.K. Murthy/ ISBN: 1-59140-049-X; eISBN 1-59140-081-3, © 2003
- **Adaptive Evolutionary Information Systems**, Nandish V. Patel/ISBN: 1-59140-034-1; eISBN 1-59140-082-1, © 2003
- **Managing Data Mining Technologies in Organizations: Techniques and Applications**,   Parag Pendharkar/ ISBN: 1-59140-057-0; eISBN 1-59140-083-X, © 2003
- **Intelligent Agent Software Engineering**, Valentina Plekhanova/ ISBN: 1-59140-046-5; eISBN 1-59140-084-8, © 2003
- **Advances in Software Maintenance Management: Technologies and Solutions**, Macario Polo, Mario Piattini and Francisco Ruiz/ ISBN: 1-59140-047-3; eISBN 1-59140-085-6, © 2003
- **Multidimensional Databases: Problems and Solutions**, Maurizio Rafanelli/ISBN: 1-59140-053-8; eISBN 1-59140-086-4, © 2003
- **Information Technology Enabled Global Customer Service**, Tapio Reponen/ISBN: 1-59140-048-1; eISBN 1-59140-087-2, © 2003
- **Creating Business Value with Information Technology: Challenges and Solutions**, Namchul Shin/ISBN: 1-59140-038-4; eISBN 1-59140-088-0, © 2003
- **Advances in Mobile Commerce Technologies**, Ee-Peng Lim and Keng Siau/ ISBN: 1-59140-052-X; eISBN 1-59140-089-9, © 2003
- **Mobile Commerce: Technology, Theory and Applications**, Brian Mennecke and Troy Strader/ ISBN: 1-59140-044-9; eISBN 1-59140-090-2, © 2003
- **Managing Multimedia-Enabled Technologies in Organizations**, S.R. Subramanya/ISBN: 1-59140-054-6; eISBN 1-59140-091-0, © 2003
- **Web-Powered Databases**, David Taniar and Johanna Wenny Rahayu/ISBN: 1-59140-035-X; eISBN 1-59140-092-9, © 2003
- **E-Commerce and Cultural Values**, Theerasak Thanasankit/ISBN: 1-59140-056-2; eISBN 1-59140-093-7, © 2003
- **Information Modeling for Internet Applications**, Patrick van Bommel/ISBN: 1-59140-050-3; eISBN 1-59140-094-5, © 2003
- **Data Mining: Opportunities and Challenges**, John Wang/ISBN: 1-59140-051-1; eISBN 1-59140-095-3, © 2003
- **Annals of Cases on Information Technology** – vol 5, Mehdi Khosrowpour/ ISBN: 1-59140-061-9; eISBN 1-59140-096-1, © 2003
- **Advanced Topics in Database Research – vol 2**, Keng Siau/ISBN: 1-59140-063-5; eISBN 1-59140-098-8, © 2003
- **Advanced Topics in End User Computing – vol 2**, Mo Adam Mahmood/ISBN: 1-59140-065-1; eISBN 1-59140-100-3, © 2003
- **Advanced Topics in Global Information Management – vol 2**, Felix Tan/ ISBN: 1-59140-064-3; eISBN 1-59140-101-1, © 2003
- **Advanced Topics in Information Resources Management – vol 2**, Mehdi Khosrowpour/ ISBN: 1-59140-062-7; eISBN 1-59140-099-6, © 2003

Critical Reflections on Information Systems: A Systematic Approach

Table of Contents

Preface

The information technologies have become a differentiating factor of modern organizations. During the last decade, multiple organizational effects like virtual structures, flat organizations, network structures, among others, have been the constant that confronts the business communities as opposed to the challenge that raises a new interconnected and demanding world, where the competitive advantages and the value generation are the most wanted treasures.

While the information technology offers different alternatives to perceive and to construct the businesses, its users remain expectant to the possibilities that it can offer. In this sense, the potentiality of the information systems and their bonds with the individuals' realities become key factors for developing the information resource through the technology.

Recent studies show that the IS in the organizations are integrated with the business functions looking for reaching greater productivity and innovation, both translated in ad value for the clients. Although experiences, in this sense, show important levels of integration and satisfaction of the clients, the technology users often do not recognize real possibilities to enrich their work environment, generating a conceptual and mental division of the individuals' behavior in the organization.

According to the above, the incorporation of a complementary approach allows the review of the organization in specific and required aspects as in its general context. It is in this way, that the systemic thought appears to be a way to see the global vision of the organization's reality and its relations and interaction of its components. This approach looks to identify the relations between the components and their behaviors, to understand the reality in context of the phenomena under study.

Therefore, the use of a systemic perspective offers to the researchers new distinctions of the problematic reviewed. In the context of the IS and the information technology, it deepens in the relations of creation of value of the individuals based on the technology and its presence in the organization processes. Thus, the discovery of behaviors that are not inherent to the components of the organization, but are the fruits of the studied and analyzed relations, is allowed.

The systems thinking applied to the IS has peculiarly short extended in this area, though the same origin of these two takes the connotation of systems in its own creation. This situation allows us to explore the ideas of the systemic thinkers and their concepts to approach the technology problematic in the organizations, understanding in a detailed way, its impacts and implications for the business communities of the 21st century.

Therefore, before establishing strategic guidelines for the technology and its relation with the business function, it is necessary for the leaders to review the different relations between the technology, the individual and the processes as a validation and reflection strategy that allows the management to watch those emergent properties that have always been in their reality, which up to the moment had not become explicit, to improve its advantages and innovative relations, reconstructing those that do not add to the expected value.

Finally, though the previous studies on systems information contribute critical and important findings and recommendations that generate new options and possibilities for the present businesses, their review and analysis in light of the systems thinking offer a new horizon of expectations and distinctions that they discover in the relations organization-individual-technology—a complementary way where the IS and the technology arise like emergent properties in the organizations of the new millennium

In this sense, the chapters of this book gather the findings, reflections and investigations in the IS and IT reviewed subjects from the systemic perspective, which offers a spectrum of conceptual and practical analysis, as well as a reference for future investigations and projects, where the relations between the technology, the individuals and the business allow for the discovery of the emergent source of knowledge and ad value in the organizations.

Chapter 1 entitled "A Systemic Approach for the Formalization of the Information Systems Concept: Why Information Systems are Systems ? by Manuel Mora, Ovsei Gelman, Francisco Cervantes, Marcelo Mejía andAlfredo Weitzenfeld, shows researchers the need to study the IS object and practitioners the need to use the same common conceptual knowledge about what Information Systems are. In this sense, this research offers improvements in the overall understanding about how organizations operate, the integration of disperse knowledge related to the way IS and IT leverages the management process, and the establishment of standard bases for contrasting research findings.

Also shown is how *IS* are systems that are included in business processes, and these, in turn, are included in organizations, and finally, the latter are included in their environment. Business processes and organizations, according to the hierarchy property of systems, can also be conceptualized as systems.

Chapter 2 entitled "Technological Frames Recursive Construction Approach: A Systemic Theory for Information Technology Incorporation in Organizations" by Jeimy Cano who, based on the assumption that information technology is the result of an individual's social interaction, explores the benefits of individuals' structural relations understanding in the process of information technology incorporation for integrating the findings of causal research, the systemic elements (the study of relations), focusing the information technology understanding in the organizational tasks.

Chapter 3 entitled "Extending Checkland's Phenomenological Approach to Information Systems" by Hernán López-Garay, introduces a new image of organizations as holistic practices —an image based on these developments— and examines how this image may enrich Checkland's phenomenological design of information systems.

In chapter 4 entitled "A Validation Test of an Adaptation of the DeLone and McLean's Model in the Spanish EIS Field," by José Luis Roldán and Antonio Leal develop a research model adapting the DeLone and McLean's information systems success model to the executive information systems (EIS) field. They test the validity of their adaptation, studying the interdependencies among the variables and examining its predictive power.

Chapter 5 entitled "A Systemic Approach of Electronic Commerce" is by Roberto Vinaja, who applies several concepts from classical Systems Theory to the growing area of E-commerce and agents. His purpose is to demonstrate how General Systems Theory principles are widely applicable to the state-of-the art field of Electronic Commerce.

Chapter 6 entitled "Information Systems as Social Systems" by Niek du Plooy argues that the "human" or sociological side of information systems is of such importance that it should be seen as the core of the discipline, and that information systems are best understood when viewed as social systems. Current thinking on systems (especially soft systems methodology) and its place in supporting information systems in a constantly changing environment are also referred to.

Chapter 7 entitled "The SoSM Revisited—Critical Realist Perspective" is by Philip Dobson, who revisits the System of System Methodologies (SoSM) and suggests that use of the SoSM as a framework for defining methodological assumptions is difficult when the concerned methodologies have significantly different meanings for one axis of the framework—"system" complexity. It is suggested that the purpose of the underlying system can provide a more appropriate frame for defining system approaches, with such purpose being defined as interaction or transformation.

Chapter 8 entitled "Soft Evaluation: A Systemic Approach for Post-Implementation Review" by Ala Abu-Samaha describes an alternative approach to evaluating Information Technology (IT) projects, which involves developing a holistic view of IT interventions. The main methodological problem in evaluating any intervention is to choose the right indicators for the measurement of success or lack of it.

In Chapter 9 entitled "Addressing Organisational and Societal Concerns: An Application of Critical Systems Thinking to Information Systems Planning in Colombia," José Rodrigo Cordóba and Gerald Midgley present a methodology for IS planning based on critical systems thinking an—approach that encourages the critical analysis of stakeholder understandings of social contexts prior to the selection and/or design of planning methods. Also, this methodology uses a combination of the systems theories of autopoiesis and boundary critique, which deepen our understanding of what it means to reflect on participation, values and social concerns during IS planning.

Chapter 10 entitled "The Information System Within the Organization: A Case Study" by Bruce Campbell and G. Mike McGrath introduces a case study where a particular technique was used to gain some understanding of a messy organizational situation that was, it was suspected, impacting the performance of the IS. The technique, using causal loop diagrams (CLD), is described and then applied to the case study.

In chapter 11 entitled "Implementation of Collaborative Technologies as a Learning Process," Tatyana Bondarouk and Klaas Sikkel present ideas about influence of group learning on ongoing use of collaborative technologies and propose a model, in which implementation is regarded as a learning process that takes place at different levels, reaching from the individual user to the entire organization.

In chapter 12 entitled "A Framework for Building Learning Organizations," Sushil K. Sharma and Jatinder N.D. Gupta suggest a framework for building learning organizations and show the use of systemic approach to implement their proposed framework to create learning organizations.

In summary, understanding in a systemic way the different elements involved in the IS and IT suggest an alternative and enriched vision of the managerial reflections on added value and strategy supported with technology in the organizations, as well as conceptual and critical land for academic, students, researchers and practitioners in IS/IT area. In this order of ideas, the chapters presented in this book review and explore diverse systemic facets of the IS and the IT, founding a knowledge base with which to understand in a holistic way the technical issues, human implications and business relationships that exhibit IT in the organizations.

Acknowledgments

The editor would like to acknowledge all the help of all involved in the collation and review process of the book, without whose support this international project could not have been satisfactorily completed. A further special note of thanks goes also to all the staff at Idea Group Publishing, especially Ms. Michele Rossi, Ms. Jan Travers and Dr. Mehdi Khosrow-Pour, whose contributions throughout the whole process from proposal of the initial idea to final publication have been invaluable.

Special gratitude is due to Iván Reyes, M.Sc. and Jorge Gil, M.Sc. for ongoing sponsorship in terms of generous spiritual support and critical reflections about all chapters of this book.

Deep appreciation and thankfulness to all reviewers who provided constructive and comprehensive reviews. Relevant reviewers who provided the most comprehensive, critical and constructive comments include: Anabela Sarmento, Instituto Superior de Contabilidade e Administração do Porto, PORTUGAL. Margherita Pagani, Bocconi University, ITALY. James L. Ritchie-Dunham, Executive Director of Institute for Strategic Clarity, USA. Iván Reyes, Independent Research in Systemic Thinking, COLOMBIA. Murray Jennex, California State University San Marcos, USA; and El-Sayed Abou-Zeid, Concordia University, CANADA.

In closing, I wish to thank all of the authors for their insights and excellent contributions to this book. I also want to thank all the people who assisted me in the review process and ongoing professional staff support at Idea Group Publishing mentioned above. Finally, I want to thank God, for his constant support in my life, my family, for its constant praying and my girlfriend, for her patience and support in grammatical and style revisions throughout this project.

Jeimy J. Cano, Ph.D.
Bogotá, Colombia
March, 2002

Section I

Systemic Concepts on Information Technology/ Information Systems

Chapter I

A Systemic Approach for the Formalization of the Information Systems Concept: Why Information Systems are Systems?

Manuel Mora
UAA & DEPFI-UNAM, Mexico

Ovsei Gelman
Centro de Instrumentos, UNAM, Mexico

Francisco Cervantes, Marcelo Mejía and Alfredro Weitzenfeld
ITAM, Mexico

ABSTRACT

In the new economic context, based on Information and Knowledge resources, the concepts of Information Systems and Information Technology (IS&IT) are fundamental to understand the organizational and managerial process in all levels: strategic, tactic and operational. From an academic and practitioner perspective, we pose that the correct use of the concept of IS&IT, and in specific of Information Systems, is critical. First ones need to study the same object and second ones need to use the same common conceptual knowledge about what are Information Systems. Nevertheless, uniquely informal and semiformal definitions of Information Systems have been reported in the literature and thus a formal definition based on core systemic foundations is missing. For these reasons, the conceptualization and formal definition of what are Information Systems acquires a relevant research and praxis status. This chapter addresses this problematic situation posing a formal definition of the term Information Systems based on core theoretical principles of the Systems Approach. For that, we firstly review the foundations of Systems Approach to establish the basis for our conceptual development. Then, an updated formal definition of the core concept System originally developed by Gelman and Garcia (1989) and that incorporates new insights from other systemic researchers is presented. With these theoretical bases, we proceed to review the contributions and limitations of main informal and semiformal definitions of the term Information Systems reported at the literature. Then the new formal definition of this term is developed using the updated formal definition of the term System. We continue with a discussion of how the definition posed formalizes systemic concepts of previous definitions, of how these are partial cases of the new definition and of how it can be used to model and study Information Systems in organizations. Finally, we conclude with main remarks and implications of this definition and with directions for further research.

INTRODUCTION

Information Systems and Information Technology (IS&IT) are essential components of organizations. Their role for providing support to the business operational processes, as well as to the management activities performed on tactical and strategic levels has dramatically increased in the last 15 years (Alter, 1996; McNurlin & Sprague, 1998; Mora & Cervantes, 1999). Furthermore, the industrial-based economy has suffered a shift to a new Information and Knowledge based economy (Druker, 1988; Nolan, 1991; Nonaka, 1991). In this new economic context, IS&IT have become core concepts for understanding the management process in organizations, and their right conceptualization is critical for assuring their acceptance and use, as well as for improving their design and management. From an academic and practitioner perspective, we pose that the correct use of the concept of IS&IT, and in specific of *Information Systems*, is critical. Researchers need to study the same object, and practitioners need to use the same common conceptual knowledge about what are *Information Systems*. Benefits for researchers are the improvement of the overall understanding about how organizations operate, integration of disperse knowledge related with how IS&IT leverage the management process and the establishments of standard bases for the comparisons of research findings. Benefits for practicioners are the gains of common knowledge to promote, plan, design, develop, implement, evaluate, update and, in its case, upgrade *Information Systems*, to assure to the organizations the expected benefits by their usage. For these reasons, the conceptualization and formal definition of what are *Information Systems* acquires a relevant research and praxis status.

However, despite the growing relevance of the term *Information Systems* for academicians as well as for practitioners, few formalizations of the term *Information System*, based on the core and substantial concepts from the *Systems Approach* (Ackoff, 1974), have been reported. Some of the current available definitions founded in the literature, despite being comprehensive due to the consideration of core elements, are informal (Seen, 1989; Hoffer, Burch, & Grudnitski, 1989; George & Valacich, 1996; Yourdon, 1993; Zatzinger, Jackson, & Burd, 2000) or semiformal (Alter, 1999, 2000, 2001). Others' proposals (Wand & Weber, 1988, 1990), being notwithstanding formal and with strong philosophical roots based on ontology (Bunge, 1977, 1979 referenced by Wand & Weber, 1990), are supported only by a mathematical structural relational approach (Mesarovic, 1964, 1975) of graph theory that has been criticized in the Systems Fiel for offering a partial view of what systems are—sets of connected parts. As Trist (1970, quoted by Sachs, 1976, p. 145) points out, the formal graph approach leads to the conceptual equation of a system = aggregation (objects, relations, attributes). This graph-like approach is not enough to represent all primary intuitions agreed in the *Systems Approach*, and therefore, it fails in capturing the essence of the notion of systems: "a system is more than the sum of its parts" (Angyal, 1941 and Trist, 1970, both referenced by Sachs, 1976). In this work, we do not reject completely this approach, but we complement it with a teleological and pragmatic approach posed by Singer (1959), Sachs (1976), Ackoff (1971) and Ackoff & Emery (1972), which focuses more on the content than on the structural form. For that, we extend a definition of the term *system*, developed by Gelman & Garcia (1989), who detected the incompleteness of the current definitions of this term. The definition posed here, as its root definition developed by Gelman & Garcia (1989), is also based in both perspectives: teleological and structural. This new definition has been recently demanded as an intellectual construct necessary to model an organization in order to help understand and manage it (Paton, 1997, p. 71). Furthermore, the use of the *Systems Approach*, as a theoretical base, has not been extensively reported, as it should seem in the research and design of *Information Systems* (Eom, 2000; Xu, 2000; Checkland, 2000). This lack of formal knowledge about why *Information Systems* are *systems* has motivated us to pursue the formalization of this core term in our field from the core principles of the *Systems Approach* discipline.

With these antecedents, this chapter has the following general objectives: (i) to assess the contribution of the *Systems Approach* in the field of Information

Systems, (ii) to pose a formal definition of *Information System,* and (iii) to illustrate the importance and conceptual productivity of the new definition for theory and praxis. The first part is dedicated to present an overview of the field of *Systems Approach,* where definitions and properties of the term *system* are analyzed. This section is based on the works of Ackoff (1973, 1976), Sachs (1976) and intensely on the study from Gelman & García (1989), who developed a formal definition of the term *system* and tested that it included the main formal definitions available at the time of publication (Kalman & Arbib, 1969; Arbib & Manes, 1974; Klir, 1968; Zadeh, 1969; Mesarovic, 1964; all referenced in Gelman & Garcia, 1989). Then, a discussion of the contributions of the *Systems Approach* to the field of Information Systems is presented. We conclude this part with an analysis of the main current definitions of the term *Information System* and with a discussion of their limitations. Consequently, we begin the next part of the chapter with the development of a new formal definition for this concept, applying the formal definition of the concept of *system* described previously. The benefits of the new definition of the term *Information Systems* are discussed, and several examples of the contributions that it could provide for the development of Information Systems studies are offered. Finally, we conclude with a section of general conclusions and recommendations for further research.

THE *SYSTEMS APPROACH*

Origins of the *Systems Approach*

Systems Approach is a scientific research paradigm that emerged in the early 1940s as an alternative to the classic positivist scientific paradigm dominant in the research activities of natural sciences (Bertalanfy, 1968; Rapoport, 1968; Ackoff, 1973, 1976). *Systems Approach,* also named *Systems Thinking* or the *Systems Movement,* was developed in several fields, such as biology, psychology, sociology, politics and economy (Checkland, 2000). *Systems Approach* is also considered a basement of other new fields such as cybernetics and control theory (Fuentes-Zenón, 1995). In the current context, the ideas from *Systems Approach* have shaped the disciplines of operations research, management sciences and information systems (Gelman & García, 1986).

Systems Approach is a scientific paradigm suitable to study phenomena that are characterized by an extraordinary complexity, a high level of interaction of their parts and the possession of properties that are lost when the whole phenomenon is considered partially isolated from its environment. According to Ackoff (1973), the traditional scientific approach is supported by three main premises: a reductionism vision, an analytical thinking and a mechanistic or causal approach. The *Systems Approach* rejects that complex problems can be understood, when uniquely, these three premises are considered and uses, as complementary research tools, an expansionistic vision, a synthetic thinking, and a teleological approach. The reductionism vision assumes that every phenomenon can be studied by a process of its separation in simple and indivisible parts. The analytical thinking, in turn, assumes that the world can be studied, e.g., it can be described, explained, predicted and controlled, through the independent investigation of its separated and indivisible parts and the consequent definition of the whole's behavior by the aggregation of the part's behaviors. The results of this aggregation can be explained using linear cause–effect relations, where a thing or event is taken as a necessary and sufficient cause of another. In this way, this mechanistic or causal approach assumes the world is a machine and "(the world) is taken to be like a hermetically sealed clock, a self-contained mechanism whose behavior was completely determined by its own structure" (Ackoff, 1973, p. 662).

Traditional scientific approach, based on a reductionism, analytical thinking and mechanistic doctrine, had been completely successful at explaining, predicting and controlling the typical phenomenon studied during the 19th century.[1] However, biological phenomena about live organisms, as well as social, political and behavioral phenomena that are present in societies and business organizations, have additional complexities that make their study by the classic scientific approach operationally unfeasible (Bertalanfy, 1968; Gich, 1979). As Gelman & García (1989, p. 4)[2] state, "the man is aware that each activity of his daily life has a large quantity of links with objects and subjects that are located in several physical, psychological, economical, social and political dimensions and spaces."

Systems Approach uses an expansionism vision that is opposite to the reductionism view. Expansionism doctrine assumes that everything in the world is part of a larger whole and that the parts of a whole are interrelated between them and with the whole. From an expansionistic point of view, the full understanding of a phenomenon of study is impossible, and the research is an endless process (Ackoff, 1973, 1976). *Synthetic Thinking* explains the whole's behavior through the understanding of the role that the whole plays in the larger whole to which it belongs. *Systems Approach* does not reject the utility to know the parts' behavior, but it assumes that the accumulation of parts' behaviors hides behavioral properties that are exclusive of the whole. *Systems Approach* assumes also that the correct performance of the whole does not depend only on the correct and independent performance of their parts, but of the adjustment of the parts into the whole. Parts' performance optimization does not conduct to whole's performance optimization. In turn, *Systems Approach* rejects the mechanistic perspective of a deterministic world governed by laws of linear cause–effect relations and, instead of it, tries to explain the behavior of the thing of study through producer–product relations

(Singer, 1957). Producer–product relations imply that some precedent events or things are necessary but are not sufficient to produce a consequence. In this way, a mechanical view of the world is rejected. In particular, when the phenomenon under study involves functions, goals, and purposes of human beings or live organisms, the whole behavior is better explained by the ends than by the means. As Ackoff states (1973, p. 665), "in teleological thinking, behavior can be explained either by what produced it or by what it is intended to produce." Some researchers have proposed different levels of teleological systems. Ackoff (1971) and Gich (1979) make differences among goal-seeking and purposeful systems. The former are wholes that can only decide their courses of action for achieving goals, and the later are wholes that can decide their goals or purposes as well as their courses of action for obtaining them. Systems with human beings as components, such as business organizations, are considered purposeful systems. Natural or machine-based designed wholes are considered goal-seeking or multi-goal-seeking in the event of several goals.

Properties of *Systems*

Systems are wholes with exclusive properties that have values that are not necessarily similar to the values of their parts' properties. According to Ackoff (1973),[3] a *system* can be conceptualized as a set of interrelated elements of any kind, e.g., physical, conceptual or live elements, which has three basic properties: (i) parts' behaviors affect the whole's behavior; (ii) the way that parts' behavior affects the whole's behavior depends on at least the other parts' behavior; and (iii) every subset of parts has both properties and their effect on the whole's behavior cannot be reproduced by a part independently. As Ackoff (1973, p. 664) states, "a set of elements that forms a system always can display a behavior that none of its elements or subgroups can."

From a literature review on *Systems Approach* (Bertalanffy, 1968; Ackoff, 1971; Gich, 1979; Checkland, 2000; Bagh, 1990), the following properties are common to all types of systems: (i) wholeness, (ii) emergence, (iii) hierarchy, (iv) organization, (v) communication, (vi) control, and (vii) complexity. Living systems, in addition, have the following properties: (i) equifinality, (ii) purposeful behavior, (iii) adaptability, (iv) stability, and (v) diachronicity. The list of properties presented above offers a rich conceptual base for studying a phenomenon under a systemic perspective. Among them, the most relevant properties regarding the traditional positivist perspective are wholeness, emergence, hierarchy, and purposeful behavior. The first three can be summarized by the idea that systems are part of a supersystem, and in turn, they are composed of systems, and the whole and its parts have exclusive properties. Regarding the property of purposeful behavior, it is considered a central idea in the *Systems Approach* applied for studying complex phenomena such as business organizations because their behavior is not governed by simple linear cause–effect relations. In this way, the study of systems' goals and purposes in the context of the environmental goals and purposes as well as of goals and purposes of systems' parts offers a richer picture of the phenomenon of interest. Hence, we have presented the foundations of the *Systems Approach* in such form that this set of ideas will permit the review of its main contributions to the field of Information Systems. Then, we will be able to continue, with the core ideas of this study: the analysis and development of a formal definition of the term *Information System,* using a formal definition of the term *system.*

The Contribution of the *Systems Approach* to the Field of Information Systems

Several studies have assessed the theoretical and practical contributions of the *Systems Approach* to the field of Information Systems (Xu, 2000; Eom, 2000; Saraswat, 1998; Churchman, 1971; Courtney, Croasdell & Paradice, 1998; Mason & Mitroff, 1973). An exhaustive review of them is out of the scope of this study. Here, we will only trace and synthesize the main findings of these previous studies. *Information Systems* have been researched and inquired mainly by a positivist based research paradigm. Consequently, research methods that permit us to isolate and observe a partial view of the phenomenon under study are the conventionally used ones, i.e., survey and experiments. Nevertheless, the surname of *Information Systems* is precisely *Systems,* and it should be expected that the Systemic paradigm is the methodological research tool used to study them. It is important to note that *Systems Approach* does not deny the use of positivist research tools, rather it implies the use of them from a holistic perspective. As Saraswat states (1998, p. 2): "it is being recognized that the existing scientific method is fundamentally inadequate to solve the complex problems of organizations encompassing numerous social, technological, psychological and economical dimensions; ... a broad-based approach is also essential to correctly interpret the increasing volume of practical and academic discourse on this subject."

The *Systems Approach* is the paradigm used to do an interdisciplinary research. It must be noted that a multidisciplinary research did not emerge from a *Systems Approach* [Ackoff, 1973; O. Gelman 2000]. The multidisciplinary research is based on the supposition that a complex phenomenon can be separated in parts corresponding to monodisciplines. Then, they could be used to study these parts independently to find partial solutions that could be finally joined in one general solution. As it was reviewed in previous subsections, a *system* must be considered in relation with its environment, and its parts must be considered in relation with the whole. Interdisciplinary research, in turn, studies the complex phenomenon as a whole, where the different disciplines help to study the different dimensions included in the problem or mass of problems.

Specific theoretical contributions of the *Systems Approach* to the *Information Systems* field are (i) a philosophical basement to integrate diversity of themes covered in the field (Saraswat, 1998); (ii) an epistemological basement to develop a theory about *Information Systems* as a whole (Xu, 2000; Alter, 2000, 2001); and (iii) an alternative paradigm to understand the role of *Information Systems* in organizations in the search of valid knowledge (Churchman, 1971; Courtney, Croasdell & Paradice, 1998). From a practical perspective, among the main contributions reported are (i) a systems development approach and methodology (Checkland, 2000; Hirschheim, Iivari & Klein, 1998); (ii) new specific research tools to account for higher-order interrelationships (Richards & Gupta, 1985; referenced in Xu, 2000); and (iii) methodological basements for the design of specific *Information Systems* such as Manufacturing Information Systems and Decision Support Systems (Xu, 2000; Eom, 2000). Nevertheless, *Systems Approach* has received complaints (Alter, 2001, p. 14) due to the general scope of its concepts. Our position is that it is not a methodological weakness but a strength that enables researchers and practitioners to acquire an integrated perspective of the complex phenomenon of *Information Systems*. However, the right concepts of *Systems Approach* must be used in the research and praxis activities.

DEFINITIONS OF THE TERM *SYSTEM*

Classic Definitions of the Term *System*

The term *system* is critical for the *Systems Approach*. Paradoxically, while the *Systems Approach* has offered to the scientific research an unifying paradigm, there is not a standard definition for this term: *systems* (Bagh, 1990). However, a literature review can display two main approaches to define this term: a mathematical approach and a linguistic-conceptual approach. In the first approach are the works of Mesarovic (1964), Kalman (1969), Klir (1968), Zadeh (1969), Arbib (1974), and Gelman & García (1989).[4] In the second approach, the main works reported are from Rapport (1966, 1968), Churchman (1973), Bertalanffy (1976), Ackoff (1960, 1971, 1974), Lange (1975), Sachs (1976), Checkland (1981), Gich (1979), Wilson, (1984) and Wand & Woo (1991).[5] The first approach is usually used in the context of hard systems, e.g., physical and technological artificially designed systems that exhibit functional behaviors controlled by causal laws, while the second approach is preferred by systems thinkers that treat with soft systems, e.g., systems where the social, political and human behavioral issues turn the system into a messy phenomenon for study. Traditionally, mathematical and logical symbols are the notation language for the former and verbs or nouns of activities for the latter.

In this study, we are interested in showing how the *Systems Approach* is useful for understanding the behavior and structure of *Information Systems*, and because these have social, political and human behavior issues, they will be considered soft systems. It conducts us to explore the definitions from a linguistic-conceptual perspective. A review of the main definitions from this perspective shows that all definitions consider three issues: (i) parts interrelated, (ii) parts affected by the whole and vice versa, and (iii) whole's goal or purpose. Churchman (1973) adds explicitly in his definition the essential idea that any *system* is inserted in an environment. With these issues, we can define a *system* as "*a set of interrelated parts inserted in an environment, that are affecting the whole they are conforming and which has a goal or purpose to fulfill as well as they are affected by their belonging to the whole.*" Nevertheless, this definition of the term *system* is similar to the definitions found in the literature. Therefore, it also has the same limitations when being used as a conceptualization tool to specify a *system* and to express the basic properties of it. In this way, these definitions do not help to specify the structure of a system or to consider the *system* as a unit with their exclusive properties. Gelman & García (1989) noted this, and they developed a robust and formal definition of the term *system* that considers both perspectives: a *system* as a unit and a *system* as a set of related parts. They called the former "a system-I thing" and the latter "a system-II thing." Furthermore, in their work, they developed conceptual and mathematical definitions of the term *system*. Nevertheless, despite the authors stating that the conceptual definition was used uniquely as a base to develop the formal definition, we consider this semiformal definition as highly consistent with the conceptual approach and as offering a rich set of ideas to extend it. For this reason, we pose in this work a more formal extension of it. Also, we will show in the next section, that this definition is useful for a better description and understanding of soft systems, such as *Information Systems*.

An Updated Formal Definition of the Term *System*

In a previous subsection, we noted that definitions of the term *system* based on logical-mathematical notation are preferred in the context of hard systems. This is due to the fact that such *systems* usually permit a direct mapping of the phenomenon to their conceptualization as a *system*. According to Wilson (1984), soft systems are better mapped using a linguistic-conceptual notation. Both approaches have advantages and disadvantages. Logical-mathematical notations are precise, but relationships and properties found in soft systems could not be translated directly in equations or logical expressions.[6] In turn, linguistic-conceptual notations are easily understandable, but the terms and even the concepts used here can have different meanings for the systems thinkers. Another problem with this notation approach is that the relations are usually specified in a high level of abstraction, and their modeling in order to study the systems' behavior is practically unfeasible.

In this study, we pose a definition of the term *system* using a hybrid notation, conceptual and formal, based on an ontological process. This definition has four objectives: (i) to include all common features of main definitions reported in the literature, (ii) to set out a framework of concepts to identify common concepts used in previous definitions, (iii) to take advantage of the strengths of both types of notations, and (iv) to offer a useful notation to specify soft systems. The main motivation for posing this novel definition is to help practitioners and academicians of *Systems Approach* and *Information Systems* to formally specify their phenomenon or object of study. As mentioned earlier, the definition posed is an update of the systems' definition developed by Gelman & García (1989). Here, we extended it and included important issues from other studies that were not considered in it (Sachs, 1976; Ackoff, 1971; Churchmann, 1973; Checkland, 1981, 2000; and Wilson, 1984). Also, from a graph-based definition posed by Wand & Woo (1991), it is taken that the notion of properties exists independently and can be detected by external observers.

The definition posed here, viewed as a model of the world, can also be considered as an ontological development as far as ontology deals with the categorical structure of the beings of the world with an accountability purpose to specify the things of the world (The Oxford Companion to Philosophy, 2001). It is based on eight postulates and on the re-definitions of the terms: "system-I thing" in

Figure 1: Essential postulates for system's definitions

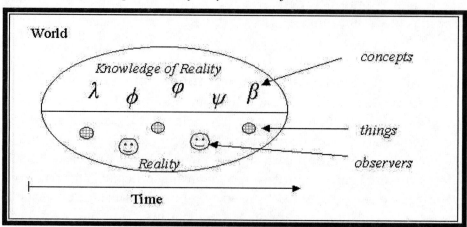

system-I, "system-II thing" in *system-II.* Finally, the original term *general system* from Gelman & García (1989) is updated, taking into account the new definitions of *system-I* and *system-II.*

Development of the Formal Definition of the Term *System*

Basic Postulates

Postulate 1. The world is composed of a real plane named *reality* and a conceptual plane named *knowledge of the reality.*

Postulate 2. The *reality* is composed of *things* that have *properties* $\rho 1, \rho 2, ...,$ ρk, both denominated by a noun and potentialities to perform *actions* $\alpha_1, \alpha_{2...}$ α_m denoted by verbs.

Postulate 3. The *knowledge of the reality* is composed of *concepts.*

Postulate 4. There is a space T named *time*, which is totally ordered with the relation "less than."

Postulate 5. In the *reality*, there are *things* named *observers* $\Theta 1, \Theta 2,..., \Theta k$, where some of their *actions* $\alpha_1, \alpha_{2...}, \alpha_m$, let them perceive, be aware about or suppose the existence of other *things.*

These basic postulates distinguish the objective reality from the conceptual knowledge plane. Any animate or inanimate object is conceptualized as a *thing*, and special *things*, called *observers*, with the ability to perceive or suppose and assign meanings to other *things* are also introduced. To complete the basic elements, the time space is also introduced. Figure 1 illustrates the core ideas of these postulates.

Definitions for System-I

Definition 1. A *thing* is a part of the *reality* that can be represented by a concept in the plane of *knowledge of reality.* The unions of *things* are *things,* and their parts are *things.*

Definition 2. It is said that X is *producer of* Y or X *produces* Y, and Y is *product of* X or Y is *produced by* X, and it is denominated as X $\Rightarrow$ Y, if the existence of X at time t0 < t1 is a necessary condition but not sufficient for the existence of Y at time t1. As well the expression X $\Rightarrow$ Y, it is named a relation *producer-product* between X and Y. Also, if the existence of X is a condition sufficient for Y, then it is said that X *causes* Y or X is the *cause* of Y, and Y is the *effect* of X or Y is *caused* by X, and it is denominated as X $\rightarrow$ Y. If X and Z *produce* Y, then X and Z are named *co-producers* of Y, and it is denominated as (X,Z) $\Rightarrow$ Y. All *co-producers* of Y are the *cause* of it.

Definition 3. A *property* $_x\rho$ of a *thing* X is a substantial feature of it that can be or not be perceived by an *observer* Θ. A *property* has the potentiality to be a *producer* or *cause* or to be a *product* or *effect.*

Figure 2: Diagram of System-I

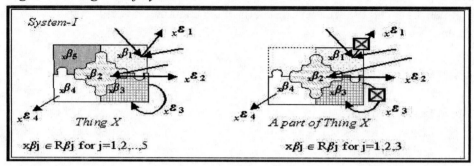

Definition 4. An *action* $_x\alpha$ of a *thing* X is an act performed by the thing when it uses one of their potentialities due to their *properties*. The *action* $_x\alpha$ can be performed on itself or on other *things* $Y_1, Y_2, \ldots Y_k$.

Definition 5. An *action* $_x\alpha$ of a *thing* X that was *caused* by itself is named a *self-action*. When the *action* $_x\alpha$ is co-produced by other *things* $Z_1, Z_2, \ldots Z_k$., the *action* is named *reaction*. When the *action* $_x\alpha$ is *produced* by another *thing* Z, the *action* is named *response* of X to Z.

Definition 6. An *attribute* $_x\beta$ of a *thing* X is a feature assigned by an *observer* Θ to a *property* $_x\rho$ of the *thing* X.

Definition 7. An *event* $_x\varepsilon$ is an *action* $_x\alpha$ performed by a *thing* X that is perceived by an *observer* Θ directly or through its consequences on other(s) thing(s).

Postulate 6. For each *attribute* $_x\beta$ of a *thing* X, there is a set finite or infinite of values possible for the *attribute* $_x\beta$ denominated by $_xv_i$. This set is named the *range* of the *attribute* $_x\beta$ and is denominated by the set $R\beta(X)$.

Definition 8. Given the sets $B(X) = \{ _x\beta_1, _x\beta_2, \ldots, _x\beta_k \}$, $E(X) = \{ _x\varepsilon_1, _x\varepsilon2, \ldots, _x\varepsilon_m \}$, and $RB(X) = \{R\beta j(X)$ for $j = 1, 2, \ldots k, \}$ respectively, as the sets of *attributes*, *events* and *range of attributes* of a *thing* X, then the expression $\S(X) = B(X) \cup E(X) \cup RB(X)$ is named the *conceptual structure* of the *thing* X.

Definition 9. A *thing* X is a **system-I**, and is denominated as $S_I(X)$ if given its *conceptual structure* $\S(X) = B(X) \cup E(X) \cup RB(X)$, any subset $B'(X)$ of *attributes* of $B(X)$ are not able to *co-produce* the set of *events* $E(X)$.

Despite that the basic definitions of the term system-I presented above could seem to be difficult to assimilate they carry out simple ideas. Figure 2 shows a graphical representation of them.

Figure 2 shows that a *system-I* is a whole of *attributes* and *events* and that any subset of *attributes* is not able to *co-produce* the same set of *events*. Figure 2 also illustrates the three types of *actions*: *responses* such as $_x\varepsilon_1$, *reactions* $_x\varepsilon_2$ and *self-actions* $_x\varepsilon_3$ and $_x\varepsilon_4$. It must be noted that the self-actions can be performed on the *thing* or another *thing*. Now, we continue with the development of the formal definition of the term *system*.

Definition 10. The set $W(X) = \{S_I(W1), S_I(W2), ..., S_I(Wk)\}$ that has a *reaction* or *response* to at least some *action* $_x\alpha$ of a $S_I(X)$, or that $S_I(X)$ has a *reaction* or *response* to at least some *action* $_j\alpha_m$ of some $S_I(Wj) \in W(X)$, is called the *environment* of $S_I(X)$.

Definition 11. Given a set $\S(X) = B(X) \cup E(X) \cup RB(X)$, for a $S_I(X)$, where $B(X) = \{ _x\beta_1, _x\beta_2 ..., _x\beta_k\}$, $E(X) = \{ _x\varepsilon_1, _x\varepsilon2..., _x\varepsilon_m \}$ and $RB(X) = \{ R\beta j (X)$ for $j = 1,2,..,k\}$, then the $k + 1$ tuple $\Omega(X,T) = <_x\nu_1, _x\nu_2 ... , _x\nu_k, t >$, where t $\in$ T, and each $_x\nu_j \in R\beta j (X)$ for $j = 1, 2..., k$, is called the *state* of $S_I(X)$.

Definition 12. The set of all possible *actions* $_w\alpha$ of the *environment* $W(X)$ of a $S_I(X)$ is named the *input components* of $S_I(X)$, and it is denominated as $I(X) = \{ _x\lambda_1, _x\lambda_2..., _x\lambda_n\}$. Any element $_x\lambda j$ of this set is named an *input* of $S_I(X)$.

Definition 13. The set of all possible *self-actions, reactions* and *responses* $_x\alpha$ of a $S_I(X)$ on its *environment* $W(X)$ is named the *output components* of $S_I(X)$, and it is denominated by $O(X) = \{ _x\varphi_1, _x\varphi_2..., _x\varphi_p\}$. Any element $_x\varphi j$ of this set is named an *output* of $S_I(X)$.

Definition 14. Given a $S_I(X)$ and its set of *inputs components* $I(X) = \{ _x\lambda_1, _x\lambda_2..., _x\lambda_n\}$ and its set of *output components* $O(X) = \{ _x\varphi_1, _x\varphi_2..., _x\varphi_p\}$, the set $IOR(X)$ of all the relations *producer-product* that exist between the *input* and *output* elements of $I(X)$ and $O(X)$ respectively, is called *input-output relation* of $S_I(X)$.

Definition 15. Given a $S_I(X)$ and its set of *input components* $I(X) = \{ _x\lambda_1, _x\lambda_2, ..., _x\lambda_n\}$ and its set of *output components* $O(X) = \{ _x\varphi_1, _x\varphi_2..., _x\varphi_p\}$, the sets $IC(X) = \{ _x\nabla_1, _x\nabla_2..., _x\nabla_n\}$ and $OC(X) = \{ _x\Delta_1, _x\Delta_2..., _x\Delta_p\}$ are named, respectively, the set of input channels and the set of output channels. An *input channel* $_x\nabla_j$ is a transmission mean of the *environment's actions* toward the

Figure 3: Diagram of a system-I and its environment

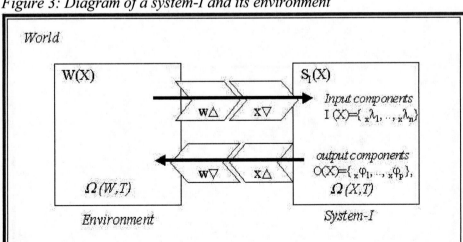

system X. An output channel $_x\Delta_i$ is a transmission mean of the *systems self-actions, reactions* or *responses* toward its *environment* W(X).

Figure 3 shows the relations between a *system-I* and its environment, through the input and output components and input and output channels. Also, in Figure 3, it is shown that the general input channel for system $S_I(X)$ corresponds to the general output channel of its environment W(X) and vice versa. A very important feature defined is that the *system-I* $S_I(X)$ and its *environment* W(X) are also systems, and both have a systems' state: W(X,T) and W (W(X),T) respectively.

Definitions for System-II

Definition 16. Given two *systems-I*, $S_I(X)$ and $S_I(Y)$, and their sets of *output components* $O(X) = \{ _x\varphi_1, _x\varphi_2, ..., _x\varphi_p\}$ and of *input components* $I(Y) = \{_y\lambda_1, _y\lambda_2, ..., _y\lambda_n\}$, respectively, if at least one output component $_x\varphi_j$ exists that is equal to some $_y\lambda_k$, then $S_I(X)$ *is related with* $S_I(Y)$, and it is denominated as $\Re(X, \propto, Y)$ in long form, where $\propto = _x\varphi_j = _y\lambda_k$ or as $\Re(X,Y)$ in short form. These types of relations are called *item relations*. Must be noted that $S_I(X)$ *is related with* $S_I(Y)$, does not imply that $S_I(Y)$ *is related with* $S_I(X)$.

Definition 17. Given a set $C = \{S_I(X_1), S_I(X_2), ..., S_I(X_k)\}$, any subset C' of C, where every item into C' is *related with* another item into C' or other item into C' is *related with* itself, is called a *set relation*, and is denominated as $\Re_s(C) = \{ \Re_1, \Re_2, ...\}$.

Definition 18. Given a set $C = \{S_I(X_1), S_I(X_2), ..., S_I(X_k)\}$ and a *set relation* $\Re_s(C) = \{\Re_1, \Re_2, ...\}$ on a subset C' of C, and two any items $S_I(Xi)$ and $S_I(Xj)$ of C', the sequence of *item relations* $\Re_1, \Re_2, ..., \Re n$, such that (i) $Xi \in \Re_1$ (ii) $Xi \in \Re n$ and (iii) for every $\Re_m$ and $\Re_{1m+1}$ for $m = 1, 2, ..., n - 1$, the *output or input component* in $\Re_m$ is the *output or input component* in $\Re_{1m+1}$ is called a *nondirected path* among $S_I(Xi)$ and $S_I(Xj)$. Must be noted that a *non-directed-path* among two items $S_I(Xi)$ and $S_I(Xj)$ of a *set relation* implies that there are no segments isolated.

Figure 4: Diagram of a System-II

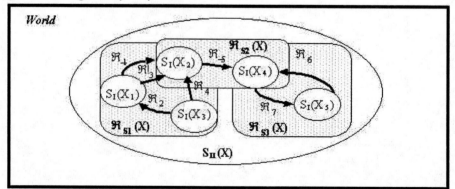

Definition 19. A *thing* X is a ***system-II*** and is denominated as $S_{II}(X)$, if (i) X is a set of things $X_1, X_2, ..., X_k$, where they are $S_I(X_i)$ or $S_{II}(X_i)$, for i = 1,2,...k, called a *set of subsystems*; (ii) there is a collection non empty of *set relations* $\Re_{S1}(X), \Re_{S2}(X), ..., \Re_{Sm}(X)$ on C; and (iii) there exists at least a *nondirected path* among two any item Xi and Xj in the set ($\Re_{S1}(X) \cup \Re_{S2}(X) \cup ... \Re_{Sm}(X)$). It must be noted that it is a recursive definition to say that a *subsystem* has *subsystems*.

Figure 4 illustrates main ideas of *system-II*. In this figure it is shown, for example, that a *system* $S_{II}(X)$ has five *subsystems* $S_I(X_1), S_I(X_2), ..., S_I(X_5)$.

In Figure 4, appears also three *set relations* $\Re_{S1}(X)..., \Re_{S3}(X)$. It must be noted that $\Re_{S2}(X)$ is necessary to account for the *item relation* $\Re_5$. Also, it must be noted that condition (iii) of Definition 19 is satisfied, i.e., for any two subsystems $S_I(X_i)$ and $S_I(X_j)$, there is a *nondirected path,* or in plain words, both subsystems are connected. With these previous definitions, we can now continue with the formalization process to arrive to the concept of *general system*.

Definition 20. A *thing* X is a *general system* and is denominated as $S_G(X)$, if (i) X is a $S_I(X)$ that can be mapped to a $S_{II}(X)$ or (ii) X is a $S_{II}(X)$ that can be mapped to a $S_I(X)$.

Definition 21. Given a *general system* $S_G(X)$ and at least another *general system* $S_G(Y)$, the *general system* $S_G(Z)$, where $S_G(X)$ and $S_G(Y)$ are items of its *set of subsystems*, is called the *suprasystem* of $S_G(X)$ and it is denominated as $SS_G(X)$.

Definition 22. The *general-system* $S_G(R)$ that contains to the *suprasystem*

Figure 5: Diagram of a General-System

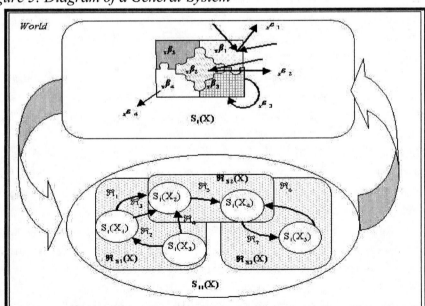

$SS_G(X)$ of a *general-system* $S_G(X)$ is called the *envelop* of the *system* $S_G(X)$ and it is denote as $ES_G(X)$. Must be noted that the *environment* $W(X)$ of a $S_G(X)$, is its *suprasystem* of $SS_G(X)$, and its *envelop* $ES_G(X)$.

Postulate 7. Very *general system* $S_G(X)$, which is or can be conceptualized as a $S_{II}(X) = \{S_I(X_1), S_I(X_2), ..., S_I(X_k)\}$, there is at least an item $S_I(Xj)$ *related with* its environment $W(X)$ and at least an item in its environment *related with it*.

Similar to the term *system-I*, basic definitions of the term *system-II* and the term *general system* carry out simple ideas. Figure 5 shows a graphical representation of them.

A set of rules about how to transform a $S_I(X)$ to a $S_{II}(X)$ or vice versa is out of the scope of this study. Here, we can only indicate that the problem consists in establishing the correspondences between *attributes* and *events* present in the $S_I(X)$ perspective to the *subsystems* and *item relations* present in the $S_{II}(X)$ conceptualization. Hence, we have posed a formal and conceptual definition of the term *system*. In the next section, we will review the current definitions of the term *Information Systems* to show that they are based on definitions of *systems* not precisely specified. Limitations of them will also be indicated.

ANALYSIS AND DISCUSSION OF CURRENT DEFINITIONS OF THE TERM *INFORMATION SYSTEMS*

The term *Information System (IS)*, is the essential concept in the field of Information Systems. It refers to the main *whole* to be studied, developed and managed in the field. However, the majority of textbooks (Seen, 1989; Hoffer, Burch, & Grudnitski, 1989; George & Valacich, 1996; Yourdon, 1993; Satzinger, Jackson, & Burd, 2000) refer to some systems concepts, such as input-process-output components, control mechanisms and open systems, using a broad and nonstandard definition of the term *system*. Furthermore, recent studies have pointed out that the field of Information Systems has (i) a lack of a set of fundamental standardized concepts (Alter, 2001), (ii) a lack of macro-structures to cumulate theories (Farohoomand & Drury, 2001), and (iii) a large number of theories used only once that produce a poor vision of a grand or unified theory of Information Systems (Barkhi & Sheetz, 2001). Therefore, the term *Information System*, that is critical in aiding academicians and practitioners in perceiving the same *whole,* is a term with multiple meanings. A sample of these definitions is as follows: (i) an *IS* is a *system* composed of subsystems of hardware, programs, files and procedures to get a shared goal (Senn, 1989, p. 23); (ii) an *IS* is a *system* composed of software application, support software, hardware, document and training materials, controls, job roles and people that use the software application (Hoffer, George, & Valacich, 1996, p. 8); (iii) an *IS* is composed of hardware, software, data, procedures and people (Yourdon, 1989, pp. 18–19); (iv) an *IS* is a *system* composed of inputs, models, outputs, technology, databases and controls (Burch & Grudnitski, 1989, p. 58); (v) an *IS* is a collection of interrelated components that collect, process, store and provide as output the information needed to complete a business task (Zatzinger, Jackson, & Burd, 2000, p. 6); and (vi) an *IS* is a *system* that uses Information Technology to capture, transmit, store, retrieve, manipulate, or display information used in one or more business processes (Alter, 1996, p. 2).

From an informal perspective, all definitions above reported have been enough to account for the core components and the purpose of an *IS*. However, a science requires the formal definition of its fundamental concepts, in order to be considered mature. Main efforts in this direction include the works developed by Alter (1996, 2000, 2001) toward the formalization of core concepts in this field, and where the term *IS* is one of the most important to be developed. Another important effort is developed by Wand & Weber (1991), but it will not be not discussed here because of two reasons: (i) its systems definition is based on a partial perspective of the term system already criticized from the 1940's (Angyal, 1941 and Trist 1970; both referenced by Sachs, 1976) and (ii) with its definition, the term *Information System* is reduced to considering a system as a graph of software components or modules useful to analyze uniquely graph-based properties such as coupling and good decomposition to be articulated. As they point out: " ... the primary contribution of our model is that it allows a precise analysis of our notion of a good decomposition to be articulated" (Wand & Weber, 1990, p. 1289). Main core and universal components of an *Information System*, founded in informal definitions, are not considered or were not developed in this study. Alter (1999, 2000, 2001) defines the term IS using the general term: Work System. In turn, it is based in the term system that is defined by Alter (2001, p. 14) as: "a set of interacting components that operate together to accomplish a purpose." Also, Alter (2001, p.14) defines a Work System as a *"system* with human participants and/or machines perform a business process using information, technology and other resources to produce products and/or services to internal or external customers." The main contribution of Alter's work is the integration of partial views of the term *IS* in a practical and parsimonious framework that covers the four key components usually found in previous definitions: participants, information, technology and the business process. Also, Alter's definition identifies adequately specific system outputs as products or services and environmental components called infrastructure and context. However, despite the benefits for the praxis, Alter's definition uses the fundamental systems concepts partially, and therefore, it loses generality. For example, system's inputs are not specified in Alter's framework and furthermore are equaled with the internal components: participants, information and technology. In a similar way, the system environment is misinterpreted, according to the *Systems Theory*, in two terms vaguely defined: context and infrastructure. The term context, in Alter's framework, is (2001, p. 23) "everything that matters to be mentioned even though it is outside of the work system and does not contribute directly to the work's systems operation ... the context included funding disputes, delays and political pressures." If it is true that Alter's definition recognizes the relevance of the environment in the component context, it fails in suggesting that the system environment is composed justly by the components that have relations with the system, i.e., they have reaction or responses to the system events or the system reactions or responses to their events, and that must be justly outside of the system. Another anomaly detected in this model, is that other components outside of the system are not considered part of its environment, such is the case of the system customers. From a formal perspective, system customers must be inside or outside of it, but it is not specified. Hence, we have claimed that the literature in the field of Information Systems is lacking a formal definition of the term *IS* that is standard and is based on formal principles of *Systems Approach*. The majority of definitions found in textbooks are vague and ambiguous. Also, core concepts of *Systems Theory*, the assumed theoretical basement for the field of IS, are denied or misunderstood. Therefore, academicians and practitioners perceive different meanings of the same term. Earlier works to reduce the fuzziness of core concepts, such as the term *IS*, are adequate, and must be enhanced. This study claims to formalize this concept, being coherent with the core principles of *Systems Theory*. Part I of this chapter has been dedicated to presenting the core concepts of the *Systems Approach* and the current definitions of the term *Information Systems* to show that main systemic concepts have been deployed incompletely or with vagueness. In part II, we will pose the formalization of the term *IS*, and we will discuss how main previous definitions fit into it. Also, potential uses and its limitations will be presented.

THE FORMALIZATION OF THE TERM *INFORMATION SYSTEMS* BASED ON A FORMAL DEFINITION OF THE TERM *SYSTEM*

According to the principle of hierarchy from *Systems Theory*, any *system* is part of another larger *system*. In this sense, *IS*, cannot be understood if we consider them isolated from other larger *systems*. *IS* are *systems* that are included in *business processes* and these, in turn, are included in *organizations*, and the latter finally are included in their *environment*. *Business process* and *organizations*, according to the hierarchy property of *systems*, can also be conceptualized also as *systems*. Therefore, before formalizing the concept of *IS*, we must formalize the concepts of *organization* and *business process*.

Formalization of the Concepts of *Organization* and *Business Process*

Definition O-1.1. An *organization* X is a *general system* and is denoted as $S_G(X)$. Therefore, an *organization* can be conceptualized as a *system-I* denoted as $S_I(X)$ or as a *system-II* denoted as $S_{II}(X)$.

Definition O-1.2. An *organization* X, conceptualized as a *system-II* $S_{II}(X)$, fulfills the following conditions: (i) is a set X of at least two *subsystems* $S_{II}(X1)$ and $S_{II}(X2)$, named *management subsystem* and *productive subsystem* respectively; (ii) is a set X with at least a *set relation* $_0\Re_{S1}(X) = \{\Re_{1,0}\Re_{2,0}\Re_{3,}$ $_0\Re_{4,0}\Re_{5,0}\Re_{6,0}\}$ where $_0\Re_1 = \Re$ (management, $\propto$-control, productive), $_0\Re_2 = \Re$ (productive, $\propto$-information, management), $_0\Re_3 = \Re$ (management, $\propto$-M-outputs, W(X)), $_0\Re_4 = \Re(W(X), \propto$-M-inputs, management), $_0\Re_5 = \Re$(productive, $\propto$-P-outputs, W(X)) and $_0\Re_6 = \Re(W(X), \propto$-P-inputs, productive). It must be noted that condition (iii) of the general definition of *system-II* is also fulfilled.

Auxiliary Definition O-1.2.1. A *Business Process BP* is a *system-II* $S_{II}(BP)$ that contains three *general systems* $S_G(BP.1)$, $S_G(BP.2)$ and $S_G(BP.3)$, called respectively, *control-subsystem-of-business-process*, *operational-subsystem-of-business-process* and *information-subsystem-of-business-process*, or CSS(BP), OSS(BP) and ISS(BP), and has the following *set relation* $\Re_{S1}(BP) = \{\Re_1, \Re_{2...}, \Re_{11}\}$ where $\Re_1 = \Re$(CSS(BP), $\propto$-control, OSS(BP)), $\Re_2 = \Re$(CSS(BP), $\propto$-C-outputs, W(BP)), $\Re_3 = \Re$(W(BP), $\propto$-C-inputs, CSS(BP)), $\Re_4 = \Re$(ISS(BP), $\propto$-information, CSS(BP)), $\Re_5 = \Re$(CSS(BP), $\propto$-support, ISS(BP)), $\Re_6 = \Re$(ISS(BP), $\propto$-I-outputs, W(BP)), $\Re_7 = \Re$(W(BP), $\propto$-I-inputs, ISS(BP)), $\Re_8 = \Re$(OSS(BP), $\propto$-data, ISS(BP)), and $\Re_9 = \Re$(ISS(BP), $\propto$-support, OSS(BP)), $\Re_{10} = \Re$(W(BP), $\propto$-O-inputs, OSS(BP)) and $\Re_{11} = \Re$(OSS(BP), $\propto$-O-Work, W(BP)). Also, it must be noted that condition (iii) of the general definition of *system-II* is also fulfilled.

Auxiliary Definition O-1.2.2. The *management subsystem* X1 of an organization X, is a system-II $S_{II}(X1)$, that contains at least one *general system* $S_G(X1.1)$ of type *business process*.

Auxiliary Definition O-1.2.2. The *productive subsystem* X2 of an organization X, is a a system-II $S_{II}(X2)$, that contains at least one *general system* $S_G(X2.1)$ of type *business process*.

Figure 6: Diagram of the system organization using business process subsystems

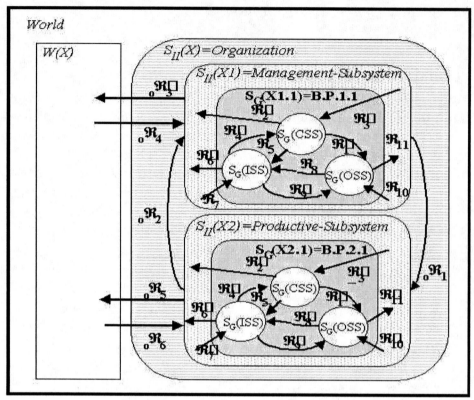

These previous formal definitions of *organization* and *business process* are illustrated in Figure 6. In it, we can observe that an *organization* has the two *subsystems* called *management* and *productive,* respectively. Both *subsystems* perform the functions posed by Negroe & Gelman (1981) based on features of Cybernetics Theory. *Management subsystem* has the responsibility to plan the goals of the system, make managerial decisions and control the *productive subsystem.* In turn, it has the responsibility to perform the main system's work: a design, a product, a service, etc. *Item relations* in the *set relation* $\Re_{s_1}(X) = \{$ $_o\Re_1, _o\Re_2, _o\Re_3, _o\Re_4\}$ among both *subsystems* account for the control actions performed from *management subsystem* to the *productive subsystem,* i.e. $_o\Re_1$, and information actions in the inverse way, i.e. $_o\Re_2$. The rest of item-relations, i.e., $_o\Re_3, _o\Re_4$, account for the actions performed by both *subsystems* toward its *environment* W(X) and from it toward the *system.*

Figure 6 also shows that *management* and *productive subsystems* have at least *one subsystem* of type *business process.* For example, in the *management subsystem* $S_{II}(X1)$, *the system* $S_G(X1.1)$ accounts for that. In an informal way, an *organization* is a set of *business process* performed into the two main *subsystems*: the *management* and the *productive*. Now, we can arrive at the formalization of the term *IS*, the core idea of this study.

Formalization of the Concept of *Information Systems*

Definition I-1-A. An *Information Systems IS* is a *general system* denominated as $S_G(IS)$, which fulfills the following conditions: (i) it is part of a *business process system* $S_{II}(BP)$ and corresponds to the Information Subsystem ISS(BP) of it; (ii) it has at least four subsystems of general type— S_G(Technology), S_G(Procedures), S_G(Information Workers) and S_G(Information Resources) denominated as $S_G(T)$, $S_G(P)$, and $S_G(IW)$ and $S_G(IR)$; (iii) it has at least the following *set relation* $\Re_{S1}(IS) = \{_I\Re_1, _I\Re_{2...I}\Re_{10}\}$, where $_I\Re_1 = \Re(S_G(P) \propto\text{-procedures}, S_G(IW))$, $_I\Re_2 = \Re(S_G(T) \propto\text{-applications}, S_G(IW))$, $_I\Re_3 = \Re(S_G(IW) \propto\text{-user-actions}, S_G(T))$, $_I\Re_4 = \Re(S_G(IW), \propto\text{-information}, S_G(CSS))$, $_I\Re_5 = \Re(S_G(T), \propto\text{-support}, S_G(OSS))$, $_I\Re_6 = \Re(S_G(T), \propto\text{-T-outputs}, W(IS))$, $_I\Re_7 = \Re(W(IS), \propto\text{-T-inputs}, S_G(T))$, $_I\Re_8 = \Re(S_G(OSS), \propto\text{-data}, S_G(T))$, $_I\Re_9 = \Re((S_G(T), \propto\text{-accesses}, S_G(IR))$ and $_I\Re_{10}$

Figure 7: Diagram of an information systems and its suprasystem and environment

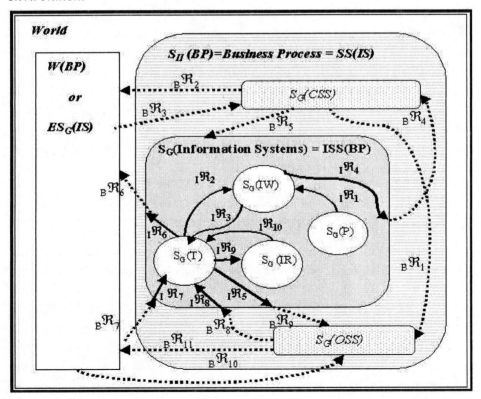

$= \Re((S_G(IR), \propto\text{-info-delivering}, S_G(T)))$.

Because an IS is considered a *general system* that can be conceptualized as *system-II*, it must be noted that condition (iii) of the general definition of *system-II* is also fulfilled.

Figure 7 presents a graphical interpretation of this definition. In this figure, the IS is presented into its *suprasystem*: a *business process*. The definition posed indicates that in order to formally conceptualize an *IS* as a *system*, it must also be considered a part of a larger *system*, i.e., a *business process system*, that, in turn, is the *suprasystem* of the *IS* denoted as SS(IS). Also, in Figure 7, are presented the other *subsystems* that are part of the SS(IS), as well as their *item relations* denominated as $_B\Re_{1, B}\Re_{2...B}\Re_{11}$. They are necessary to understand the output actions of the *system IS*, and therefore, its role in the larger *system* to which it belongs. Goals of the *system IS* can be specified for using a definition of the term *IS as system-I*, through the definition of its attributes.

However, this aim is out of the scope of this work and will be part of further research recommended. It must be noted, in Figure 7 that some *item relations* of the *system IS*, when they go into or go out of the *system*, they become in *item relations* accounted for in the *system business process*. For example, the *item relations* $_I\Re_4$ and $_I\Re_5$ that belong to the *system IS*, when they go out, become part of the *item relations* $_B\Re_4$ and $_B\Re_9$ of the *system BP*. In turn, the item-relation $_B\Re_8$ of the system BP, when it goes into the *system IS*, becomes part of the *item relation* $_I\Re_8$. The ten *item relations* $_I\Re_{1, I}\Re_{2, ..., I}\Re_{10}$, account for the actions performed among the minimal components of an *IS*. As the same way, those informal definitions, the component of *Information Resources*, is considered an independent component from *Technology*. Also, direct users, called *Information Workers*, and *Procedures*, are considered, as well as in previous informal definitions analyzed. Hence, we have posed a formal definition of the term *Information System*, based in a formal definition of *system*. In next section, we will discuss the potential uses of it.

DISCUSSION

The formal definition of *IS* posed offers a flexible framework to model and specify an *Information System* in the level of detail demanded by the researchers or practitioners. The term *IS*, defined as a *system*, allows us to use the previous systemic definitions and postulates in order to study the phenomenon from a different optical. For example, the systemic properties of *organization* and hierarchy, mapped into the concept of *IS*, help to resolve the "Siamese twin problem" stated by Alter (2001, pp. 30–31) about the fallacy to study the *Information Systems* without studying the *Work System,* in that formerly it is included. *Hierarchy* property and *expansionism* approach, prevent us from studying the *IS* in an isolated way, and they obligate us to observe the phenomenon of an *IS*, included in a larger system, i.e., the *Business Process System* or Alter's *Work System* concept. We claim, in agreement with the Synthetic Thinking, that the behavior of any system only can be understood, when its role that it plays in its *suprasystem* is considered. For that, the formal definition posed in this study establishes in its first condition (i) that any *IS* is a *subsystem* of another.

We claim also, that our formal definition offers a flexible framework to fit previous definitions of the term *IS*. We will analyze two examples of them: an informal definition (Hoffer et al., 1996, p. 8) and a semiformal (Alter, 2001, pp. 21–23). Hoffer's et al. definition of *IS* accounts for software application, support software, hardware, document and training materials, controls, job roles and people that use the software application. These components are considered by the posed formal definition of *IS*, in the following way: the *subsystem* S_G(Technology) accounts for software support and hardware; the *subsystem* S_G(Procedures) accounts for document, training materials and controls; the *subsystem* S_G(Information Workers) accounts for people that uses the software application.

Furthermore, some *item relations* from the formal definition are useful to model, the way that these subsystems perform actions to make the components work as a *system*. For example, Hoffer et al's definition makes mention to the components: job roles and software applications. In this case, the first feature can be specified through the *item relation* $_1\Re_3 = \Re(S_G(IW), \propto\text{-user-actions}, S_G(T))$, where it accounts for the different patterns of actions that define the roles of direct users or *Information Workers*. Furthermore, even though the current definition is not developed totally in the study reported here, this *subsystem*, i.e., S_G(Information Workers), according to its definition of *general-system*, can be modeled as well a *system-II* as a *system-I*. Therefore, from definitions 8 and 9, to specify the job roles potentially performed by people in an IS, the S_G(Information Workers) can be modeled as a *system-I* and can define these features, i.e., the job roles, as system's attributes $B(IW) = \{_{IW}\beta_1, _{IW}\beta_2,...\}$, if they are considered as nouns or as system's events $E(IW) = \{_{IW}\varepsilon_1, _{IW}\varepsilon2, ...\}$, if they are considered as verbs. Hoffer et al's definition of *IS*, does not account for the Information component per se. It could be considered as the main output of the system in Hoffer's et al definition. In our formal definition posed, this component is modeled as a subsystem of general type denoted as S_G(Information Resources). And as pointed out for the component S_G(Information Workers), the S_G(Information Resources) can be modeled as a *system-I* and specify *system's attributes* $B(IR) = \{_{IR}\beta_1, _{IR}\beta_2,...\}$, such as quality, clarity, accuracy, accessibility, appropriateness, among others (Burch, Strater & Grudnitski, 1979).

In turn, Alter's framework defines the term *IS* through the concept of Work Systems (Alter, 2001, p. 15). This definition is one of the most comprehensive definitions reported at present. Alter states (2001, p. 14) that "Information Systems (and projects) are work systems on their own right since they consist of human participants, and/or machines performing a business process using information, technology, and other resources to produce products and/or services to internal or external customers."

However, as reviewed in the previous section, Alter's framework used partially systemic principles and present ambiguity in delimit appropriately an *IS* from its *environment*. Furthermore, this ambiguity brings the problem of distinguishing the *IS* from its *suprasystem*: the Work Systems. In Alter's framework, the overlap is possible (Alter, 2001, p. 30), which is not in agreement with the principles of *Systems Theory*. However, Alter's framework accounts for critical components in any *IS*. We claim that this model, fits also in our formal model of *IS*. The *subsystems* S_G(Technology), S_G(Information Workers) and S_G(Information Resources), can be mapped directly to the Alter's components participants, information and technology. The SS(IS), i.e., the suprasystem of the *IS* for that it justifies its existence and role according to *Systems Theory* principles, accounts for the business process noted in Alter's framework.

It must be noted that while in the semiformal model of *IS*, the *business process* is seen as an independent component it could sometimes be overlapped on the IS. In the formal model is clearly established that a *business process* has two *subsystems* directly associated with it: the control and the operational *subsystems*. In the former, all the management activities and tasks performed in *the business process* can be specified, as well as the operational level in this specific business process. This definition avoids the ambiguity to overlap Work Systems with *IS*. Products and services made in the business process, can specified through the *item-relations* $\Re_2 = \Re(CSS(BP), \propto\text{-C-outputs}, W(BP))$ and $\Re_{11} = \Re(OSS(BP), \propto\text{-O-Work}, W(BP))$.

Furthermore, these *item relations* let us distinguish outputs from control and managerial activities performed in the *business process*, from those generated at the level of the operational *subsystems* of it. It must be noted that the current model posed does not use parameters of $\propto$-actions, but it can be extended in further research to consider the flow of materials, information and energy (Gich, 1981), and therefore, to specify attributes of the products and services generated by the *business process*.

Internal and external customers of the *business process*, i.e., people that receive the products or services generated by the *business process* supported by the *IS*, are counted in the formal model through the specification of subsystems of the environment W(BP) of the *business process* considered. If the formal model does not establish them explicitly, include them. Similarly, attributes of the Information component can be specified, and the formal model lets us specify attributes of the interests of clients, i.e., knowledge, aptitudes, beliefs, etc. Finally, with regard to the environmental component presented separately in the Alter's framework, i.e., context and infrastructure, the formal model allows for the model of social, technical and political features, through the specification of *attributes* and *events* assigned to subsystems in the *system's environment* W(BP). For example, soft features such as top management support, environmental hostility and dynamism and organizational climate, once the *systems'* modeler can identify how to measure them, are easily assigned to subsystems' *attributes* of W(BP).

In summary, we claim that the formal definition of the term IS, developed from the formal definition and principles of *systems*, lets us (i) avoid ambiguity from informal definitions, (ii) account for practically all informal definitions reported at the date of this study, (iii) specify and customize a structure of the concept *IS* with the level of detail demanded by the modelers, and (iv) build complex systemic models of organizations that uses *IS*.

In the next section, we will conclude with the main remarks of this chapter, and we will present the limitations and suggestions for further research in this direction— the formalization of the term *IS*.

CONCLUSION

We have reviewed the principles of *Systems Approach* and showed that these should be considered theoretical foundations for studying *Information Systems*, because this phenomenon is a *system*. After reviewing main philosophical doctrines of *Systems Approach*, properties of systems were analyzed. Then, a formal definition of the term *system* was posed, based strongly on a previous work developed by Gelman & García (1989). Later, we claimed that the literature of *Information Systems* has failed to report a comprehensive and formal definition of the term *Information System*. Comprehensive definitions available are informal or semiformal Alter (1999, 2000, 2001) and the few formal definitions (Wand & Weber, 1998, 1990) are limited in their abilities to capture the essence of core principles of *systems* (Sachs, 1976).

These definitions were analyzed, and their limitations of vagueness and ambiguity were accounted for in the former case. In turn, were identified the limitations of a reduced scope for capturing the main primary intuitions widely agreed upon in the field of *Systems* for the latter case. Next, using the formal definition of the term *system*, a formal definition of the term *Information Systems* was developed and it was shown that its definition must be related to the larger whole to which it belongs. In this sense, the definition posed establishes that an *Information System* is a subsystem of a larger system called *Business Process*, that in turn, belongs a larger whole called *Organization*. With this definition, we showed that previous definitions can be explained formally. Also, it was shown that the formal definition is a base for any *systems* modeler who specifies a more detailed structure of an *Information Systems*, through the utilization of the concepts of *system-I*, *system-II* and *general system*, and the definitions of *attributes*, *events* and *item relations*.

Finally, we claim that the formal definition posed in this study let us (i) avoid ambiguity from informal definitions, (ii) account for practically all informal definitions, (iii) specify and customize a structure of the concept of *Information Systems* with the level of detail demanded by the modelers, and (iv) build complex systemic models of organizations that use *Information Systems*. This definition, due to its formal foundation, offers a nontrivial way to understand an *Information System*. However, we consider that further research must address empirical studies of practical cases to assess the strengths and weaknesses of the usaging it as a praxis tool. From an academician perspective, the field of *Information Systems* requires the formalizations of core concepts, and this work is a forward step in this direction.

ACKNOWLEDGMENTS

The main author thanks Professors Ovsei Gelman and Francisco Cervantes for sharing their experience and knowledge in the Systems field and their valuable guidelines to structure this chapter. Also, the main author thanks Professors Marcelo Mejia and Alfredo Weitzenfeld for improving and validating the content of this paper from the expertise of their fields of study, Computer Sciences and Software Engineering, respectively. Finally, all the authors give thanks to anonymous reviewers for their valuable insights.

ENDNOTES

1   The Industrial Revolution is proof of it.
2   The original text of Gelman & García is in the Spanish language. Translation is adapted.
3   Please note that this definition covers more essential properties than those that refer only to sets of interconnected parts.
4   All of these references were taken from the work of Gelman & García (1989).
5   In particular, the work of Gelman & García (1989) offers an excellent and detailed review of these definitions and a nonformal definition of the term *system*, in addition to the formal and mathematical-based definition.
6   Some systemic disciplines can offer useful soft modeling tools as Systems

Dynamics, but the translation of soft relationships will still require a strong validation process of them.

REFERENCES

Ackoff, R. (1960). Systems, organizations and interdisciplinary research. *General System Yearbook, 5*, 1–8.

Ackoff, R. (1971). Towards a system of systems concepts. *Management Science, 17*(11), July, 661–671.

Ackoff, R. (1973). Science in the systems age: Beyond IE, OR and MS. *Operations Research, 21*(3), 661–671.

Ackoff, R. (1976). *The aging of a young profession: Operations research.* Philadelphia, PA: University of Pennsylvania.

Ackoff, R. and Emery, F. (1972). *On purposeful systems.* Chicago, IL: Aldine Atherton.

Alter, S. (1996). *Information systems: A management perspective.* New York: Prentice Hall.

Alter, S. (2000). A general yet useful theory of information systems. *Proceedings of the AMCIS Conference,* Long Beach, CA, August.

Alter, S. (2001, Apr). Are the fundamental concepts of information systems mostly about work systems? *CAIS, 5*(11). Retrieved from the World Wide Web: http://www.ais-net.org.

Angyal, A. (1941). A logic of systems. Referenced in Emery, F.E. (1969). *Systems thinking.* Middlesex, England: Penguin Books.

Arbib, M. and Manes, E. (1974). Foundations of systems theory: Decomposable systems. *Automatica, 10.* England: Pergamon Press.

Bagh, C. (1990). Major systems theories through the world. *Behavioral Science, 35*(2), April, 79.

Barkhi, R. and Sheetz, (2001). The state of theoretical diversity of information systems. *Communication of the Association for Information Systems, 7*(6). Retrieved from the World Wide Web: http:www.ais-net.org.

Bertalanffy, L. (1968). *General systems theory: Foundations, development, applications.* New York: Braziller.

Bunge, M. (1977). *Treatise on basic philosophy: Vol. 3: Ontology I: The furniture of the world.* Boston, MA: Reidel.

Bunge, M. (1979). *Treatise on basic philosophy: Vol. 4: Ontology II: A world of systems.* Boston, MA: Reidel.

Burch, J. G. and Grudnitski, G. (1989). *Design of Information Systems.* New York: John Wiley & Sons. Checkland, P. (1981). *Systems Thinking, Systems Practice.* New York: John Wiley & Sons.

Checkland, P. (2000). Soft systems methodology: A thirty year retrospective. *Systems Research and Behavioral Science, 17*(11), S11–S58.

Churchman, W. (1971). *The design of inquiring systems: Basic concepts of systems and organizations*. Basic Books, referenced in Courtney et al. (1998).

Courtney, J., Croasdell, D. and Paradice, D. (1998). Inquiring organizations. *Foundations of information systems*. Retrieved from the World Wide Web: http:www.cba.ub.edu/~parks/fis/inqorg.htm.

Davis, G. and Olson, M. (1985). *Management information systems*. New York: McGraw-Hill.

Eom, B. S. (2000). The contributions of system science to the development of decision support systems subspecialities: An empirical investigation. *Systems Research and Behavioral Science, 17*(2), March, 117.

Farohoomand, A. and Drury, D. (2001). Diversity and scientific progress in the information systems discipline. *Communication of the Association for Information Systems, 5*(12). Retrieved from the World Wide Web: http://www.ais-net.org.

Gelman, O. and García, J. I. (1989). Formulation and axiomatization of the concept of general system. *Booklet of the Operational Research Mexican Society*. Mexico.

Gigch, van J.P. (1979). Applied general system theory. Harper and Row.

Gigch, van J. P. and Le Moigne, J. L. (1989). A paradigmatic approach to the discipline of information systems. *Behavioral Science, 34*(2), 128–150.

Hirschheim, R., Iivari, J. and Klein, H. (1998). A comparison of five alternative approaches to information systems development. *Foundations of information systems*. Retrieved from the World Wide Web: http://www.cba.uh.edu/~parks/fis/sad5.htm.

Hoffer, J., George, J. F. and Valachi, J. S. (1996). *Modern systems analysis and design*. Menlo Park, CA: Benjamin/Cummings.

Kalman, Falb, and Arbib. (1969). *Topics in mathematical systems theory*. New York: McGraw-Hill.

Klir, G. (1968). An approach to general systems theory. *General systems yearbook, 13*, 13–20.

Mason, R. and Mitroff, I. (1973). A program for research on management information systems. *Management Science, 19*(5), January, 475-487.

McLeod, R. (1997). *Management Information Systems*. Englewood Cliffs, NJ: Prentice-Hall.

McNurlin, B. C. and Sprague, R. H. (1998). *Information Systems Management in Practice*. Englewood Cliffs, NJ: Prentice Hall.

Mesarovic, M. D. (1964). *Views on general systems theory*. New York: John Wiley & Sons.

Mesarovic, M. D. and Takahara, Y. (1975). *General systems theory*. New York: Academic Press.

Mora, M. and Cervantes, F. (1999). The role of IS/IT in the organizations for the next decade: Toward a conceptual grounded theory. *Proceedings of the 10th IRMA Conference*, 919–923, Hershey, PA, May.

Negroe, G. and Gelman, O. (1981). *Papel de la planeación en el proceso de conducción.* Master thesis report, Institute of Engineering, México: UNAM Press (in the Spanish Language).

Nolan, R. (1991). The strategic potential of information technology. *Financial Executive,* 25–27, July–August.

Nonaka, I. (1991). The knowledge-creating company. *Harvard Business Review,* 96–104, November–December.

Paton, G. (1997). Information system as intellectual construct–its only valid form. *Systems Research and Behavioral Science, 14*(1), 67–72.

Rapoport, A. (1968). Systems analysis: General systems theory. *International encyclopedia of the social sciences, 15.* New York: McMillan and Free Press.

Richards, L. and Gupta, S. (1985). The systems approach in information society: Reconsideration. *Journal of the Operational Research Society, 36*(9), 833–843, referenced in Xu (2000).

Sachs, W. M. (1976). Toward formal foundations of teleological systems science. *General Systems, 21,* 145–153.

Saraswat, P. (1988). A historical perspective on the philosophical foundations of information systems. Retrieved from *Foundations of Information Systems* on the World Wide Web: http://www.cba.uh.edu/~parks/fis/saraswat3.htm.

Satzinger, J. W., Jackson, R. B. and Burd, D. S. (2000). *Systems analysis and design in a changing world.* Cambridge, MA: Course Technology.

Senn, J. A. (1989). *Analysis and design of information systems.* New York: McGraw-Hill.

Singer, E. (1959). Experience and reflection. In Churchman, W. (Ed.), Philadelphia: University of Pennsylvania Press, referenced in R. Ackoff (1973).

Trist, E. L. (1970). Organization et systeme: Quelques remarques theoriques se rapportant plus particuliereise aux recherches d'Andras Angyal. *Revue Francaise de Sociologie,* 11–12.

Wand, Y. and Weber, R. (1990). An ontological model of an information systems. *IEEE Transactions on Software Enginering,* 16(11), November, 1282-1292.

Wand, Y. and Woo, C. (1991). An approach to formalizing organizational open systems concepts. Retrieved from *ACM Digital Library* on the World Wide Web: http://www.acm.org.

Wilson, B. (1984). *Systems: Concepts, methodologies and applications.* New York: John Wiley & Sons.

Xu, L. (2000). The contributions of system science to information systems research. *Systems Research and Behavioral Science,* 13(12), March, 105.

Yourdon, E. (1980). *Modern Structured Analysis.* Englewood Cliffs, NJ: Yourdon Press.

Zadeh, L. and Polak, E. (Eds). (1969). *Systems Theory.* New York: McGraw-Hill.

Section II

Systemic Theoretical Models in Information Technology/Information Systems

Chapter II

Technological Frames Recursive Construction Approach: A Systemic Theory for Information Technology Incorporation in Organizations

Jeimy J. Cano
Newport University—Colombia Branch, Colombia

ABSTRACT

Information Technology, during the last few years, has turned into a determining factor of modern organization development. In this line, a lot of studies have been conducted aimed at explaining the possible relations to company's productivity and competitiveness, which to some extent, leads to causal conclusions, casting structural individual relationships into a background in the organizational tasks. In this direction, social researchers have incorporated valuable elements to understand the individuals' position in the construction of technological artifacts and the comprehension thereof in the organization scope. Such research led to the statement of the concept of so-called technological frames, which explicitly incorporate an individual's social and cognitive distinctions around the technological context in a community. Subsequent studies, however, fail to delve into the way such frames are constructed or influenced in a significant extent by the companies's tasks or technology incorporations. For such reasons, this paper, based on the assumption that Information Technology is the result of individuals' social interaction, is intended to explore the benefits of individuals' structural relations understanding in Information Technology incorporation to integrate the findings of causal research and systemic elements (the study of relations), focusing on information technology understanding in the organizational tasks.

INTRODUCTION

During the last two decades, Information Systems and Information Technology (IS/IT) have turned into the key factor of organizational development (Brancheau, Jan, & Wetherbe, 1996). This situation has been evidenced through a significant number of successful and nonsuccessful exercises (Ginzberg, 1981) made in several different organization around the world by using Information Technology (IT), all of which, based on the belief that organizations are outperforming in the business world, are just those using in a right way the state-of-the-art technologies (Niederman, Brancheau, & Wetherbe, 1991). It is, therefore, necessary to identify the elements allowing for diagnosing and stating the recommendation to incorporate information technology into the organizations, to successfully develop competitiveness and productivity elements. (Mata, Fuerst, & Barney, 1995) in the business functions context.

In this direction, investigations focused on understanding those aspects allowing the proper technology to support business functions to incorporated, and hence, to bring about the dynamics to make easy organization productivity easier have been conducted (Henderson & Sifonis, 1988; Brown, 1997; S'Tnan, 1991; Mata, Fuerst & Barney, 1995).

An overview of studies conducted to identify the factors leading to IT successful implementation and use in the organizations, shows that, usually, they make reference to top management directives concerning technology, alignment of the business strategic plan to the IT plan, market strategies development using IT, frequency of technology use, and process improvement by computer science (Henderson & Sifonis, 1988; Brown, 1997; Weil & Olson, 1989; Goodhue, 1995; Andrew & Ciborra, 1996), which involve an understanding of the business linked to information technology.

While this IT vision is a sine qua non condition to develop new options in the organizational business context, it is also an essential part of an individual's perspective vision about technology, because through the individuals IS/IT will make easy the actions and possibilities usually devised and planned by top management.

Therefore, an individual's vision about technological phenomenon provides the strategies devised by organizational top management with meaning. Each individual establishes some way to observe, understand, and use technology, and such ways have been re-created in literature as a technological frame. This term comes from a revision of technological phenomenon in the social scope (Bijker, Hughes, & Pinch, 1987; Barley, 1990), whereby the common perspective and technology social construction are analyzed.

Gash and Orlikowsky (1994) use the term *technological frames* to identify the subset of existing organizational frames concerning knowledge, expectations, and assumptions the members of the organization use to understand technology. This includes the nature and role of technology by itself, and the specific conditions, applications, and consequences of technology in specific contexts.

This perspective offers an additional manner with which to understand an individual's expectations, assumptions, and knowledge about technology purpose, context, significance, and role as a factor complementary to business strategies supported by technology.

As Pinch and Bijker (1987) argue, inasmuch as technology is a technological artifact, constructed and interpreted by multiple social groups, answers and interpretations will vary and are arranged according to social groups in function to their context, power, base-knowledge, and artifact. That is, technology takes up a connotation to the social group in function of its shape or image. (Morgan, 1996), relying on the fact that community is supported by systems of shared meaning, resulting from individuals interrelationships and surrounding environment.

Therefore, this paper intends to explore social and strategic implications when technological frames constructions are acknowledged in a recursive manner as a complementary way to understand incorporation processes or information technology use in the organizations, by challenging and reviewing management's traditional ideas, which without being aware of, or knowing the individual's work, have failed to notice the significant change of individual and social relationships as a result of IT usage.

Below, some reflections about technological frames constructions are given starting with the introduction of duality and dualism terms in the information technology context, followed by the introduction of technological frames and the eigenbehavior, this latter coined by cybernetic theorists (Mateus, 1996; Reyes, 1996; Espejo, 1996), and concluding with the proposal for *technological frames recursive construction* as a way to understand recurrent reconstruction of relationships and conversions relative to technology in the social environment, thus offering a new way to establish and understand technology and its relations to the organization.

DUALISM AND DUALITIES: INDIVIDUAL AND TECHNOLOGY

Paraphrasing Morgan (1996, p. 119) when referring to organization culture, being faced with technology means to disclose the worldly as well as the smartest aspects of the reality construction process. Under technology influence, organizations and individuals become investment cores, bringing about expenses and profits, and at the same time, the source of creativeness as requirements re-creating organization reality.

By virtue of the above, a possible paradox is posed, whereby technological phenomenon by itself is dependent on those people noticing or using it. That is, by understanding technology as a technical possibility that operates a social reality, as a result of human acknowledgment in the same social context, we may understand that any such technology is not subordinated to, or constricted by, a process of acceptance and usage of technical elements, and by contrast, technology integrates tangible technical possibilities as a means for social systems construction.

That is, the institutions and individual actions world proposed by Giddens (1995), mirrors a complementary reality allowing to contextualize dualities around information technology making attempts to diminish a construction based on dualism (cause-effect), leading many researchers to antagonistic concepts that may be the consequence of their Cartesian vision of world associated to orthodoxy.

In order to make a more in-depth approach around the complementary process proposed by dualities, we will discuss the basic idea of *distinction* proposed by Spencer-Brown (1972). As human beings, we frequently elaborate distinctions. This is just one of the most important human activities; this is the means whereby we know surrounding world.

A distinction divides the world into two portions: *"This"* and *"That."* The object divided is taken out from its "background." To put it simply, a basic distinction may plot drawing a circle in any surface. The circle is made up of two sides, the one inside and the other outside. It is evident both sides are complementary, i.e., the one side specifies the other one, and conversely, one can say that the

Figure 1: Distinctions

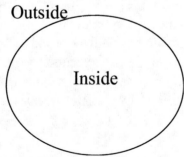

Outside

Inside

circle should not be that what it is, but in relation to both two sides (Reyes 1996, Chap.3).

An *indication* is built when looking at a side of the distinction. After establishing a distinction, we can choose to become concentrated in the (external or internal) environment of the system defined by distinction. In the first instance, we are considering the system as a simple entity with its properties and the study of its interrelations to the environment. In this direction, the system is seen as a set of inputs and outputs limited by the environment. This visions leads to the problem of system control (idem).

In the second instance, the properties of the system emerge from its component interaction with its environment, which is acknowledged as the origin of disturbances. The system has neither inputs nor outputs (idem).

Early description responds to the system presentation as a black box. In this way, system is described in accordance with the interaction means it has with the surrounding environment, which defines a set of inputs and transfer functions. The second description suggests a more appropriate way to understand stand-alone systems. It specifically concentrates on the internal natural coherence describing its constitutive interlinking elements. This view leads us to consider that future behavior of system is defined by the internal coherence of its relations, thus acknowledging external forces as disturbances potentially taken or not as such system (idem).

The above distinctions are complementary, and each define and discriminate the observer in the system under revision.

In this line of views, and in order to analyze these concept implications in technology incorporation process, an overview of such concepts will be made in the information technology (IT). Orlikowski (1992, 1991) states technology is created and changed by human action. This view suggests a complementary idea the researcher names technology duality. That is, actors working in any social context physically build technology, and technology is socially built through several different meanings they attach to their activities and the various features they emphasize and use.

If the above claims are true, the studies completed by individuals around the context of technology acceptance, usage, or usefulness (Dickinson, 1998; Brown, 1997) fail to acknowledge the effect of technological social construction making sense of the information technology use, because individual, in its social acting defines and builds the meaning of information technology. Otherwise, we would be feeding a dualism potentially and inexorably leading to opposing positions: the society and the individual.

In this connection, Orlikowski (1992) argues it is necessary to develop a constructive flexibility of technology design, use and construction, as a degree whereon users have incorporated into their (physical and/or social) constitution.

Such view constitutes an attribute of the relationships among human beings and technology, and in the same way, it states its influence on material artifact features (hardware, software), on individual characteristics, and on context characteristics (social relations, job allocation, resources location).

Individuals, as technology producers, are under the obligation to interpret technology in the social context. Individuals, in their relations to the others, establish ways allowing them to review and enhance their products, as a consequence of the indication at the social community inside that defines the technological phenomena as a property emerging from participants' relationships, as a response to a structural condition changing their acting to evolve and rework their interpretation about how the things are made. In the same way, the individual delivers meanings, which then are disseminated and established in the relations alongside the interlinking of all of the participants. Specifically, this interpretation establishes that technology emerges as a property of the community based on the several different relations built, rather than on specific use of technological artifacts implemented by the organization. This distinction draws our attention about the existence of an array of individual perceptions demanding to become established to turn technological incorporation into a natural process of the business social evolution rather than as a result of machine commands or digital devices.

In the same way, as Orlikowski (1992) suggests, technology defines the influence of individual's social role in the organization, leading to practices and actions bearing meaning only through organization players' relationships. Additionally, it is important to note that information technology, as a social product, fails to suggest an exclusive and static model, and instead, this property created and evolved in function of the relations defined by individuals in any community. This claim is supported in Maturana and Varela's (1980) works, according to which, organizations, as well as living beings, hold the capability of autoreproduction and self-conservation, i.e., they have the capacity to produce themselves through a closed relations system. Such closed relation defines the system objective, its identity as an organization, which becomes shaped in function of their relations.

In this context, information technology establishes and assigns variation models and organization reference expressions, thus integrating the IT environment, attempting to modify its actions around its needs and relations defined among individuals.

The above enables us to question that technology incorporation into the organizations is not a function only of physical (hardware, software) technology manifestations, but it is also an internal searching of the understanding of social doing allowing for the organization to understand and learn about its identity, as an opportunity to pursue a self-revision and understand its relations with the world.

All those ideas allow us to observe in more detail, that an individual, as making part of a dual (complementary) relation with technology, expresses its doing and thinking throughout the social reality, of which technology is not detached. That is, by knowing information technology as a social property emerging from an individual's action, we are faced with the organization identity attempting to evolve and understand its surrounding environment as part of an array of relations and templates that get transformed by themselves. Each individual, every relation among individuals, defines a technological action evidenced in the organization operations. In other words, every individual defines a way to face technology, such a way is shared and spread with others relations developing what Orlikowski and Gash (1994) call a technological frame. This concept will be reviewed below, integrated to the eigenbehavior as a preamble, to establish a recursive construction of technological frames in the individuals.

THE EIGENBEHAVIOR AND TECHNOLOGICAL FRAMES

Elements thus far proposed have questioned "Hegelian Dialectics," whereby a synthesis is achieved by contrasting the opposites: "Thesis and Antithesis," attempting to establish a complete and effective way to inquire about a situation, through dualities submersed in the concepts.

Autopoiesis theory (Maturana & Varela, 1980), encourages the understanding of transformation or evolution of living systems as a result of internal changes, provides a manner of exploring the way an organization or individual can influence the appearance or development of any change through an interacting cyclic model. That is, it is an invitation to think of circles or loops instead of lines, looking for substituting mechanical causality idea—A is the cause of B—to reciprocal—by suggesting A and B may be defined as the result of belonging to the same relations cyclic causality system (Morgan, 1996, p. 235).

In this connection, Heinz Von Foerster in 1977 (Mateus, 1996, p. 371) hypothesized the existence of solution of an indefinite recursive equation based on Jean Piaget's recursive structure that describes the amount of interactions between object and subject made by an observer. Specifically, the expression that initiates without an initial condition or starting point, tells us that a specific instance of an observation will be the result of an indefinite succession of cognitive operations. This cautions us about the existence of a chain of cognitive operations done in a while in the time that defines the observed objects. (Mateus, 1996, p. 371).

$$\text{Obs(t)} = \text{COORD (Obs(t-1))}$$

where COORD stands for a set of cognitive operations produced in a prior instant about an object (Obs).

In other words, for a cognitive operations succession, the structure of the object observed does not change and when this occurs, the object (Obs) exhibits its own behavior (*eigenbehavior*). That is, the eigenbehaviors are self-defined behaviors or self-referenced in the object structure via the operator COORD, which implies a complementary relation of closure between the eigenbehaviors and operator COORD: the one implies or defines the other one. (Mateus 1996, p.372)

The eigenbehaviors stand for the observable external manifestations of the array of cognitive operations developed, which is used to define autonomous behavior in cognitive systems through a closure of cognitive operations disclosing regular perception of the objects (idem).

According to the above, interactions of each individual in the organization in its cognitive domain define the organization. In other words, interactions have ascribed purposes and meanings, which have been constructed in the relations defined by each member in the organization. This allows us to observe that any community is structurally *closed* in the array of relations, and *open* to receive information from the environment, as a manner to integrate and acknowledge its identity in the business setting where the organization operates.

In any organization, as suggested by Espejo (1994, p. 205) and in line with the previous development about eigenbehaviors, this a complex network of interpersonal relationships with closure. In this connection, organization emerges when recurrent interactions of action coordination are produced between the participants, which brings about an order within the chaos. This situation shows the degree of self-organization generated inside the organization (Espejo 1994, 1996).

As noted, the above definition concentrates on the relations among the parties rather than in the parties, which allows for painstakingly analyzing the implications of the eigenbehaviors submersed in the individuals' relations to construct their social reality and an organizational systemic vision.

Specific, human and other (technological) resources account for the relations in the time and the specific context that define the organizational structure. That is, the organization is made starting from its relations between individuals and its resources instead of under authority lines defined and imposed by an external interpretation. The organization perceives itself through the actions with defined purposes in order to create a shared reality.

If such statements are true, in the same way the individuals create and share cognitive domains through their relationships in connection with information technology. As Orlikowski and Gash (1994) suggest, several different groups of any organization may hold different cognitive structures about technology, i.e., different *technological frames*.

Many social perception discussions are not focused on technology *per se*, rather they emphasize strategy, innovation, or change management. Orlikowski and Gash (1994) think it is useful, at least analytical guide interpretations about technology and its role in the organization. The *"Technological Frames"* term is used to identify the subset of institutional frames existing related to knowledge, expectations, and assumptions used by the organization members to understand technology. This includes, technology and the ideas the authors like to preserve in treating technological frames, and specially the latter meaning.

Technological frames hold a powerful effect on individual's expectations, assumptions, and knowledge about technology purpose, context, significance, and role, because, as earlier mentioned in the development of this chapter, technology is a social artifact integrated to individuals' chores to construct objectives, values, interests and time, establishing conscious or unconscious assumptions which are internalized by organizational roles, directly influencing the organization, and hence, each individual's interpretation of information technology.

Congruity notion is defined in technological frames as an alienation of frames in the key elements or categories. Congruity does not mean identical, but rather related in structure and contents. Congruity, in the technological frames, e.g., similar expectations about technology role in the business process, the nature of technology use, or the type and frequency of support and maintenance. Incongruity involves major disparities in expectations, assumptions or knowledge about technology key aspects. For instance, an incongruent frame apparently appears when managers intend for the technology to transform the way the deals are made, and users believe technology only will increase the speed and control over their work (Orlikowski & Gash, 1994).

Gash and Orlikowski (1994) believe in the organizations where incongruities in technological frames appear, and there exists a high possibility to experience difficulties and conflicts around the technology development, implementation, and use. When authors review some cases, the findings showed significant gaps in communications, lack of users' participation in the design process, and a potential project interruption (idem).

The Orlikowski and Gash proposal, discusses the concepts shared about technology as an interesting means to link and maintain the follow-up of information technology's influence on organizations. This bearing in mind, it is possible to set the elements allowing us to acknowledge a cognitive inertia to limit organization adaptive process to the surrounding environment where business operates.

While this research contributes key elements to understand information technology in the organization, a more in-depth contention is necessary of the problems posed by information technology. In such connection, inputs by Orlikowski and Gash (1994) require painstaking discussion about the way the frames constructed around technology agree or disagree, and examination of the incongruent areas among the key players in the organization.

Additionally, researchers fail to offer the way to review technological frames, construction process and any way or approach to identify the organization technological frames and in the same way assess the congruence thereof a way to lift up a diagnosis of technological incorporation process.

The following section, a recursive construction of technological frames is proposed as a way to understand the process whereby organization's technological understanding is constructed, based on the eigenbehavior understanding, as described in this section, and the complexity concept assumed by cybernetic theorists.

A RECURSIVE INTERPRETATION OF TECHNOLOGICAL FRAMES

In our daily tasks, we usually associate complexity with difficulty. In such a connection, we claim some is complex when we are faced with difficulty to understand or explain it. If we fall back on the Oxford Dictionary to find a more accurate definition of complexity, there appears that something is complex when made up by a closed array of linked parts. Therefore, complexity relates to our ability to discriminate the part some object is made of. In clearer words, *complexity* is defined as the number of distinctions we can make in any situation (Reyes 1996, chap.5).

And then, complexity is not an intrinsic property of any situation. As observers, we see several different complexities in any situation, depending on causality between its associated purposes and the process construction in its action domain (idem).

This bearing in mind, it is important to acknowledge individual complexity as a key factor in connection with information technology incorporation, inasmuch as are just the individuals who acknowledge such incorporation and usually integrate it with the individual when creating the organization.

In this context, the strategy to analyze and promote individual's complexity development around technology, makes sense, because this way, it is possible to ease the process of technology incorporation, or otherwise, identify the would-be failures potentially resulting in the organization.

Information technology, as a social phenomenon emerging from individuals, establishes a series of distinctions, which have to be negotiated and identified to reach an adequate array of agreements around IT. Every participant establishes and acknowledges in its daily work, several different manners to understand technology, allowing for complexity to astringe or increase.

In this connection, each individual builds a specific way to understand technology, by shaping a technological frame in the specific context of the organization work. This situation suggests the organization, as an entity shaped from the array of relations among individuals who define the community identity, has also a corporate technological frame emerging from the understanding and relations of the several different individual technological frames.

Should this be a correct assumption, it will be possible to identify a way whereby organizations understand and use technology, not just in an excluding manner, individual–organization, and rather as an emergent process appearing or emerging from technological frames shared by individuals. That is, we could say that:

$$MT(t) = MT(t-1)$$

Technological frame in the moment t, $(MT(t))$, is the result of the acknowledgment of interaction prior to $(t-1)$ from other individuals. Specifically, we could say that the technological frame of a set of individuals emerges or appears at a higher level $MT(t)$ thanks to prior construction of other players who share their technological understanding associated with a specific context.

So to speak, there exists an eigenbehavior associated with technology object, which is built by each individual recurrent interaction.

$$MT(t) = MT(MT(...MT(t-1))..)$$

Each technological frame defines the technology interpretation at the individual level related as well to others' interpretation, thus bringing about again the possibility of technological understanding, and so on, until establishing a shared vision as the result of the structural individual relations.

This interpretation suggests that it does not suffice to know to what extent technology is used to understand technological incorporation processes (causal relations), but it is also necessary to take into account the complexity developed by each participant around the technological topic, in order to acknowledge the several different distinctions (structural relations) allowing to come to terms in the several different technological frames identities, to decrease incongruities and increase the possibilities of business knowledge and understanding through reflection about information technology.

The proposal stated shows a facet incorporating early research related to the use, resistance to changes, and quality of information technology use (Brown, 1997; Dickinson, 1998; Malhotra, 1998), and it delves into revision of technological understanding construction, making up an integrated frame which, through individual relations, establishes a structure with closure (i.e., defines an identity of players' relationships) around technological phenomenon, thus offering a way to review technology not just as a phenomenon external to the organization, but rather as the result of a recurrent revision of individual technological frames, which limit and define the institutional technological frame.

That is, individuals as information technology depositaries, developers, and users set out organization technological paradigms according to the understanding or technological frame identified in any given time, looking for, through their daily work, a way to evolve in the social context, and hence, to understand technology in each of their activities.

DISCUSSION

This paper proposes a different way to confront information technology incorporation into the organizations. The proposal of a recursive way for technological frames construction invites us to devote more time to identify the several different individuals' about technology as a way to line up and set out the more adequate schemes to incorporate technology into the companies.

Recursive interpretation establishes, in a natural way, that it is necessary to an understanding of technology in the business context and a revision and understanding of the way the individuals in their daily work, modify and establish distinctions leading to the technological artifact generations which rework their way to become related to the several different aspects of their tasks. In this connection, organizations, leaving out these types of issues usually challenge potential problems of rejection or resistance to change, because the new technological elements pose relation structures, most of which are in conflict with the business hierarchical relations, thus bringing about social incongruities rather than alignment with the business purposes.

Therefore, technological incorporation processes have to consider, within their strategic context, as a sufficient and sine qua non condition, the identification of the business existing technological frame, allowing for the organization to establish the technological supporting alignments proposed by the company in order to review the current status of technology understanding and the way technology influences the processes. For such purposes, research developed in Colombia (Cano, 2000), based on a theoretical approach that sets out an array of technological frame templates, reviewed in the light of the organizational work context, offers an array of technological strategies lined up with the current technological understanding. In the same way, such a method provides the organization with guidelines to promote the evolution of the existing technological frame toward the desired frame, warning about the structural changes required to obtain such a frame. Investigation results are focused to verify the advantages of technological frames understanding in a recursive way at individual and corporate levels, providing a new proposal of strategic alignment supported on technology to bring about competitive advantage in the organizations.

Should identification of the existing technological frame be considered within organization planning and strategic direction processes, investment in technological artifacts (software and hardware) could become concentrated in those aspects or the organizational work proposed by individuals, materializing the expectations of technological understanding. Possibly increasing operations effectiveness of the several different businesses, because technology responds to social understanding of its work.

This acknowledgment leads, in a collateral manner, to rethink conversations and communication structures among individuals and business purposes, providing the corporate strategies with meaning, and importantly, guidance and direction to individual's tasks in each of their roles.

According to the above considerations, recursive interpretation of technological frames poses a new view to acknowledge technology within the social context, making attempts to more deeply understand the issues related to use and incorporation of information technology into the several different individuals' relations and the complexity developed around the technological artifacts, thus paving the way toward productivity and competitive advantage, claimed in the promise made by information technology during the last few decades.

REFERENCES

Andrew, R. & Ciborra, C. (1996). Organisational learning and core capabilities development: The role of IT. *Journal of Strategic Information Systems*, 5(1), 111–127.

Barley, S. (1990). Technology as an occasion for structuring: Evidence from observation of CT Scanners and the social order of radiology departments. *Administrative Science Quarterly*, (31), 78–108.

Bijker, W., Hughes, T. & Pinch, T. (1987). *The social construction of technological systems*. Cambridge, MA: MIT Press.

Bostrom, R. P. & Heinen, J. S. (1977). MIS problems and failures: A socio-technical perspective, Part 1. The causes. *MIS Quarterly*, 1(3), 17–32.

Brancheau, J. C., Jan, B. D. & Wetherbe, J. C. (1996). Key issues in information systems management: A shift toward technology infrastructure. *MIS Quarterly*, 20(2).

Brown, S. (1997). *Knowledge, communications and progressive use of information technology. Doctoral thesis*. University of Minnesota. USA.

Cano, J. (2000) *A diagnostic theoretical framework for information technology incorporation in organizations. A systemic approach. Doctoral thesis*. School of Business Administration. Newport University. USA

Dickinson, L. (1998). *Can computer users really be managed? Individual factors and organization context as influences on resistance to information technology. Doctoral thesis*. Graduate Faculty. Rensselaer Polytechnic Institute.

Espejo, R. (1996). *Organizational transformation and learning. A cybernetic approach to management*. New York: John Wiley & Sons.

Espejo, R. (1994). What is systemic thinking? *Systems Dynamic Review, 10*(2/3), Summer-Fall, 199–212.

Espejo, R. & Harden, R. (1989). *The viable system model. Interpretation and application of Stafford Beer's VSM*. New York: John Wiley & Son.

Giddens, A. (1995). *La constitución de la sociedad*. Amorrortu Ediciones.

Ginzberg, M. J. (1981). Early diagnosis of MIS implementation failure: Promising results and unanswered questions. *Management Science, 27*(4), 459-478.

Goodhue, D. (1995). Understanding user evaluations of information systems. *Management Science, 41*(12), December.

Goodman, P., Griffith, T. L. & Fenner, B. (1990). Understanding technology and the individual in an organizational context. *Technology and Organizations*, 45–86. San Francisco, CA: Jossey-Bass.

Henderson, J. & Sifonis, J. (1988). The value of strategic IS Planning: Understanding, consistency, validity and IS markets. *MIS Quarterly*, June, 187–199.

Henderson, K. (1991). Flexible sketches and inflexible data bases: Visual communication, conscription devices, and boundary objects in design engineering. *Sci. Tech. Hum, 16*(4), 448–473.

Malhotra, Y. (1998). *Role of social influence, Self-determination and quality of use of information technology acceptance and utilization: A theoretical framework and empirical field study. Doctoral thesis*. Katz Graduate School of Business. University of Pittsburgh: USA.

Mata, F., Fuerst, W. & Barney, J. (1995). Information technology and sustained competitive advantage: A resource-based analysis. *MIS Quarterly, 19*(4), December.

Mateus, L. (1996). Eigenbehavior and symbols. *Systems Research, 3*(3), 371–384.

Maturana, H. & Varela, F. (1980). *Autopoiesis and Cognition: The Realisation of the Living*. Boston, MA: Reidel.

Morgan, G. (1996). *Imágenes de la organización*. Alfaomega.

Niederman, F., Brancheau, J. C. & Wetherbe, J. C. (1991). Information systems management issues for the 1990s. *MIS Quarterly, 15*(4), 474–500.

Orlikowski, W. (1992). The duality of technology: Rethinking the concept of technology in organizations. *Organization Science, 3*(3), August.

Orlikkowski, W. & Baroudi, J. (1991). Studying information technology in organizations: Research approaches and assumptions. *Information Systems Research, 2*(1), March.

Orlikowski, W. & Gash, D. (1994). Technological frames: Making sense of information technology in organizations. *ACM Transactions on Information Systems, 12*(2), April, 174–207.

Reyes, A. (1996). *A theoretical framework for the design of a social accounting system. Doctoral thesis.* Management Cybernetics. Humberside University, UK.

Spencer-Brown, G. (1972). *Laws of form* (second edition). New York: Dutton.

S'Tnan, A. R. (1991). Rigid politics and technological flexibility: The anatomy of a failed hospital innovation. *Sci. Tech. Hum., 16*(4), 419–447.

Weil, P. & Olson, M. (1989). Managing investment in information technology: Mini case examples and implications. *MIS Quarterly*, March.

Chapter III

Extending Checkland's Phenomenological Approach to Information Systems

Hernán López-Garay
Universidad de los Andes, Venezuela

ABSTRACT

Recent developments in systems thinking (Fuenmayor & López Garay, 1991; Fuenmayor, 1991a,b,c; Fuenmayor, 1997; López-Garay & Suárez, 1999) linked to the phenomenological *perspective, are changing our understanding of systems, and organizations. In this chapter, we will introduce a new image of organizations as* holistic practices—*an image based on these developments— and examine how this image may enrich Checkland's* phenomenological *design of information systems*

The application of a phenomenological *approach to information systems design (ISD) is not a new idea. Boland (1985) and Checkland & Scholes (1990), among others, brought the attention of information systems designers to this fruitful approach years ago. To phenomenology, reality is socially constructed, the product of continuous social interaction. Sense-making becomes then the focus of the systems designer, rather than the positivistic search for the "true" organization and the "true" requirements of the system to be designed (usually the main concern of the classical systems expert in every study). In the phenomenological perspective, organizations are socially constructed. Such systems can be described in relation to different particular world views of the members of the organization (Checkland & Scholes, 1990) and their interpretations. Therefore, information is the* meaning *that results from an engagement with the different perspectives a human organization handles. In this connection, information systems have to be designed as systems to support the organization's central meaning-creation processes, and hence, their social construction of organizational reality (Boland 1987).*

THE PHENOMENOLOGICAL APPROACH IN INFORMATION SYSTEMS DESIGN: INTRODUCTION[1]

Phenomenology is considered by information systems designers the philosophical base of interpretive research (Boland, 1985). Its ontology is based on the idea that reality is not a given, structured "out there" independently from the observer or its social and cultural contexts. Rather, reality is socially constructed and the outcome of continuous social interaction. In particular, human organizations are the outcome of the complex processes of sense-making carried out by its members. Therefore, when a systems designer asks for the objectives and purposes that an information system is to serve, in a particular organization, this question cannot be answered merely by reading the organization's annual report or asking management. Understanding the ends of an organization requires an understanding of the sense-making processes which constitute them. Similarly, the objectives of an information system can only emerge as part of the organization's processes of social construction. This implies that the role of the designer is not only to get involved with the organization's sense-making processes but also help its members and future users of the system clarify and find their preferred views. In this connection, Hirschheim and Klein (1989) point out: "Through interaction, objectives emerge and become legitimized through continuous modification. Systems cannot be designed in the usual sense, but emerge through social interaction. The mechanism of prototyping or evolutionary learning from interaction with partial implementations is the way technology becomes embedded into the social perception and sense-making process." (p.1205). In other words, ISD must emerge as part of the organization's actors' struggle to make sense of their organizational reality.

Now, in order to have a better idea of this approach, it is important to understand the historical context within which it arose, that is, to display what was the state of the art in ISD before phenomenology made its appearance.

ORGANIZATIONS, INFORMATION AND INFORMATION SYSTEMS IN THE SIXTIES AND SEVENTIES

Throughout the sixties and seventies, a powerful image of reality was emerging and gradually dominating the Western world. It was a hybrid image made up of two metaphors, namely, the metaphor of a living organism and that of a machine. The outcome, an "organismic machine," or rather a cybernetic machine,[2] is a machine designed to behave similarly to a living organism in a given environment: It is a goal-seeking machine that through input, output, and feedback processes of communication and control seeks to attain its goals in an effective and efficient manner in a given environment. The computer is a paradigmatic exemplar of this sort of machine.

Now, the human understanding of this metaphor gradually changed from an image that helps to explain reality to reality itself. Accordingly, we came to adopt the positivistic view that there is an external reality independent from the observer, and such reality is "actually" structured by cybernetic processes that follow their own cybernetic laws which any objective observer (i.e., an observer who does not influence with his feelings, ideas, or interpretations, the observed) is able to discover. Thus, industry, economics, politics, education, and most human endeavors were considered constituted by these input-output feedback processes or "systems" as they were called.[3] Ludwig von Bertalanffy (1976), an organismic biologist, contributed greatly to popularize this metaphor in the sciences and the professions, with his General Systems Theory. The fields of organizations and information did not escape these influences. In fact, in some ways, one can say they were their offsprings (Boland, 2001).

According to the cybernetic view, organizations are seen—and designed—as goal-seeking machines. They are designed to reach their stated goal in the most effective and efficient manner in a given environment. In order to do so, hundreds of vital decisions have to be made by different subsystems that constitute the organization. A vital resource for these decision-making processes is information, which is considered to be basic raw data. The role of information systems is to provide data needed by the organization (e.g., data about the organization's environment, market share, performance of competitors, market suppliers, general tendencies of the industry, consumer behavior, etc.).

Similar points are made by Hirschheim and Klein (1989), who point out that for the classical systems analyst who holds a positivistic view of the world "...[i]nformation systems are developed to support rational organizational operation ...Requirements specification builds on the notion of a manifest and rational organizational reality. Information systems development proceeds through the application of a 'naive realism'—the notion that the validity of system specifications, data models, decision models, and system output can be established by checking if they correspond to reality. Reality consists of objects, properties, and processes that are directly observable" (p. 1203).

Put otherwise, information needs and organization's goals are assumed to be rationally and uniquely definable. Therefore, the design of an information system can be structured following what is known as the "project life cycle," It consists of five phases, namely, "...analyzing the information requirements of some organization, department or section, designing, constructing and implementing a *computer system* to provide these requirements, and monitoring its operation." (Checkland & Scholes, 1990, p. 307, italics added). Because nowadays it is hard to imagine that an information system could be implemented by any other means than a computer, the image of information as equivalent to structured data and information system as a computerized provider of structured data have become highly influential in organizations and institutions throughout the Western world (Boland, 1987, p.364–365).

ORGANIZATIONS, INFORMATION AND INFORMATION SYSTEMS IN THE EIGHTIES: THE EMERGENCE OF A *SYSTEMIC-PHENOMENOLOGICAL* APPROACH

In the eighties, the social sciences, in particular, their interpretive phenomenological schools (Burrel & Morgan, 1979), entered the fields of information systems, organization theory, systems thinking, and management science in general. What was the influence of phenomenology in these fields, in particular, in information systems? As Boland (2001) has pointed out, in the early cybernetic period of information systems, the sense-making process of organizations was not a problem to be considered in information systems design. But with the introduction of the phenomenological perspective in this field, information systems' researchers and designers began to be aware of the vital importance of meaning and the processes of social construction of reality in the life of the organization and systems design. Information systems designers are now aware that people sharing a human situation interpret their reality in different ways, not because we humans have some inherent perception defect, but because we are historical and cultural beings. As mentioned before, contrary to scientific positivism which assumes that there is a world of things out there, independent from us, and that we hang on things meanings and values, from the phenomenological perspective, things are meaningful per se because they are in their essence co-constructed by us. Therefore, one cannot do as positivists would like, namely, get rid of the subjective aspects of our being—in other words, take off the labels, meanings, etc., one assumedly hangs on neutral things— and thus obtain true objective knowledge of the world around us. The phenomenological perspective forcefully argues that the very subjectivity of humans is our fundamental possibility of access to reality (Gadamer, 1977).

How does this perspective change our understanding of organizations, information, and information systems?

As one can expect, organizations cannot be seen anymore as objective realities "out there" waiting to be studied by a scientist who can determine objectively their laws of behavior, goals, information needs, etc. The organization, its objectives, and its needs are nothing but continuous social constructions of organizational reality carried out by its members. Furthermore, an external observer cannot understand what the organization's objectives or information needs are if he or she does not get involved with these meaning-creating processes.

How then can one approach such phenomena? Boland (2001) has proposed use of the notion of "narrative." Actors involved in the social construction of an organization seek to make sense of their world through a continuous narration of their experience: "Our narrative capacity is our ability to see ourselves in situations populated by agents in which things happen. We understand our experience of duration as an unfolding sequence of events into which we are able to read a meaningful plot" (p. 2). We make sense of our reality, because "we get the story that is being played out" (ibid.). Accordingly, in an organization, these different narratives are coherently weaved into a larger narrative that explains organizational life and makes meaningful communication between agents possible (although they may have different perspectives of the situation).

Similarly, Checkland & Scholes (1990) interpretive phenomenological approach to organizations seeks to disclose the social construction of organizational reality through the use of a systemic notion called "human activity system" (HAS). The idea of this "construct" is inspired by the fact that—from the phenomenological perspective— something which characterizes an organization as a whole is purposeful activity, i.e., people and resources gathered together to realize meaningful activity. Checkland's action research studies of organizations in the seventies led him to conclude that a set of activities so linked as to form a purposeful whole "…could be regarded as a kind of system [construct], a *'human activity system'* [HAS]. Then came the hard-won learning that such systems could be adequately clearly described only in relation to a particular world view, or *Weltanschauung*: purposeful activity which one observer perceives as 'a terrorist system' is to another observer 'a freedom-fighting system'. *Meaning attribution* is crucial, so that it is essential to declare a world view when giving an account of any purposeful activity" (Checkland & Scholes, 1990, p. 309, emphasis added).

HAS is a systemic construct structured as an activity system, i.e., as sets of interrelated activities to achieve a meaningful purpose according to a declared *Weltanschauung*. Now, the way these constructs can help to disclose the social construction of organizational reality is by using them to promote a learning process about such reality. This works as follows. HAS are conceptual models, not of real-world activity, but models relevant to debate it. They cannot be models— mathematical or of any other type— for the simple reason that the reality of an organization is a dynamic social construction carried out by its members. What a systems designer can do, according to the interpretive view we are discussing here, is set up a process of disclosing and *learning* about these processes of meaning-construction. Because each HAS makes explicit the particular world view that makes meaningful its system of activities, it can be used to trigger debate among organizational actors with regard to the different meanings they attribute to their roles and the activities of the organization. In this way, one can disclose the meanings and "stories" whereby people not only make sense of their organizational life but actually construct such reality!

What is information according to this phenomenological view? For Checkland, *information is the transformation of data into meaning. Hence, an information system is an organized attempt at meaning-creation from data.* Similarly, for Boland (1987, p. 363), information is that which *in-forms.* It is the meaning — or *inward-forming* of a person — that results from an engagement with data. For Boland, an organizational information system's fundamental role is to aid dialogue, interpretation, and the individual's search for meaning within the organization. In other words, the systems designer has to pay serious attention to the processes of inward-forming. If we just sidestep the issue of meaning and proceed to design information systems as if the processes which transform data into meaning were simply a standard set of structures that can be determined by scientific method, then what is substantial and vital to an information system is lost. Furthermore, without really wanting it, systems designed with this positivistic view of reality contribute to develop and reinforce an image of the world in which "…the human meaning of knowledge and action are unproblematic, predefined and pre-packaged." (Boland, 1987, p. 365). According to this view, organizations are not seen as intentional human communities based on dialogue and the search for meaning. Humans in such communities are considered beings void of meaning, input-output decision-making machines, starving for data to achieve a given goal in a given environment.

From the phenomenological perspective, a different picture of systems design emerges. For instance, Checkland proposes the use of HAS in information systems design. He points out that for each HAS, one can ask the following question: What data is required in principle to fulfill the HAS's purpose? We can ask the same question of each activity which constitute the HAS. When these HAS are used to trigger debate among organizational actors about their interpretations of organizational life, different information systems can then be outlined. Hence, for Checkland, the first stages of information systems design have nothing to do with identifying needed data, hardware, or software. Rather, they concern "…perceptions and politics, the interpretations of their world by the organizations in question: they concern the meanings attributed to the flux of events and ideas through which the organization lives. Analysis has to start there, and has to accept that the meanings (and hence the conversions of data into information) will remain static only for the most basic mechanical processes" (Checkland & Scholes, 1990, p. 313). Recent developments of systems thinking related to the phenomenological view can help us to further enrich ISD approaches as Boland's and Checkland's. Before explaining how, let us summarize some of these developments.

RECENT DEVELOPMENTS IN
SYSTEMS THINKING

Just like Boland (1985) brought phenomenology into the field of information systems, to critically examine this field of endeavor, raise consciousness, and clarify its path, so has Checkland (1981, pp. 264–284) done in the field of systems thinking. In so doing, sense-making and the social construction of reality have become central notions in their respective fields. With regard to systems thinking, phenomenology has allowed systems thinkers to understand that *systems thinking* is not about a reality considered independent from the observer and constituted by interconnected cybernetic processes or elements, or about emergent processes. Rather, systems thinking is about how we attribute meaning to the world and construct the unity of our reality. This is an important lesson Checkland's systems thinking teaches us. In the context of human organizations, we have seen how Checkland addresses the problem of understanding the unity of organizational phenomena by uncovering the plurality of interpretations and learning to see how they constitute such a unity (through the use of HAS).

But, there is another even more important lesson. This idea of "uncovering" the plurality of interpretations implies a deeper notion, namely, the common plane or perspective on which they can stand and be compared. Taking into account this perspective of perspectives is what really characterizes the new noncybernetic systems thinking that Checkland and others (for instance Churchman's 1968) inaugurated. However, as Fuenmayor (2000) has pointed out, this idea was not further developed by their originators. What was the nature of this "supra" perspective? Surely, we are not implying our acceptance to an infinite regress of perspectives. If not, then what is the nature of the common plane or ground where various perspectives are displayed? Recent developments of systems thinking (see for instance, Fuenmayor, 1997) have displayed the nature of such a common ground as a cultural order. It is in relation to that *order* that different perspectives find their unity. Systems thinking, then, is to insert phenomena harmoniously in such an order. However, Checkland's systems thinking stops at the organizational level and did not relate phenomena to its wider cultural ground: "his [Checkland's] point of view is that of a manager who is concerned with 'good' management. This means that he is concerned with the good or well-being of a given organization [and with openly discussing what it may mean for different organizational actors]...harmony beyond the organization is not the focal point [of his systems approach]." (Fuenmayor, 2000, p.767).

Nonetheless, followers of the Checklandian-Churchmanian tradition (see for instance, Fuenmayor, 1997, 2000; López-Garay, 1999a), guided by a phenomenological framework of ideas, have gone beyond the organizational systemic level to explore the wider social and cultural *Weltanschauung (W)*. *Placing what-ever-is the-case in the context or the perspective of this W is to make holistic sense*. Making holistic sense is the business of systems thinking and any systems approach.

HOLISTIC PHENOMENOLOGICAL SYSTEMS THINKING IN ORGANIZATIONS AND INFORMATION SYSTEMS

Let us see now how some of these recent developments in systems thinking can change or improve the work of those, who like Boland or Checkland, have introduced the phenomenological approach to the field of information systems. In particular, let us revisit Checkland's approach to information systems, and see how it can be enriched. As we recall, organizations are seen by him as social constructions carried out by the organization's actors. In light of the new developments, we could also seek *to display the ground which makes possible such constructions*. Put differently, the holistic phenomenological stand demands to unfold the holistic sense of organizations by displaying the social sense of them— which implies to unfold different interpretations of the organization's social role— and seek their unity in the cultural order which makes them possible and gives them some unity.

In light of this wide context of meaning, different information systems could be discussed, whose aim would be to support various ways of integrating organizational life, the life of the community, and that of the individual in a holistic unity.

In order to pursue this task, we propose that a designer could use a systemic construct similar to a Checklandian HAS but more evolved. Let us explain. We recall that Human Activity Systems (HAS) were systemic constructs that encapsulated a particular *Weltanschauung* (W) which makes completely meaningful the system's activities. However, Checkland's approach did not take the (W) in its full dimension, i.e., it was not really considered a world view that gives meaning and orders life as a whole.

However, we could widen the scope of a HAS so as to take into account the good of the organization in terms of the wider social context. The construct *organization-as-practice* (OAP) intends to do so. Let us see what is an OAP and how it can be used to extend Checkland's approach to information systems design.

Organizations as Practices (OAP)[4]

A *practice-organization* may be defined as a form of cooperative human activity with an *internal good* that is to make a particular product or render a service with excellence, where the standards of excellence and their development are also a main concern of the practice itself. In a practice-organization, work is not a mere instrument for organizational members' own ends but a form of life whose good is to cultivate the development of the practice-organization itself, providing each member with all the necessary conditions to become an excellent *practitioner* (craftsman). The latter implies that one major activity of a practice-organization is *learning*: the more virtuous practitioners educate those who are less or new. Their learning will not be merely technical but also will involve the education of character and love for their practice. In so doing, the ends of the organization —make a product or render a service with standards of excellence constantly developed by the practice itself— are realized. On the other hand, the organization has to be conceived as part of a larger social whole to whose major good it should contribute. This social good would be no other than enabling every citizen the pursuit of a good life —i.e., the realization of his or her practice (craft) with excellence and not just for mere profit. Furthermore, all practice-organizations in a given community must be coordinated by the political practice which constitutes and sustains that community. The role of politicians is to motorize the search for the good life of the community, by displaying exemplars of different practice-organizations, support their development, and help to distill the essence of the good which is manifest in each practice (so as to have a general referent of the good to orientate the community as a whole). Hence, in this ideal organization, there is no conflict between what is good for the individual and what is good for the organization or society at large.

Notice how different this image of organizations as practices (OAP)[5] is from current organizational life. Organizations are usually conceived as "organs," i.e., as instruments to produce a good or service as profitable as possible. In highly developed capitalistic societies, the individual-organization relationship is usually of a mutual exploitation: managers see individuals as instruments which, properly managed can help the organization's products to attain a high level of profits and the managers to get a good control of the market. Similarly, organization's members see the organization as an instrument which can help them —through salaries and other rewards (e.g., power, social status)— to pursue their own personal interests. The qualities of skill and character valued by management in current organizations are those which allow the organization to achieve high profits. Equally, each member of the organization values those qualities of character in himself or herself and in his or her work mates, which can help him or her to achieve a high level of reward. However, as MacIntyre (1994) says, in this form of organizational life when "...the level of reward is insufficiently high, then the individual whose motivation and values are of this kind will have from her or his own point of view the best of reasons for leaving this particular [organization] or even taking to another trade" (p. 285). In sum, actual organizations tend to be nonsystemic: their members' lives are separated from that of the organization and the latter's from that of society's and its general good.

Let us see now how OAPs can be used in ISD orientated by the holistic phenomenological view.

Information Systems Design: Extending Checkland's ISD Approach

As we recall, in Checkland's phenomenological approach to information systems, the first stages of design have nothing to do with data, hardware, or software. Rather, they are concerned with bringing forth different interpretations of organizational life and possible systems ends. Instrumental, in these earlier stages of systems design, is the use of HAS. However, as mentioned before, HAS are not holistic enough because they do not encapsulate reflections about the social sense of organizations and what role information systems may play under a holistic phenomenological perspective of man, organizations, and society.

We propose to extend Checkland's approach in this direction, by the use of OAPs. In the design of an information system we conducted for a prison in Mérida, Venezuela, we carried out the first stages of systems design, bringing forth the inmates and managers' perceptions of the organization, its social role, and the system's objectives by means of OAPs This process of design turned out to be a learning process which sought to raise the holistic consciousness of the participants (i.e., how their lives are inserted into the organization's and society's at large). From this holistic awareness, organizational changes were proposed, and based on them, the design of several information systems to support these changes were considered.

In the next section, we will present a sample of this case study to illustrate some of the ideas introduced in this chapter and show how Checkland's approach was actually extended in practice.

INFORMATION SYSTEMS TO SUPPORT PRISON SELF-MANAGEMENT: A CASE STUDY[6]

In this section, we will present only the first stages of information systems design, which have to do with perceptions and interpretations and setting up a learning process to raise holistic awareness at the individual, organizational, and societal levels. We will see how the objectives and the general outlines of possible information systems are then discussed. We are going to show how awareness was raised in the inmates and prison management in the context of a systems project with the aim of supporting the development of an organization managed by the prisoners themselves. We will begin by describing the client organization and the initial formulation of the information systems project. Next, we will design an OAP which (like HAS) will be used to compare it with actual organizational life, in order to raise a debate among the inmates and managers about the social role of the prison. Finally, organizational changes and ideas for possible information systems to support these changes will be discussed.

Becoming Familiar with the Client Organization and Its Social Background

"Bloody riots throughout Venezuela's overcrowded and dilapidated prison system this year have erupted like a running sore on this once oil-rich nation. The sheer number and brutal nature of the deaths have turned the country's captive underworld into a perverse mirror-image of Venezuela's current social and economic ills" (*Guardian Weekly*, May 15, 1994).

In 1993, a project to investigate the social role of prisons in Venezuela was launched in the Department of Interpretive Systemology of the University of Los Andes in Mérida, Venezuela. A male prison in the city of Mérida was chosen as the target organization of the study. In the context of this investigation, we were initially approached by the prison's warden, some members of his staff, and some inmates to ask whether we would be able to help them with an information system that could support the tasks of the self-management program they were about to implement. This program was the prison's warden contribution to help ameliorate the difficult situation of inmates in the prison he was managing. If this program worked, he said, it could serve as a model for other prisons in the country.

We began this project by conducting a set of interviews aimed at becoming familiar with the client organization and its sense-making processes.

In our first interviews with the prison's warden, he explained that he felt the prison was not fulfilling its formal mission. He said the prison was not rehabilitating the inmates. As a result, when they returned to civil life, they were not fit to take their place in a democratic society. As he saw the situation, jails had become micro-societies ridden with problems of violence and repression. So, he wondered how prisons could be changed in order to make them more appropriate for fulfilling their social mission. The idea came to him that in order to help delinquents become men able to live in a participatory democratic society, the prison should somehow resemble a democracy. To accomplish this goal, inmates' participation in the management of the prison was vital: "We must not cast out the inmates of any participation in decision making but give them a chance to contribute to the solution of the major problems that they have to endure. In so doing, they will learn to be active participants in a democratic society." Hence, a radical change in jail management was required. The plan to do so was the warden's *self-management program*!

The basic strategy of this program was *the formation of self-management groups to steer two major change projects*. One project had as its main target the formal education of inmates at all levels (primary, secondary, university) and a closer interaction with the community outside the prison through different *socio-cultural* activities.

The second project was orientated toward organizational and administrative aspects of prison self-management (e.g., inmates improving arrangements to get legal advice, improving pavilion conditions, running campaigns for program funding, etc.).

Unfolding the Social Construction of Organizational Life with OAP's

Designing OAPs for the Prison Study
Our next step in our holistic phenomenological approach was to unfold the social construction of organizational life by means of OAPs. Following similar steps to those of Checkland's information systems design, we wanted to build a systems construct that could be used to trigger a debate among the prison's actors, in order to reveal their interpretations of the prison and the relation of it to the wider social context.

Accordingly, we developed the rough sketch of an OAP with its main mission being educational, that is to say, an organization in which inmates and management could have the chance to learn to live in a *participatory democracy*. The internal good of this practice organization (which we must not forget is a systemic construct, not a description of reality) is *the continuous sustenance of a self-governing community focused entirely on deliberation about the good life for the whole community of inmates.*

In this community, all members will be encouraged and allowed to participate in its government, and their main focus will be on deliberation about what is the common good of the prison. This form of democratic organization and practice should be distinguished from representative democracy, because the latter cannot be considered a political practice. This is due to the fact that, in general, representative democracies remove the individual too far from day-to-day decision making. However, as we have seen in previous sections, a practice-organization demands from each of its members active participation. This is the only way a member can learn the knowledge and the virtues of the practice, and thus to appreciate its good and contribute to its attainment. A good painter cannot become so just by sending a representative of his/her to the master's studio. In like manner, a good citizen has to develop, as far as he can, the virtues of a good citizen and governor. Hence he has to participate in the running of his government and be gradually educated in part by watching and working with living role-models of good citizens and governors which can both be imitated and serve as teachers of those who are just beginning or are less advanced. Economic practices (e.g. farming, crafts, etc.) will help not only to generate basic resources to support the community, but also, as long as they are run as practices, will also help to develop the basic virtues common to any practice, including the political one.

Comparing the OAP with Actual Organizational Life

As we began to compare our ideal OAP with the actual organization, serious differences arose. For instance, inmates pointed out that they were not allowed to participate in important decision-making processes. For example, they could not sit in the disciplinary committees or in those which granted legal benefits for good behavior, and they were they not allowed to participate in crucial administrative chores (e.g., decisions related to food supplies, punishments, etc.).

Two internal organizations managed by the inmates attracted the attention of the researchers. One of them, a Literary Society, spent a great deal of effort awakening critical awareness among its members, with regard to prevailing social order in Venezuela, and the members' future role in that social order. The other organization, a society to study and reflect on the thought of Bolívar—the Venezuelan hero that fought the independence wars against the Spaniards in America—was actually dedicated to help the inmates in all sorts of legal matters, e.g., making sure legal benefits were granted on time to those who were legally entitled to receive them.

When management was confronted with these facts, an undercurrent *power game* was revealed: the prison management was willing to give the "societies" a share in decision making if they could obtain in return a more peaceful environment through the good offices of the societies' leaders. On the other hand, the "societies" were willing to play the role of organizers of educational and cultural activities, because these gave their leaders the opportunity to get to know the "ins" and "outs" of the jail's actual organization and its relations with the judicial system. It also allowed them to become known to the public (for their "good" work in improving the image of jails). These actions were strategically important to gain power for future struggles against the prison and judicial system of which the former was a part!

But why did they have to hide their actions and discourse behind the façade of a self-management program? A possible explanation was this. It is clear that, in general, prison management in Venezuela is not really in the business of rehabilitation. Moreover, statistical studies (*SIC*, 1993, 1994, a Venezuelan monthly journal) show that there is a high recidivism rate in Venezuela, which clearly indicates the failure of the jail to fulfill its established social role. Yet management's discourse is casting an image to society that jails are in the business of rehabilitation. So, what is the jail's actual role in society, and why has this role to be *hidden* behind a formal discourse, for instance of the kind portrayed by the self-management program?

Further interviews and discussion with the inmates brought to the surface the perception the members of the organization had of a very unjust and undemocratic social system. In this system, the jail is, together with the police, the courts, and other parts of the judicial system, a *defense* machinery of those in power. *It helps keep a large part of the population of Venezuela which "rebel" against its unjust social order —by becoming delinquents— out of the streets for long periods of time.* The "inefficiency" of the Venezuelan judicial system, including its prisons, is part of its mission of keeping the marginal "rebels" out of circulation as long as possible. If the "prison societies" were really allowed to make the judicial system function, many of these "rebels" (some of whom have committed minor faults) would soon be back to the streets. But having no future in the current Venezuelan unjust social order, they soon return to the "old path," only this time better prepared to continue their self-appointed "revolutionary mission." And, this is precisely what neither the judicial system and the jail cannot permit, otherwise the dominant power system would be destabilized.

Ideas for Possible (Desirable? Feasible? Ethical?) Information Systems

Having unfolded together with the prison's actors their processes of social construction and how they perceive the relationship with their social environment, we had to decide now, how they wanted to proceed with their organization and the design of their information system. Did they still think it was worthwhile to carry on with the self-management project? It was clear that such a program was not about creating a model of a democratic society within the prison. It was clear also for them that their organization was very far from the ideal practice organization portrayed by our OAP. It was also revealed that the larger society was not only far from being a participatory democracy, but that its unjust social order contributed to the very delinquency it was trying to stop and obliterate by means of a corrupt judicial system. Now, if they redesigned their organization to actually create a small participative democratic society, thus approaching the prison to the OAP model, what sense did this make, in light of a very undemocratic and unjust social order?

It will amount to be educating inmates for a nonexistent society! It would not work unless management and the inmates were prepared to make prisons the beachheads of a radical societal change (something which at first sight sounds paradoxical if not absurd).

These and other similar questions brought forth startlingly the ethical context within which our design process was unfolding. In this regard, Hirschheim & Klein (1994)[7] had pointed out not only the unavoidable emergence of ethical issues in information systems design, when one makes human beings the center of design, but also suggested various ways of beginning to deal with them. As they say "...the scope of information systems development (ISD) practices should not only embrace rules of skill, but also rules of prudence and rules for rational discourse about competing value standards. Without warranted value standards (design ideals) the choice among conflicting goals in the development of information systems cannot be based on reason." (p. 1).

It was clear for us that our design process had reached a point where different interpretations and values about the prison and the society where the former was embedded were displayed, and a decision had to be made as to how to continue unfolding our design process. Following Hirschheim and Klein, we tried to set up a debate between the different interpretations unfolded. Although we could not finally do it, our conversations and informal debates let transpire a basic feeling in the inmates: their fundamental value was that of justice, and hence, they would be happy with less ambitious projects (as that of becoming a model of democracy for the larger society) if only they could promote the gradual construction of a just community within the prison.

In this direction, we discussed with the inmates possible information systems that could help in this project. *One proposal was related to the implementation of an information system that could help minimize the conditions for oppression or injustice in the prison.* In this regard, a system that could keep track of what is happening in court with each inmate's legal case (e.g., which judge is handling his case, in which court, how long this process is taking, etc.) was very much welcomed. This system could be run by the inmates themselves and supply reports to the warden, so that management felt pressed to take action and speed up the course of justice.

In sum, the first stages of our design process had disclosed to us that the actual organization with its "participative democracy" was really about helping the "misfits" fit the dominant social order. But as our design project was unfolding, a different objective for our information system emerged. For the inmates far more meaningful was the realization of a just community within the prison. In sum, what other roles could information systems play in the construction and maintenance of such a community?[8]

After the project was finished, someone pointed out to the author that maybe the conceptual framework of a *learning organization* could have given us greater light on how to orientate more clearly our design. In particular, the author was told that because (according to Senge's work) creating a learning community requires, among other things, the development of a "...culture based on transcendent human values of love, wonder, humility, and compassion" (Kofman and Senge, 1993, see Section on Operating Principles), then justice would, per force, emerge from such a culture. In addition, a learning community had to develop an holistic view of life, i.e., a capacity to see and work with the flow of life as a system" (ibid.).

Unfortunately, we could not continue evolving the project in this direction. Our research agenda called us to focus our efforts on the interpretive phenomenological study of prisons in Venezuela. However, for the purposes of this chapter, we believe we have managed to illustrate with our case study the potential of the systemic ideas described above for the practice of ISD. They provide a solid ground to understand the human aspects of organizations and how information systems design can help organizations become more human and integrated to society for pursuing the common good. In this way, information systems design might help to reverse the dehumanizing process that the cybernetic era has helped to propel in the modern world (Boland, 1987).

CONCLUSION: THE ROLE OF *ISD* IN THE PRESENT

Coming to the conclusion of this chapter, one idea crossed the author's mind. It is related to *the role that organizational information systems design and other management sciences can play in the present.* The idea is that they could be the ushers of what Koffman and Senge (1993) call a systems culture revolution. As a matter of fact, for them, organizations have embodied a mechanistic *Weltanschauung*, the instrumental paradigm of modern society. Being the most important institutions of modern times, they could become the beachheads of a cultural revolution, the laboratories where the development of a holistic systems culture could be tried. What *learning organizations* have to learn is to go from a mechanistic, fragmented, and highly individualistic view of the world to a systems view. The latter requires the development of new capabilities, such as the capability to "...*recover 'the memory of the whole'*, the awareness that wholes actually precede parts; [realize that] [c]*ompetition* becomes cooperation when we discover the 'community nature of the self' [i.e., its systemic or holistic character] ... [and realize that] *[r]eactiveness* becomes creating when we see the 'generative power of language', how language brings forth distinctions from the undivided flow of life" (ibid. p. 2, emphasis added).

How can information systems design contribute to this cultural change? Our chapter intends to be a small contribution in a direction that might start a deep reflection on this question and the future role of IS.

ACKNOWLEDGMENTS

My deep thanks to professor Kristo Ivanov, former Head of the Department of *Informatics* of the University of Umeå, Sweden, for providing the academic niche where the basic ideas of this chapter were developed.

ENDNOTES

1   See, for instance, *Qualitative Research in IS* edited by Trauth and, in particular, Klein and Myers' (2001) chapter on Interpretive Research. There are also various places on the internet that can be searched for information on this subject. One of them, used in this research and which has various useful links is: **http://www.auckland.ac.nz/msis/isworld.** The editor is Michael D. Myers (mentioned above), and the place is called **Qualitative Research in Information Systems**.

2   This is given that cybernetics arose from merging biology (in particular, a sector of this discipline dedicated to the study of feedback regulatory systems of living beings) and information theory (Shannon's).

3   In this regard, see *Systems Behavior*, edited by John Beishon and Geoff Peters.

4   The idea of seeing organizations as *practices* has been suggested by Reed (1992, 1993).

5   An image which, incidentally, is beginning to have some popularity among various management scientists such as Kofman & Senge (1993), Senge (1990, 1998), Spinosa, Flores, & Dreyfus (1997), Suárez (1998).

6   For a full development of this study see Contreras & López-Garay (2000a, b), López-Garay (1999b), and Suárez (1999).

7   My referenced page numbers are based on an earlier draft I got from the authors of this paper.

8   Balasubramanian (1995) has explored the role that information systems can play in learning organizations.

REFERENCES

Balasubramanian, V. (1995). *Organizational learning and information systems (draft)*. Graduate School of Management, Rutgers University, Newark, New Jersey.

Beishon J. & Peters G. (Eds.). (1976). *Systems behaviour* (second edition). The Open University.

von Bertalanffy, L. (1976). General systems theory. In Beishon, J. & Peters, G. (Eds.). *Systems behaviour* (second edition). The Open University.

Boland, R. (1985). Phenomenology: A preferred approach to research in information systems. In Mumford, E., Hirschheim, R. A., Fitzgerald, G. and WoodHarper, T. (Eds.), *Research methods in information systems*, 193–201. Amsterdam: North-Holland.

Boland Jr., R. (1987). The information of information systems. In Boland Jr., R. J. & Hirschheim, R. A. (Eds.), *Critical issues in information systems*. New York: John Wiley & Sons.

Boland Jr., R. (2001). *The everyday experience of virtuality. Short paper for the social study of information technology workshop*. Weatherhead School of Management, Case Western Reserve University.

Burrell, G. & Morgan, G. (1979). *Sociological paradigms and organizational analysis*. London: Heyneman.

Checkland, P. (1981). *Systems thinking, systems practice*. New York: John Wiley & Sons.

Checkland, P. & Scholes, J. (1990). Appendix in *Soft systems methodology in action*. New York: John Wiley & Sons.

Churchman, C. W. (1968). *The systems approach*. New York: Delta.

Contreras, J. & López-Garay, H. (2000a). El Sentido histórico de la prisión rehabilitadora en Venezuela (II): Una interpretación foucaultiana de su devenir. Revista *Capítulo Criminológico de Venezuela, 28*(1).

Contreras, J. & López-Garay, H. (2000b). El sentido histórico de la prisión rehabilitadora en Venezuela (II): Una interpretación foucaultiana de su devenir. Revista *Capítulo Criminológico de Venezuela, 28*(2).

Fuenmayor, R. (1991a). The roots of reductionism. *Systems Practice, 4*(5). New York: Plenum Press.

Fuenmayor, R. (1991b). The self-referential structure of an everyday-living situation: A phenomenological ontology for interpretive systemology. *Systems Practice, 4*(5), 449–472.

Fuenmayor, R. (1991c). Truth and openness: An epistemology for interpretive systemology. *Systems Practice, 4*(5). New York: Plenum Press.

Fuenmayor, R. (1997). The historical meaning of present systems thinking. *Syst. Res. Behav. Sci., 14*(4).

Fuenmayor, R. (2000). A brief crack of light? *Systemic Practice and Action Research, 13*(6).

Fuenmayor, R. & López-Garay, H. (1991). The scene for interpretive systemology. *System Practice, 4,* 401–418.

Gadamer, H. (1977). *Philosophical hermeneutics.* Berkeley, CA: University of California Press.

Hirschheim R. & Klein, H. (1989). Four paradigms of information systems development. *Communications of the ACM, 32.*

Hirschheim, R. & Klein, H. (1994). Realizing emancipatory principles in information systems development: The case for ethics, *MIS Quarterly, 18*(1).

Klein, H. & Myers, M. (2001). A classification scheme for interpretive research in information systems. In Trauth, E. (Ed.), *Qualitative research in IS: Issues and trends.* Hershey, PA: Idea Group Publishing.

Kofman, F. & Senge, P. (1993). Communities of commitment: The heart of learning organizations. http://deming.eng.clemson.edu/pub/tqmbbs/prinpract/comcom.txt. *Organizational Dynamics,* Autumn, *22*(2).

López-Garay, H. (1999a). Guest editorial. *SPAR, 12*(1).

López-Garay, H. (1999b). The holistic sense of prison phenomena in Venezuela (I). *SPAR, 12*(1).

López-Garay, H. & Suárez, T. (1999). The holistic sense of prison phenomena in Venezuela (III). *SPAR, 12*(1).

MacIntyre, A. (1994). *After MacIntyre.* Horton, J. & Mendus, S. (Eds.). NY: Polity Press.

Myers, D. (2002). *Qualitative research in information systems.* (A Reference Web Page.) Retrieved from the World Wide Web: http://www.auckland.ac.nz/msis/isworld.

Reed, M. (1992). *The Sociology of Organizations. Themes, Perspectives and Prospects.* New York: Harvester.

Reed, M. (1993). Organizations and modernity: Continuity and discontinuity in organization theory. In Hassard, J. & Parker, M. (Eds.), *Postmodernism and organizations.* Thousand Oaks, CA: Sage.

Senge, P. (1990). *The fifth discipline.* New York: Currency Double Day.

Senge, P. (1998). Some thoughts at the boundaries of classical system dynamics: Structuration and Holism. *Proceedings 6ᵗʰ International Conference of the System Dynamics Society,* Quebec, Canada.

Spinosa, C., Flores, F. & Dreyfus, H. (1997). *Disclosing New Worlds.* NY: MIT Press.

Suárez, T. (1998). An inquiry into the historical meaning of "The fifth discipline." *SPAR, 11*(5).

Suárez, T. (1999). The holistic sense of prison phenomena in Venezuela (II). *SPAR, 12*(1).

Section III

Information Systems and Business Strategies: Holistic Approach

Chapter IV

A Validation Test of an Adaptation of the DeLone and McLean's Model in the Spanish EIS Field[1]

José L. Roldán and Antonio Leal
University of Seville, Spain

ABSTRACT

This chapter offers a reflection about systems thinking, models and validation tests. In this way, starting from the recognized model of information systems success created by DeLone and McLean, the authors develop an adaptation in the executive information systems (EIS) area. Their research aim is to carry out a validation test of the adapted model applying the Partial Least Squares approach. The study is based on a survey involving 100 managers in 55 Spanish organizations. The results show this model has an adequate predictive power for most implied variables, demonstrating the existence of significant links among information systems success dimensions. The model helps to understand the influence of EIS on both individual and organizational impacts. Finally, as a consequence of the validation process, new ideas for the redesigning of the model are proposed.

INTRODUCTION

From a systemic approach, we develop a research model adapting the DeLone and McLean's information systems success model to the executive information systems (EIS) field. We aim to test the validity of our adaptation, studying the interdependencies among the variables and examining its predictive power. Applying the Partial Least Squares (PLS) technique, we test the model using data from a survey conducted on 100 Spanish users in 55 organizations.

BACKGROUND

Systems and Models

The systems thinking has always borne in mind the idea of complexity (Espejo, 1994). According to Flood and Carson (1988), the complexity concept is associated with people and things or systems (situations as perceived by people). In relation to the former, it comprises the following aspects concerning individuals: perceptions and notions, interests, and capabilities. With regard to systems, complexity includes the ideas of the number of parts and the number of relationships between the parts.

Because we cannot deal with the entire complexity of our environment, we use abstractions of the latter, i.e., we develop models. In this sense, "models are representations of real-life phenomena, situations or systems" (Faucheaux, Laurent, & Makridakis, 1976, p. 108). Therefore, models help us to understand, research, and act on systems or phenomena (Ortigueira, 1987) (Figure 1). Besides, a model can have three general types of purposes (Finkelstein & Carson, 1985): description, prediction, and explanation of the modeled system.

Models are defined by groups of variables and links between these variables (Figure 1). Each variable can be observed as a bridge between a theoretical concept (which provides the variable with meaning) and observable magnitudes. In empirical models, each variable can be expressed by one indicator or several.

On the other hand, model and system are inseparable entities. In fact, a model is a system. A model is a representative system of another specific system or phenomenon. In a complementary way, Flood and Carson (1988) state that since a system can be defined as an abstraction from the world, a system is a model.

Figure 1: System and model [Source: adapted from Ortigueira (1987, 1995)]

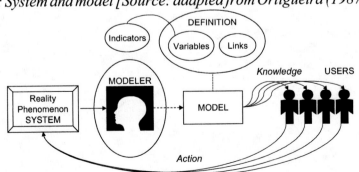

It is a utopia to think that it is possible to build models with all attributes, properties, and characteristics of a specific system (Ortigueira, 1995). If this situation were possible, it would mean both systems (model and represented system) are isomorphous. However, in the real world, all the models and their respective systems are homomorphous, because it is impossible to obtain a total correspondence between the attributes of the system and the model. Notwithstanding, in each science, every researcher should aim to come close to the perfect isomorphous model in relation to the represented system. "The effectiveness of any model used to describe and understand behavior of a particular system as a whole ultimately depends on the degree to which that model accurately represents that system" (Ackoff, 1999, p. 34).

DeLone and McLean's Model of Information Systems Success

Information systems (IS) success is one of the most researched topics in IS literature. DeLone and McLean (1992) become aware of the complex reality that surrounds the identification and definition of the IS success concept. They organize the large number of studies on IS success and present a comprehensive and integrative model. DeLone and McLean, in their study, identify six main dimensions for categorizing the different measures of IS success: system quality, information quality, use, user satisfaction, individual impact, and organizational impact. They develop an IS success model in which these categories are interrelated, shaping a process construct. Their model proposes that "system quality and information quality singularly and jointly affect both use and user satisfaction. Additionally, the amount of use can affect the degree of user satisfaction as well as the reverse being true. Use and user satisfaction are direct antecedents of individual impact; and, lastly, this impact on individual performance should eventually have some organizational impact" (DeLone & McLean, 1992, pp. 83, 87) (Figure 2).

DeLone and McLean (1992) state that their model is "an attempt to reflect the interdependent, process nature of IS success" (p. 88), undertaking to describe the IS success concept and the causes for the success.

Figure 2: DeLone and McLean's IS success model

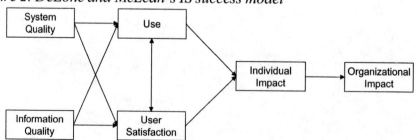

According to Ballantine et al. (1996) and Seddon (1997), DeLone and McLean's work makes several important contributions to the understanding of IS success. First, it consolidates previous research. Second, it provides a scheme for classifying the different measures of IS success that have been proposed in the literature into six dimensions. Third, it suggests a model of temporal and causal interdependencies between the identified categories. Fourth, it makes the first moves to identify different stakeholder groups in the process. Fifth, it has been considered an appropriate base for further empirical and theoretical research. Sixth, it has met general acceptance in the IS community.

Nevertheless, this model has received different critical reviews from different points of view (Ballantine et al., 1996; Seddon, 1997) and modifications (Fraser & Salter, 1995; Pitt, Watson, & Kavan, 1995; Wilkin & Hewett, 1999).

Executive Information Systems

Executive information systems (EIS) have, in recent years, become a major IS topic. An EIS is defined as a computer-based information system designed to provide executives with easy access to internal and external information relevant to their management activities. This kind of information system has experienced a great expansion since the 1980s as a consequence of facilitating and pressuring (internal and external) factors (Watson, Rainer, & Koh, 1991). In Spain, EIS has become widespread since 1990. Although, at the beginning, the target public for this type of IS was the top managers, nowadays, this system has often spread to other nonexecutive users such as middle managers, support staff, analysts, and knowledge workers (Frolick, 1994). Because of this common use, it has been suggested that the EIS acronym should actually stand for everyone information system. Accordingly, EIS have increased their applications available to users, including some or all of the following capabilities (Watson, Houdeshel, & Rainer, 1997): support for electronic communications, data analysis capabilities, and organizing tools.

MAIN THRUST OF THE CHAPTER

Models play a linking role between two fields, connecting, on the one hand, a theoretical area (which is interpreted by the model), and, on the other, an empirical sphere (which is synthetically represented by the model) (Ortigueira, 1995). Referring to the second field, the validation question arises; it is necessary to corroborate the model with empirical data. This validation of a model can be inserted in the process of the scientific method (Rivett, 1980) with phases that are as follows (Ackoff, 1999): (1) formulating the problem, (2) constructing the model,

(3) testing the model, (4) deriving a solution from the model, (5) testing and controlling the solution, and (6) implementing the solution. This process is usually cyclic. If, when testing a model, it is found to be deficient, i.e., the facts fail to fit some of the proposed hypotheses, the model could be re-examined and modified, for instance, incorporating new factors that had not been taken into account. Following Espejo's arguments, it could originate the emergence of holons or insightful ideas with the purpose of allowing us to think more creatively about the world (Espejo, 1994).

In this chapter, we will play a modeler and tester role. We have developed a research model adapting the DeLone and McLean's IS success model to the EIS area. We aim to test the validity of our adaptation, studying the interdependencies among the six categories and, at the same time, examining its predictive power.

Research Model and Hypotheses

The conceptual model used to guide this study is shown in Figure 3. This one is based on the DeLone and McLean's IS success model, adapting it to the EIS context. Because of the difficulty in defining the impact concepts, we have opted to use different variables to study the individual and organizational impacts. In this sense, we have followed the works of Leidner (1996) and Leidner and Elam (1994, 1995) on EIS to select the different variables subsumed, both in the individual and organizational impact dimensions.

Our conceptual model proposes the following linkages: EIS system quality and information quality affect both EIS use and user satisfaction. According to the Attitude Theory of Fishbein and Ajzen (1975), user satisfaction influences EIS use. Both EIS use and user satisfaction are direct antecedents of individual impact variables. The organizational impact variables are affected by the individual impact of the EIS. We are going now to define all these variables.

Figure 3: Conceptual model

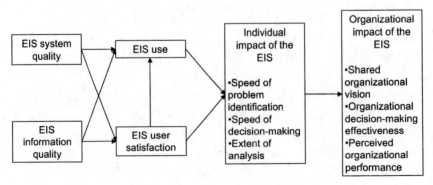

EIS system quality refers to the desired characteristics of the EIS which produces the information. EIS information quality relates to the quality of the executive information system output. This construct is also related to issues such as the relevance, timeliness, and accuracy of information generated by an EIS. EIS user satisfaction refers to the recipient response to the use of the output of an executive information system. EIS use is defined as recipient consumption of the output of an EIS. Use also means to employ the executive information system.

The individual impact dimension is defined by DeLone and McLean (1992) as "the effect of information on the behavior of the recipient" (p. 69). Following Leidner and Elam (1994, 1995), we have selected three variables for analyzing the influence of the EIS on the individual: speed of problem identification, speed of decision making, and extent of analysis. These variables are congruent with the cognitive perspective identified by Isenberg that is useful in understanding how an EIS may affect the management process: manager as decision maker (Rockart & DeLong, 1988). The article of Leidner and Elam (1995) presents the following definitions: (1) Speed of problem identification is defined as "the length of time between when a problem first arises and when it is first noticed" (p. 142). (2) The speed of decision making refers to "the time between when a decision maker recognizes the need to make some decision to the time when he or she renders judgment" (p. 142). (3) Extent of analysis is defined as "time spent on interrelating symptoms to get at the root cause of problems and the effort spent to generate solutions" (p. 142).

DeLone and McLean (1992) define organizational impact as "the effect of information on organizational performance" (p. 74). We have followed the work of Leidner (1996) to select two variables that indicate potential benefits of the EIS on the organization as a whole: shared organizational vision and organizational decision-making effectiveness. Moreover, we have included a third construct from the strategic management area: perceived organizational performance. Therefore, we can define shared organizational vision as "a shared perspective of what is important for managers at all levels, indicating what areas need their attention" (Leidner, 1996, p. 5). Organizational decision-making effectiveness is concerned with the enhancement of the organizational decision-making process. Finally, perceived organizational performance refers to the business performance, which embraces financial performance (sales growth, profitability, earnings per share, and so forth) and operational performance (market share, new product introduction, product quality, etc.) (Venkatraman & Ramanujam, 1986).

In Figure 4, we depict the hypotheses to be tested. These derive from the DeLone and McLean model and are outlined in Table 1. In addition to the theoretic support provided by the DeLone and McLean model, we have added a relation of supplementary references from IS literature that support the different hypotheses.

Figure 4: Research model and hypotheses

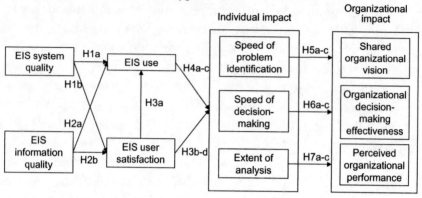

Table 1: Hypotheses to be tested

Conceptual model	Hypotheses	Supplementary supporting references
System quality and information quality of the EIS singularly and jointly affect both use and user satisfaction	H1a: EIS system quality will be positively related to EIS use	Davis (1989); Hwang, Windsor, & Pryor (2000); O'Reilly (1982)
	H1b: EIS system quality will be positively related to EIS user satisfaction	Barki & Hartwick (1989); Fraser & Salter (1995); Hwang, Windsor, & Pryor (2000); Igbaria & Nachman (1990); McGill, Hobbs, & Klobas (2000); Seddon & Kiew (1996); Sherman (1997)
	H2a: EIS information quality will be positively related to EIS use	Hwang, Windsor, & Pryor (2000); O'Reilly (1982); Szewczak (1988)
	H2b: EIS information quality will be positively related to EIS user satisfaction	Gluck (1996); Hwang, Windsor, & Pryor (2000); Fraser & Salter (1995); McGill et al. (2000); Seddon & Kiew (1996); Sherman (1997); Zviran (1992)
The degree of user satisfaction can affect the amount of EIS use	H3a: EIS user satisfaction will be positively related to EIS use	Bergeron, Raymond, Rivard, & Gara (1995); Downing (1999); Fishbein & Ajzen (1975); Fraser & Salter (1995); Igbaria & Tan (1997); McGill et al. (2000)
EIS use and user satisfaction are direct antecedents of individual impact variables	H3b-d: EIS user satisfaction will be positively related to individual impacts of the EIS.	Etezadi-Amoli & Farhoomand (1996); Gatian (1994); Gelderman (1998); Igbaria & Tan (1997); McGill et al. (2000); Sherman (1997)
	H4a-c: EIS use will be positively related to individual impacts of the EIS.	Igbaria & Tan (1997); Leidner (1996); Leidner & Elam (1994, 1995); Vlahos & Ferrat (1995)
This impact on individual performance should eventually have some organizational impact	H5a-c: Speed of problem identification will be related to organizational impacts of the EIS	Huber (1990); Leidner (1996); Mirani & Lederer (1998); Molloy & Schwenk (1995); Ragowsky, Ahituv, & Neumann (1996); Straub & Wetherbe (1989)
	H6a-c: Speed of decision-making will be related to organizational impacts of the EIS	
	H7a-c: Extent of analysis will be related to organizational impacts of the EIS	

Methodology

Procedures

A survey instrument was used to gather data to test the relationships shown in the research model. The study was conducted in Spain from January to June 1998. A pilot test of the survey was conducted in order to assess content validity (Straub, 1989). The instrument was pretested with EIS consultants (n = 4) and business and information systems professors (n = 3). Suggestions were incorporated into a second version that was then tested by two other management professors. No additional suggestions were made. Thus, bias in response from misinterpretation of the instrument should be reduced. Based on the positive feedback from pretest respondents, a survey was conducted on a cross-section of Spanish companies using EIS.

Respondents to the survey were EIS users. Contacts were made with EIS software vendors and consultants to obtain the names of organizations that had an operational EIS. In addition, we used a list of participants in an EIS seminar organized by an important Spanish business school. In each organization, we contacted the EIS or IS manager to ensure that the EIS was in full operation and to achieve their cooperation with the study. Once we obtained their commitment (n = 132), we requested them to deliver the surveys to three senior managers that used the EIS. A total of 396 questionnaires were sent to the EIS/IS contacts, and if we did not obtain any response from an organization within 45 days, we proceeded to call our contact again. As a result, we attained 100 usable user surveys from 55 organizations, representing a response rate of 25.25%. A summary of the demographic characteristics is shown in Table 2.

Table 2: Demographic characteristics of the sample

Demographic variable	Sample composition	
Departments	Planning / management control	21.7%
	General management	17.4%
	Finance / accounting	15.2%
	Marketing / sales	14.1%
	Information systems	6.5%
	Production / operations	4.3%
	Human resources	2.2%
	General management staff	2.2%
	Other	12%
Hierarchical level	Level 1	24%
	Level 2	31.3%
	Level 3	30.2%
	Level 4	12.5%
	Under level 4	2%
Experience	M = 80 months; SD = 64.76; range = 5-300	
Experience as EIS user	M = 30 months; SD = 21.71; range = 1-120	

Table 3: Measures developed or adapted by the authors

Item	Measure
	(EIS system quality). To what extent has EIS helped you?
sq1	Faster access to information
sq2	Easier and more comfortable access to information
sq3	Availability of an improved access to the organizational data base
sq4	Have the benefit of new or additional information
sq5	Enjoy an improved presentation of data
	(EIS information quality). To what extent has EIS helped you?:
iq1	Obtain more current and timely information
iq2	Have more relevant, useful and significant information
iq3	Have more concise and summarized information
iq4	Enjoy more accurate information
iq5	Obtain more orderly and clear information
iq6	Obtain more reasonable and logical information
	(Perceived organizational performance). Using a five-point scale, indicate how EIS has influenced the global performance of your organization:
pop1	Our EIS has dramatically increased our organization's productivity
pop2	Our EIS has improved our competitive position
pop3	Our EIS has dramatically increased our profitability
pop4	Our EIS has dramatically increased our revenues
pop5	Our EIS has dramatically improved our overall performance

Measures

Whenever possible, items were derived and translated from previously verified sources. However, in some cases, the items used to measure the variables of interest were created specifically for this study. Because of chapter length limits, we only show our developed or adapted measures in Table 3.

Items measuring EIS system quality were adapted from two former relations of EIS system characteristics (Bergeron & Raymond, 1992; Young & Watson, 1995), and those items measuring EIS information quality were mainly adapted from the information dimensions identified by Zmud (1978).

EIS user satisfaction was measured by five items developed by Sanders and Courtney (1985) who examined user satisfaction with DSS. Like the study of Leidner (1996), "DSS" in their instrument was changed to "EIS." EIS use was measured by one item: hours of EIS use per week.

The items measuring speed of problem identification, speed of decision making, and extent of analysis were borrowed from Leidner and Elam (1994, 1995). The items aimed at identifying the shared organizational vision and the organizational decision-making effectiveness were taken from Leidner (1996). Perceived organizational performance was measured by five items developed by Powell (1995), who studied the influence of TQM programs on the organizational performance. "TQM program" in this instrument was changed to "EIS."

Except for the use variable, the remaining ones were measured on a five-point scale ranging from "to no extent" (1) to "to a great extent" (5). On the other hand, perceived organizational performance was measured on a five-point scale, from "strongly disagree" (1) to "strongly agree" (5).

Data Analysis

A structural equation modeling (SEM) is proposed in order to assess the relationships among the constructs together with the predictive power of the research model. We have used the Partial Least Squares (PLS) technique, because this tool is primarily intended for causal-predictive analysis in which the explored problems are complex, and theoretical knowledge is scarce. PLS is an appropriate technique to use in a theory development situation (Wold, 1979), such as this research. We have used PLS-Graph software version 2.91.03.04 (Chin & Frye, 1998).

A PLS model is analyzed and interpreted in two stages: (1) the assessment of the reliability and validity of the measurement model and (2) the assessment of the structural model. This sequence ensures that the constructs' measures are valid and reliable before attempting to draw conclusions regarding relationships among constructs (Barclay, Higgins, & Thompson, 1995).

Results

Measurement Model

The measurement model in PLS is assessed in terms of individual item reliability, construct reliability, convergent validity, and discriminant validity. Indi-

Table 4: Individual item reliability–individual item loadings

EIS system quality (SQ)		EIS information quality (IQ)		EIS user satisfaction (US)		EIS use (U)		Speed of problem identification (SPI)	
Item	Loading	Item	Loading	Item	Loading	Item	Loading	Item	Loading
sq1	0.8669	iq1	0.7600	us1	0.7399	u1	1	spi1	0.8585
sq2	0.8762	iq2	0.8564	us2	0.7484			spi2	0.8450
sq3	0.7356	iq3	0.7892	us3	0.6963			spi3	0.7776
sq4	0.7342	iq4	0.7775	us4	0.8468				
sq5	0.6973	iq5	0.8103	us5	0.8166				
		iq6	0.8539						

Speed of decision-making (SDM)		Extent of analysis (EA)		Shared organizational vision (SOV)		Organizational decision-making effectiveness (ODME)		Perceived organizational performance (POP)	
Item	Loading	Item	Loading	Item	Loading	Item	Loading	Item	Loading
sdm1	0.8856	ea1	0.8268	sov1	0.8641	odme1	0.8552	pop1	0.8307
sdm2	0.9024	ea2	0.7526	sov2	0.9218	odme2	0.9051	pop2	0.8445
sdm3	0.8445	ea3	0.6962	sov3	0.8432	odme3	0.8857	pop3	0.8413
sdm4	0.7594	ea4	0.8199					pop4	0.8280
								pop5	0.8704

vidual item reliability is considered adequate when an item has a factor loading that is greater than 0.7 on its respective construct (Carmines & Zeller, 1979). Most of our individual item loadings are above 0.7 or very near (sq5, us3, ea3) (Table 4).

Construct reliability is assessed using two measures of internal consistency: Cronbach's alpha and composite reliability (ρ_c). The interpretation of both values is similar. We can use the guidelines offered by Nunnally (1978), who suggests 0.7 as a benchmark for a "modest" reliability applicable in early stages of research. In our research, all of the constructs are reliable (Table 5). They all have measures of internal consistency that exceed 0.75 (alpha) and 0.85 (ρ_c). To assess convergent validity, we examine the average variance extracted (AVE) measure, which was created by Fornell and Larcker (1981). AVE values should be greater than 0.50. Consistent with this suggestion, AVE measures for all constructs exceed 0.59 (Table 5).

To assess discriminant validity AVE should be greater than the variance shared between the construct and other constructs in the model (i.e., the squared correlation between two constructs). For adequate discriminant validity, the diagonal elements should be significantly greater than the off-diagonal elements in the corresponding rows and columns (Barclay et al., 1995). The majority of our constructs satisfy this condition with the exception of system quality in relation to information quality (Table 6). Notwithstanding, the difference between them is very

Table 5: Construct reliability and convergent validity coefficients

Construct	Cronbach's alpha	Composite reliability (ρ_c)	AVE
EIS system quality (SQ)	0.8376	0.8887	0.6171
EIS information quality (IQ)	0.8969	0.9188	0.6540
EIS user satisfaction (US)	0.8302	0.8798	0.5953
EIS use (U)	1	1	1
Speed of problem identification (SPI)	0.7701	0.8670	0.6852
Speed of decision-making (SDM)	0.8795	0.9119	0.7221
Extent of analysis (EA)	0.7877	0.8574	0.6017
Shared organizational vision (SOV)	0.8498	0.9089	0.7691
Org. decision-making effectiveness (ODME)	0.8612	0.9133	0.7784
Perceived organizational performance (POP)	0.9018	0.9247	0.7108

Table 6: Discriminant validity coefficients

	SQ	IQ	US	U	SPI	SDM	EA	SOV	ODME	POP
SQ	(0.786)	--	--	--	--	--	--	--	--	--
IQ	0.791	(0.809)	--	--	--	--	--	--	--	--
US	0.709	0.674	(0.772)	--	--	--	--	--	--	--
U	0.308	0.292	0.277	(1.000)	--	--	--	--	--	--
SPI	0.665	0.674	0.716	0.246	(0.828)	--	--	--	--	--
SDM	0.664	0.677	0.667	0.337	0.751	(0.850)	--	--	--	--
EA	0.687	0.677	0.736	0.258	0.709	0.751	(0.776)	--	--	--
SOV	0.550	0.654	0.629	0.149	0.701	0.607	0.640	(0.877)	--	--
ODME	0.585	0.617	0.674	0.051	0.663	0.666	0.606	0.698	(0.882)	--
POP	0.492	0.546	0.541	0.037	0.588	0.580	0.509	0.582	0.684	(0.843)

Note. Diagonal elements (values in parentheses) are the square root of the variance shared between the constructs and their measures. Off-diagonal elements are the correlations among constructs. For discriminant validity, diagonal elements should be larger than off-diagonal elements.

tight (0.005). For this reason, we maintain the discriminant validity of the constructs of the model, but take into consideration the special situation of system quality variable.

Structural Model

Figure 5 shows the variance explained (R^2) in the dependent constructs and the path coefficients (β) for the model. Consistent with Chin (1998), bootstrapping (500 resamples) was used to generate standard errors and t-statistics. This allows us to assess the statistical significance of the path coefficients.

Eleven of the 20 hypotheses were supported. H1b and H2b were supported. This shows that system quality and information quality of the EIS exert a significant positive influence on EIS user satisfaction. However, we have not found significant links between use (hours per week) and its predictor variables, i.e., H1a, H2a and H3a were not supported. On the other hand, the study strongly proves the hypotheses H3b-d. All the links between EIS use and individual impact variables have been rejected except H4b, which shows a weak relationship between EIS use and speed of decision making. We proved different links between individual impact and organizational impact variables (H5a-c, H6b, H7a). With regard to the subject under discussion, we should highlight the influence of the speed of problem identification on organizational impact variables (H5a-c).

Except for use variable, the research model seems to have an adequate predictive power for the majority of implied variables. Excluding EIS use variable, the mean of explained variances for the rest of the dependent constructs is 50%.

Figure 5: Structural model results

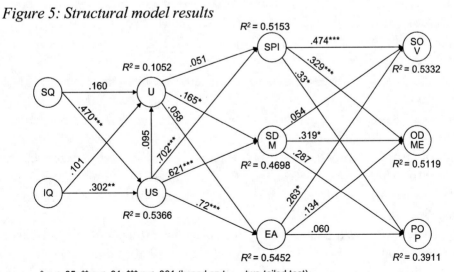

* p < .05; ** p < .01; *** p < .001 (based on $t_{(499)}$, two-tailed test)

Discussion and Limitations

The empirical results of this study indicate that information quality and system quality influence EIS user satisfaction. These factors explain more than 53% of the variance in the overall user satisfaction measure. This is consistent with the findings of Seddon and Kiew (1996) and McGill et al. (2000). However, we have not found significant relationships between use and its predictor variables, i.e., system quality, information quality, and user satisfaction. This supports the results of Fraser and Salter (1995), Klobas (1995), and McGill et al. (2000), whose works show that system quality and information quality do not significantly influence use. On the other hand, these outcomes are congruent with Collopy (1996), who didn't find a relationship statistically significant between user satisfaction and amount of use (using self-assessments). Nath (1989) offers an alternative explanation when he reports that the length of time of the usage for lower-level managers correlates to high levels of satisfaction. For upper-level managers who are the target of this study, higher levels of satisfaction are associated with frequency of use. Therefore, we think further research is necessary to identify other predictor variables of the EIS use.

Inconsistent with prior research, insufficient support was found for the influence of EIS use on individual impact constructs; the study only indicates a significant but weak relationship between use and speed of decision making. Nevertheless, the findings demonstrate that user satisfaction is a dominant construct in explaining all the individual impact variables considered. All the links between user satisfaction and individual impact variables have path coefficients greater than 0.62. This supports the conclusions of Gelderman (1998), Igbaria and Tan (1997), and McGill et al. (2000), who found that user satisfaction had a greater influence on individual performance than use construct. At the same time, these results are consistent with Seddon's (1997) opinion that the link between use and individual impact may not exist.

We have found different links between individual impact and organizational impact variables. The speed of problem identification variable is the main individual impact construct for explaining the organizational impact variables. Indeed, the results suggest significant relationships between speed of problem identification and all organizational impact constructs. This result supports the EIS contribution to problem opportunity finding, the first phase of the Simon-based process of decision making (Turban & Aronson, 1998). It suggests how the environmental scanning role of executives, supported by EIS, leads to important organizational benefits.

There are several limitations to the study that warrant mention. The first relates to organization bias. It seems likely that organizations that are unhappy with their EIS would be less inclined to participate in this study. Hence, the sample of EIS includes a larger proportion of "good" systems than is the case in the population of all EIS. Second, the study addressed only users of EIS at the point in time the survey was conducted. Users who, for various reasons, had discontinued use of the system were not included in the sample. Third, while evidence of causality was provided, causality itself was not proven. Fourth, the research relied mainly on user perceptions and a single method to elicit those perceptions. Fifth, a single data collection was used to test the structural model in the survey data analysis, assuming that a second data collection would have been more convincing. Finally, the study was conducted in a particular geographical context (Spain) focusing on a type of information system (EIS). Therefore, we must be cautious in generalizing the results to other contexts and types of information system.

FUTURE TRENDS

As future research lines, we point out the following two: (1) To identify and test other predictor variables of EIS use would be worthwhile. We think that alternative theoretical models could offer constructs that influence the use variable. In this sense, we could consider the technology acceptance model (Davis, Bagozzi, & Warshaw, 1989), the task technology fit model (Goodhue & Thompson, 1995), and the updated model of IS success (Garrity & Sanders, 1998). (2) It would also be worthwhile to adapt and analyze other information success models in the EIS domain, for instance, the approaches proposed by Seddon (1997) and Ballantine et al. (1996).

CONCLUSION

From a systemic point of view, we have developed an adaptation of DeLone and McLean's information system success model. At the same time, we have undertaken a validation test of this model using the Partial Least Squares approach. This work represents the first analysis of the complete DeLone and McLean's model in the EIS context using a structural equation modeling.

As a conclusion, we would like to highlight that our findings have the following implications for researchers and practitioners. First, our adaptation of DeLone and McLean's model to the EIS field in Spain seems to have an adequate predictive power for most implied variables (excluding the use variable): the mean of the explained variance is 50% for the rest of dependent constructs. Second, except for the use variable, several relationships among IS success dimensions have been demonstrated. Third, the research model helps us understand the influence of EIS on individual and organizational benefits. Fourth, the study shows hierarchical relationships among variable groups, i.e., connections between variables that stand out from the rest. In this matter, we would highlight that (a) the preponderance of the system quality is in the explanation of user satisfaction, (b) user satisfaction is strongly related to individual impact constructs, and (c) the EIS contribution to speed problem identification is critical for all organizational impact variables. Fifth, as a result of the validation process, new ideas and possibilities for the design of the model emerge: (a) further research is necessary to identify other predictor variables of the EIS use variable; (b) as with Seddon's (1997) model, we could question the existence of links between the use variable and the group of impact constructs; and (c) since system quality and information quality are two important predictors of user satisfaction, an adequate planning of the design, implementation, and sustaining phases of EIS is necessary in order to obtain a satisfactory level in both dimensions that contribute to EIS success.

ENDNOTE

1   An earlier version of this chapter was presented at the BITWorld 2000 Conference (Mexico City, June 1st, 2nd, & 3rd, 2000). Financial support for this work was provided by the Andalusian Research Plan (Research Group SEJ-115).

REFERENCES

Ackoff, R. L. (1999). *Ackoff's best. His classic writings on management.* New York: John Wiley & Sons.

Ballantine, J., Bonner, M., Levy, M., Martin, A., Munro, I. & Powell, P. L. (1996). The 3-D model of information systems success: The search for the dependent variable continues. *Information Resources Management Journal, 9*(4), 5–14.

Barclay, D., Higgins, C. & Thompson, R. (1995). The partial least squares (PLS) approach to causal modelling: Personal computer adoption and use as an illustration. *Technology Studies, 2,* 285–309.

Barki, H. & Hartwick, J. (1989). Rethinking the concept of user involvement. *MIS Quarterly, 13,* 53–63.

Bergeron, F. & Raymond, L. (1992). Evaluation of EIS from a managerial perspective. *Journal of Information Systems, 2,* 45–60.

Bergeron, F., Raymond, L., Rivard, S. & Gara, M. F. (1995). Determinants of EIS use: Testing a behavioral model. *Decision Support Systems, 14*(2), 131–146.

Carmines, E. G. & Zeller, R. A. (1979). Reliability and validity assessment (*Sage University paper series on quantitative applications in the social sciences. N. 07-017*). Beverly Hills, CA: Sage.

Chin, W. W. (1998). The partial least squares approach to structural equation modelling. In Marcoulides, G. A. (Ed.), *Modern methods for business research*, 295-336. Mahwah, NJ: Lawrence Erlbaum Associates.

Chin, W. W. & Frye, T. (1998). *PLS-Graph (Version 2.91.03.04) [Computer software]*. Calgary, Alberta, Canada: University of Calgary.

Collopy, F. (1996). Biases in retrospective self-reports of time use: An empirical study of computer users. *Management Science, 42*, 758–767.

Davis, F. D. (1989). Perceived usefulness, perceived ease of use, and user acceptance of information technology. *MIS Quarterly, 13*, 319–339.

Davis, F. D., Bagozzi, R. P. & Warshaw, P. R. (1989). User acceptance of computer technology: A comparison of two theoretical models. *Management Science, 35*, 982–1003.

DeLone, W. H. & McLean, E. R. (1992). Information systems success: The quest for the dependent variable. *Information Systems Research, 3*, 60–95.

Downing, C. E. (1999). System usage behavior as a proxy for user satisfaction: An empirical investigation. *Information & Management, 35*, 203–216.

Espejo, R. (1994). What is systemic thinking? *Systems Dynamic Review, 10*, 199–212.

Etezadi-Amoli, J. & Farhoomand, A. F. (1996). A structural model of end user computing satisfaction and user performance. *Information & Management, 30*, 65&73.

Faucheux, C., Laurent, A. & Makridakis, S. (1976). Can we model the wild world or should we first tame it?. In Churchman, C. W. and Mason, R. O. (Eds.), *World modeling: A dialogue*, 107–115. Amsterdam: North-Holland.

Finkelstein, L. & Carson, E. R. (1985). *Mathematical modeling of dynamic biological systems*. Letchwoth: Research Studies Press.

Fishbein, M. & Ajzen, I. (1975). *Belief, attitude, intentions and behavior: An introduction to theory and research*. Reading, MA: Addison-Wesley.

Flood, R. L. & Carson, E. R. (1988). *Dealing with complexity: An introduction to the theory and application of systems science*. New York: Plenum Press.

Fornell, C. & Larcker, D. F. (1981). Evaluating structural equation models with unobservable variables and measurement error. *Journal of Marketing Research, 18*, 39–50.

Fraser, S. G. & Salter, G. (1995). A motivational view of information systems success: A reinterpretation of DeLone & McLean's model. *Proceedings of the 6th Australasian conference on information systems, 1*, 119–140.

Frolick, M. N. (1994). Management support systems and their evolution from executive information systems. *Information Strategy: The Executive's Journal, 10*(3), 31–38.

Garrity, E. J. & Sanders, G. L. (1998). Dimensions of information systems success. In Garrity, E. J. and Sanders, G. L. (Eds.), *Information Systems Success Measurement*, 13–45. Hershey, PA: Idea Group Publishing.

Gatian, A. W. (1994). Is user satisfaction a valid measure of system effectiveness? *Information & Management, 26*, 119–131.

Gelderman, M. (1998). The relation between user satisfaction, usage of information systems and performance. *Information & Management, 34*, 11–18.

Gluck, M. (1996). Exploring the relationship between user satisfaction and relevance in information systems. *Information Processing & Management, 32*, 89–104.

Goodhue, D. L. & Thompson, R. L. (1995). Task-technology fit and individual performance. *MIS Quarterly, 19*, 213–236.

Huber, G. P. (1990). A theory of the effects of advanced information technologies on organizational design, intelligence, and decision making. *Academy of Management Review, 15*, 47–71.

Hwang, M. I., Windsor, J. C. & Pryor, A. (2000). Building a knowledge base for MIS research: A meta-analysis of a systems success model. *Information Resources Management Journal, 13*(2), 26–32.

Igbaria, M. & Nachman, S. A. (1990). Correlates of user satisfaction with end user computing: An exploratory study. *Information & Management, 19*, 73–82.

Igbaria, M. & Tan, M. (1997). The consequences of information technology acceptance on subsequent individual performance. *Information & Management, 32*, 113–121.

Klobas, J. E. (1995). Beyond information quality: Fitness for purpose and electronic information resource use. *Journal of Information Science, 21*, 95–114.

Leidner, D. E. (1996). The transition to open markets and modern management: The success of EIS in Mexico. In DeGross, J. & Jarvenpaa, S. (Eds.), *Proceedings of the seventeenth international conference on information systems*, 290–306. Cleveland, OH.

Leidner, D. E. & Elam, J. J. (1994). Executive information systems: Their impact on executive decision making. *Journal of Management Information Systems: JMIS, 10*, 139–155.

Leidner, D. E. & Elam, J. J. (1995). The impact of executive information systems on organizational design, intelligence, and decision making. *Organization Science, 6*, 645–664.

McGill, T., Hobbs, V. & Klobas, J. (2000). Testing the DeLone and McLean Model of IS success in the user developed application domain. In Gable, G.

G. & Vitale, M. R. (Eds.), *Proceedings of the 11th Australasian conference on information systems [CD-ROM]*. Information Systems Management Research Centre, School of Information Systems, Queensland University of Technology.

Mirani, R. & Lederer, A. L. (1998). An instrument for assessing the organizational benefits of IS projects. *Decision Sciences, 29*, 803–838.

Molloy, S. & Schwenk, C. H. (1995). The effects of information technology on strategic decision making. *Journal of Management Studies, 32*, 283–311.

Nath, R. (1989). Are frequent computer users more satisfied? *Information Processing & Management, 25*, 557–562.

Nunnally, J. (1978). *Psychometric theory* (second edition). New York: McGraw-Hill.

O'Reilly, C. A. (1982). Variations in decision makers' use of information sources: The impact of quality and accessibility of information. *Academy of Management Journal, 25*, 756–771.

Ortigueira, M. (1987). *Administraciones públicas: Teoría básica de las auditorías de gestión [Public administrations: Basic theory of the management audits]*. Granada: Publicaciones del CUR.

Ortigueira, M. (1995). *La Implantación de la contabilidad financiera en la administración de la xunta de Galicia. Bases metodológicas y científico-técnicas [The implementation of the financial accounting in the administration of the Galician government. Methodological and technical-scientific bases]*. Santiago de Compostela: Xunta de Galicia. Consellería de Economía e Facenda.

Pitt, L. F., Watson, R. T. & Kavan, C. B (1995). Service quality: A measure of information systems effectiveness. *MIS Quarterly, 19*, 173–187.

Powell, T. C. (1995). Total quality management as competitive advantage: A review and empirical study. *Strategic Management Journal, 16*, 15–37.

Ragowsky, A., Ahituv, N. & Neumann, S. (1996). Identifying the value and importance of an information system application. *Information & Management, 31*, 89–102.

Rivett, P. (1980). *Model building for decision analysis*. Chichester: John Wiley & Sons.

Rockart, J. F. & DeLong, D. W. (1988). *Executive support systems. The emergence of top management computer use*. Homewood, IL: Business One Irwin.

Sanders, G. L. & Courtney, J. F. (1985). A field study of organizational factors influencing DSS success. *MIS Quarterly, 9*, 77–93.

Seddon, P. B. (1997). A respecification and extension of the DeLone and McLean model of IS success. *Information Systems Research, 8*, 240–253.

Seddon, P. B. & Kiew, M. Y. (1996). A partial test and development of DeLone and McLean's model of IS success. *Australian Journal of Information Systems*, *4*(1), 90–109.

Sherman, B. A. (1997). *Operationalization of information systems technology assessment. Unpublished doctoral dissertation*, State University of New York at Buffalo.

Straub, D. W. (1989). Validating instruments in MIS research. *MIS Quarterly*, *13*, 147–190.

Straub, D. W. & Wetherbe, J. C. (1989). Information technologies for the 1990s: An organizational impact perspective. *Communications of the ACM*, *32*, 1328–1339.

Szewczak, E. J. (1988). Exploratory results of a factor analysis of strategic information: Implications for strategic systems planning. *Journal of Management Information Systems*, *5*, 83–98.

Turban, E. & Aronson, J. E. (1998). *Decision support systems and intelligent systems* (fifth edition). Upper Saddle River, NJ: Prentice Hall.

Venkatraman, N. & Ramanujam, V. (1986). Measurement of business performance in strategic research: A comparison of approaches. *Academy of Management. The Academy of Management Review*, *11*, 801–814.

Vlahos, G. E. & Ferratt, T. W. (1995). Information technology use by managers in Greece to support decision making: Amount, perceived value, and satisfaction. *Information & Management*, *29*, 305–315.

Watson, H. J., Houdeshel, G. & Rainer, R. K. Jr. (1997). *Building Executive Information Systems and Other Decision Support Applications*. New York: John Wiley & Sons.

Watson, H. J., Rainer Jr., R. K. & Koh, C. E. (1991). Executive information systems: A framework for development and a survey of current practices. *MIS Quarterly*, *15*, 13–30.

Wilkin, C. & Hewett, B. (1999). Quality in a respecification of DeLone and McLean's IS success model. *IRMA International Conference*, 663–671.

Wold, H. (1979). *Model construction and evaluation when theoretical knowledge is scarce: An example of the use of partial least squares (Cahiers du Département D'Économétrie)*. Geneva, Switzerland: Faculté des Sciences Économiques et Sociales, Université de Genève.

Young, D. & Watson, H. J. (1995). Determinates of EIS acceptance. *Information & Management*, *29*, 153–164.

Zmud, R. W. (1978). An empirical investigation of the dimensionality of the concept of information. *Decision Sciences*, *9*, 187–195.

Zviran, M. (1992). Evaluating user satisfaction in a hospital environment: An exploratory study. *Health Care Management Review*, *17*(3), 51–62.

Chapter V

A Systemic Approach of Electronic Commerce

Roberto Vinaja
University of Texas Pan American, USA

ABSTRACT

This chapter applies several concepts from classical Systems Theory to the growing area of E-commerce and agents. The purpose of this chapter is to demonstrate how General Systems Theory principles are widely applicable to the state-of-the art field of Electronic Commerce. The Systems Approach can be used as a framework to model interaction in the electronic marketplace. Software agents play an important role in this system. The chapter describes the characteristics of an intelligent agent and its applications in Electronic Commerce from a systemic perspective.

INTRODUCTION

General systems theory delineates rules that govern behaviors of a variety of entities, both living and nonliving. These rules can be conceptualized as systems with various interacting components. Laws could theoretically be formulated to describe how any system functioned. Systems theory is closely connected to cybernetics. According to Van Gigch (1991), the systems approach is a method of inquiry, which emphasizes the whole system instead of component systems. The systems approach is a useful framework in which we can analyze the role of intelligent agents and the e-commerce environment. The systems approach embodies the tenets of systems theory. The systems approach is a common conceptual framework for many disciplines, and it can be applied to the field of electronic commerce and intelligent agents.

We will apply several concepts from classical systems theory to the growing area of e-commerce and agents. Our purpose is to demonstrate how general systems theory principles are widely applicable to the state-of-the art field of electronic commerce. The systems approach can be used as a framework to model interaction in the electronic marketplace. Software agents play an important role in this system. The next section will describe the characteristics of an intelligent agent.

AGENT CHARACTERISTICS

As stated before, there is not an accord on what precisely constitutes an agent, or on its characteristics. There are dozens of definitions, and each author proposes a different set of characteristics. Franklin and Graesser (1996) propose the following properties: reactivity, autonomy, goal-oriented, temporally continuous, communicative, learning, mobile, flexible, and character. Etzioni and Weld (1994) propose a few other characteristics such as collaborative behavior.

The designer of any agent should keep the user in mind when deciding on the characteristics of an agent. The cognitive style of the user, the intended use of the agent, the user's perception of the agent, and the user's expectations play an important role in the successful implementation of an agent. These problems can be analyzed from the viewpoint of related disciplines such as human–computer interaction, cognitive psychology, and ethics. In this section, we will review the main characteristics cited by leading experts in intelligent agent technology. For the purpose of our framework, we will focus on the eight most cited characteristics.

Intelligence

Intelligence can be defined as the degree of reasoning and learned behavior. At a minimum, there can be some statement of preferences; higher levels include reasoning, planning, learning, and adaptation (Gilbert et al., 1995). Allen Newell (1990) defines intelligence as: "the degree to which a system approximates a knowledge-level system." Truly intelligent agents may use classical AI techniques, such as rule-based systems, knowledge-based systems, or neural networks.

Autonomy

An agent can be considered a system with behavior that is "goal-oriented" toward a certain ideal state. Self-regulated agents are goal-governed agents, which given a certain goal, are able to achieve it by themselves. Self-regulation is a characteristic of cybernetic systems. Another characteristic of a system is its autonomy. However, to be an agent and to be self-regulated are not sufficient conditions to be an autonomous agent. In a sense, even a simple cybernetic servo-mechanism (like a thermostat) is able to assure "autonomously" the fulfillment of a given goal-state. Autonomy is more than that; it requires "autonomous goals" (Castelfranchi, 1994).

Agents should be able to conduct transactions on behalf of their owners, such as signing an advantageous contract, finding the lowest price for an item on the Internet, entering into an agreement, or negotiating with other agents. These are actions that the agent should conduct without relying on its owner for every step. The agent should be provided with the basic parameters for operation, and then it should be left on its own. Negotiation agents have been used for electronic auctions. The user can create a negotiation agent and specify a set of parameters for a given auction. After that, the agent is on its own. According to Maes (1995), a software agent can initiate communication, monitor events, and perform tasks without the direct intervention of humans.

An agent should have a measure of autonomy from its user; otherwise, it would be just a regular algorithmic program. According to d'Inverno (1996), "A motivated agent is one which pursues its own agenda for reasoning and behavior in accordance with its own internal motivation. An autonomous agent must necessarily be a motivated agent." An autonomous agent is an agent, which has its own set of motivations.

Learning

Learning occurs as an agent interacts with its environment. The agent can be taught what to do for each individual user; it is a sort of customization (Dent et al., 1992). Because people do not all do the same tasks, and even those who share the same task do it in different ways, an agent must be trained in the task and how to do it (Mitchell et al., 1994).

Cunnyngham (1980) has developed a hierarchy for understanding intelligence, the learning hierarchy, where at each step something is added to the learning mechanisms already at hand.
1.   Learning by discovery
2.   Learning by seeing samples
3.   Learning by being told
4.   Learning by being programmed

Automated machine learning, or learning by being programmed, is the foundation upon which all cybernetic intelligence is built.

Learning by being told is simpler than learning by seeing samples, because there is no need to decide which difference is most important and what to do about it. But on both levels, there is a need for a data structure into which information about what is important can be assimilated. In order to learn by being told, there is a need to match descriptions or attributes. Thus, even below the level of learning by seeing samples, there is a need for discrimination between the characteristic patterns of attributes, which identify objects as specific types of entities.

Maes (1994) has addressed the problem of agent training based on the learning approach of a real human assistant. In addition, she has proposed a learning model highly compatible with Cunnyngham's hierarchy.

Internet consumers have distinct profiles. Some customers are more price-sensitive, some others are more concerned about quality. An agent can be customized depending on the preferences of the consumer. An agent can be trained to maximize profit or minimize costs in a transaction. In the domain of financial investments, an agent can be customized to reflect the risk adversity level of its owner.

Consumers have unique characteristics: income level, age, gender, marital status, educational level, personality type, and shopping preferences. The agent can be customized and trained on the likes and dislikes of its owner. The agent can be trained on what to do for each individual user; it is a sort of customization. Since people do not have the same shopping preferences, and even those who share the same preferences may not have the same shopping behavior pattern, an agent must be instructed in the task at hand and how to do it. In order to do this, an agent should have learning capabilities and a memory.

Mobility

A mobile agent is able to roam networks and to transport itself from one machine to another (Franklin & Graesser, 1996). Mobile agents are able to move from one network to another. In contrast, static agents are bound to a specific computer. Mobility has many advantages. Mobile agents can perform a task while the user is off-line, in other words, the agent can be instructed on a specific task and sent over the Internet to complete it. In the meantime, the user can reset the Internet connection and reduce connection costs. Mobile agents can meet and interact with other agents in electronic marketplaces or participate in auctions and on-line trading.

Cognition

The level of cognition can be from reactive to deliberative. Reactivity is the ability to selectively sense and act (Murch & Johnson, 1999). A reactive agent responds in a timely fashion to changes in the environment (Franklin & Graesser,

1996). A reactive agent is also able to modify its behavior as environmental circumstances change (Wooldridge, 1996). On the other hand, deliberative agents engage in planning and negotiation in order to achieve their goals (Nwana & Ndumu, 1998). Watcher agents such as WebWatcher, Personal Webwatcher, or agents that alert users of updates to a web page are examples of reactive agents. Some of these monitoring agents can sense changes in a web page and modify search criteria.

Cooperation

Collaborative agents are able to work in concert with other agents in order to achieve a common goal. Cooperation involves high-order messages (Nwana & Ndumu, 1998). In order to cooperate, agents need to possess a social ability, for example, the ability to interact with other agents and possibly humans via some communication language (Guha & Lenat, 1994; Wooldridge et al., 1995). To address multi agent interactions, agents should at least adhere to a common ontology. Such ontology provides a minimal basis for either direct interaction through interagent communication or indirect interaction through the modification of the environment (Giroux, 1995).

When considering cooperation and collective activities, we are concerned with both the object level and the metalevel of artificial agency. The object level is concerned with the state, rationality, and communication acts of a single agent; the metalevel refers to the society of agents with social laws and conventions among them. While the object level helps to design individual agents in a society of agents, the metalevel helps to design appropriate interaction laws that should govern the society (Haddadi, 1996).

Each agent or group of agents has knowledge about itself and about other agents (Guichard & Ayel, 1994). A category of agents called software agents or interface agents are software entities that interact in digital environments (Genesereth & Ketchpel, 1994; Crowston & Malone, 1988). A cooperative agent must have the ability to communicate with persons and other agents with human-like languages (Murch & Johnson, 1999; Haddadi, 1996). One or several mechanisms or languages could accomplish this (Lashkari et al., 1994).

Openness

Most organic systems are open, meaning that they exchange materials, energies, or information with their environments (Koehler, 1938). An open system is one that relates, interacts, and communicates with other systems (Katz, 1966). Openness is not restricted to natural systems, a software environment can also be considered as open. Intelligent agents as a special class of open systems have properties of their own, but they share other properties with all open systems.

According to Bertalanffy (1950), general properties include the exchange of information with their environment, feedback, and equifinality (that is, reaching the same ultimate goal, from different initial conditions, through diverse paths).

Intelligent agents must be open, and they need features to handle an open environment. An agent programmer must provide the agent with means to deal with the environment and interact (especially with other agents). Agents may collaborate or negotiate in a dynamic environment. Since the electronic market environment where an agent interacts is open, the behaviors or characteristics of other agents cannot be known a priori. Therefore, agents must be able to live and act in evolving and unpredictable environments. Agents with different behaviors should be able to interact and cooperate in a multiagent environment.

Purposiveness

Purposeful behavior is that which is directed toward the attainment of a goal, a final state (Van Gigch, 1991). This behavior is also called proactivity or goal-orientation. A goal-oriented agent does not simply act in response to the environment (Franklin and Graesser, 1996). According to d'Inverno (1996), "An agent is something that satisfies a goal or a set of goals." It is important to identify the goals of the agent during the design phase. According to Van Gigch (1991), the following criteria can be used to determine if a behavior is purposeful:

1.   The object to which behavior is attributed must be part of the system.
2.   Purposeful behavior must be directed toward a goal.
3.   There must be a reciprocal relationship between the system and its environment.
4.   Behavior must be related to or coupled with the environment, from which it must receive and register signals, which indicate whether behavior is conductive to making progress toward the goal.
5.   A purposeful system must always exhibit choice of alternative courses of action.
6.   Choices of behavior must lead to an end product or result.
   Intentional attitudes, usually attributed to humans, are also a characteristic of agents (Haddadi, 1996).

Adaptation

Many natural systems display a quality called adaptation. In the natural sciences, adaptation is such behavior that is "adapted": it preserves the life of the animal by keeping the essential variables within limits (Ashby, 1960, pp. 58, 60–62). An adaptive system can react in a positive way to a change in the environment, in some way to the continued operation of the system. *Adaptation can occur in several levels of an organizational hierarchy and may even apply to itself, as in "amplifying adaptation" (Ashby), which is "adaptation to adapt" and has the properties of self-organization.*

An adaptive system is one that "evolves tactics to keep the domain of stability, broad enough to absorb the consequences of change" (VanGigch, 1991). An agent should be able to adapt dynamically to its environment and improve its performance. According to Pekelis (1970), any system that can improve the algorithm of its behavior and make it flexible or adaptable to the environment is described as self-organizing. Adaptation smoothens interactions and keeps agents alive and evolutional (Giroux, 1995).

Objects that can affect a system module but are outside its boundaries constitute the frame environment of the system. A frame is also a collection of objects and relations. A conceptual frame-perspective for describing a system is called a "world view" of the system. The notion of alternative frame environments representing alternative states of the world is of fundamental importance (Cunnyngham, 1980). The frame problem can be described as the task of any agent acting in a dynamic environment to keep its model of the world and its general knowledge in synchrony with the world. In the case of an Internet environment, the agent has to detect changes in URL addresses and update links. The agent should be able to adapt to unexpected situations in the environment and be able to recover (Giroux, 1995).

Anthropomorphism is the use of metaphors ascribing human characteristics to nonhuman forms. There is a great debate over anthropomorphism in user interface design and intelligent agents (Krogh, 1995). However agency does not necessarily imply a need for anthropomorphism.

As a summary, Table 1 compares characteristics proposed in three different studies (Murch & Johnson, 1999; Franklin & Graesser, 1996; Huhns & Singh, 1998).

A TYPOLOGY OF AGENTS

A methodology to support agent design for specific e-commerce applications should provide a framework that enables the complexity of the system to be managed by decomposition and abstraction. Intelligent systems can be organized into hierarchies, or levels—the levels above inherit capabilities of the lower levels. Simon (1977) proposed that a hierarchical decomposition is necessary for the construction of any complex assembly.

Many researchers have proposed various classification schemes and taxonomies to provide a simpler way of characterizing the space of agent types. In a classical paper, Gilbert et al. (1995) from IBM described agents in terms of a space defined by three dimensions (or attributes), agency, intelligence, and mobility. The scope of intelligent agents is shown in Figure 1. This model was the first one to consider multiple dimensions.

Table 1: A comparison of proposed characteristics

CHARACTERISTICS	AUTHORS		
	(Murch & Johnson, 1999)	(Franklin & Graesser, 1996)	(Huhns & Singh, 1998)
Agency, Autonomy, Self-starters	x	x	x
Collaboration/Cooperation	x		
Communication/Social Ability	x	x	
Construction			x
Flexible		x	
Friendliness			x
Inference capability	x		
Intelligence			
Interactions			x
Learning	x	x	
Level of Cognition	x	x	
Mobility	x	x	x
Persistence,	x		x
Personality	x	x	
Purposeful	x	x	
Rugedness, Adaptation		x	
Sociability			x
Social autonomy			x
Transparency/Accountability	x		
User centered	x		

Figure 1: Intelligent agent scope

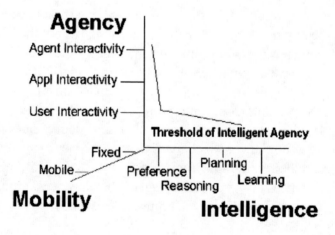

The classification criterion shown in Figure 2 was proposed by Nwana (1996). Nwana uses three attribute dimensions: mobility, reactivity, and autonomy. He combines the three attributes in a Venn diagram, resulting in four types of agents: collaborative-learning agents, collaborative agents, interface agents, and smart agents.

After proposing the previous classification criteria, Nwana describes ongoing research in seven categories: collaborative agents, interface agents, mobile agents, information/Internet agents, reactive agents, hybrid agents, and smart agents. The agent topology is illustrated in Figure 3.

Franklin and Graesser (1996) proposed a taxonomy of autonomous agents based on a biological taxonomy. This taxonomy is shown in Figure 4. Below this initial classification, they suggest that agents can be categorized by control structures, environments (e.g., database, file system, network, Internet), language in which they are written, and applications.

Figure 5 presents another framework based on the task the agent performs or the languages or protocols it is based on. This scheme proposed by Labrou et al. (1999) has a similar approach to that of Franklin and Graesser (1996).

The taxonomy shown in Figure 6 has been proposed by Brenner, Zarnekow, and Wittig (1997). At the highest level, three major categories of agents can be distinguished: human agents, hardware agents, and software agents.

Brustoloni (1991) classifies agents starting with a three-way classification taxonomy that includes regulation agents, planning agents, or adaptive agents. A

Figure 2: Nwana classification diagram

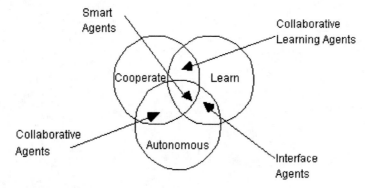

Figure 3: Nwana's agent topology

Figure 4: Taxonomy of autonomous agents

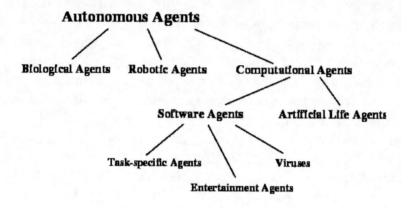

Figure 5: Software agent technologies classification

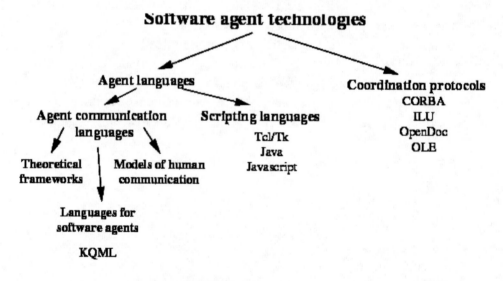

Figure 6: A taxonomy of intelligent agents

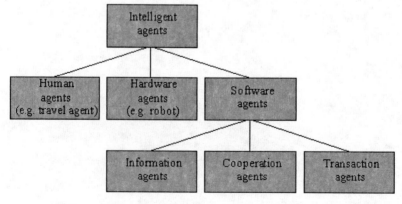

regulation agent reacts to inputs, and it always knows what to do, it never learns or plans. Planning agents plan using Artificial Intelligence techniques, case-based reasoning, or Operations Research methods. Adaptive agents can learn.

Given so many agent attributes, Gilbert et al. (1995), Nwana (1996), Franklin and Graesser (1996), Brustoloni (1991), and Brenner, Zarnekow, and Wittig (1997), have all tried to come up with a simplified framework in order to describe the space of agent types. Some models use two attributes or dimensions and classify agents in a bidimensional plane. Other models, such as Gilbert's (1995) and Zarnekow's (1997) use three attributes, resulting in a three-dimensional space where agents are categorized.

Zarnekow (1997) has also proposed a three-dimensional classification space. The three selected criteria are intelligence, mobility, and number of agents. Notice how Gilbert et al. (1995) and Zarnekow (1997) agree on including intelligence and mobility as main attributes.

INTELLIGENT AGENT AS A SYSTEM

We can conceptualize electronic commerce as a metasystem. At the whole systems level, we embrace, not only the e-commerce system but also, among others, a social system, a legal system, a technological system, and an economics

Figure 7: Three-dimensional classification space

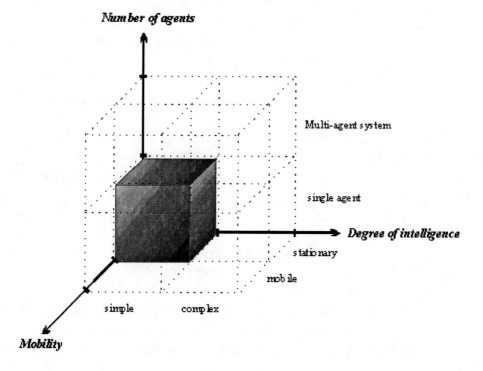

Figure 8: Description of the three dimensions

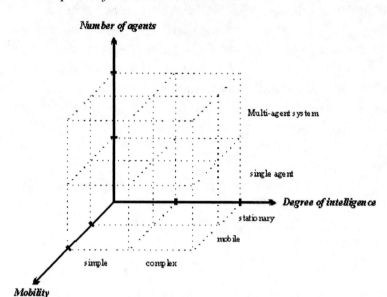

system. The social system involves the changing nature of the workforce, ethical issues, and political changes. The legal system deals with regulations, privacy issues, and legal issues. The economics system deals with the global economy, market conditions, and competition. The environment can be defined as comprising all systems not included in the total system. Within the total system, i.e., the e-commerce infrastructure, we have both human, organizational, and digital entities and agents working toward a common goal. Each agent can be considered a subsystem within the e-commerce system. Van Gigch (2000) has identified some other components of the Web system such as web sites, information, individuals, providers, companies, and organizations.

Each agent in the total system can operate as a self-contained and self-sufficient entity, pursuing a set of goals. From the point of view of the agent subsystem, all other agents, consumers, etc., are classified as the relative environ-ment. Agents exhibit many characteristics from general systems theory. If we apply some general concepts from general systems theory we can show that an intelligent agent qualifies as a system. In a classic work, Churchmann (1971), one of the System Theory pioneers, lists the necessary conditions that something (let us call it S) should fulfill to be conceived of as a system. Notice how we can apply all conditions to an intelligent agent.

1. *S (The agent) is teleological.* Systems theory uses the concept of teleology. Teleology is the philosophical doctrine that seeks to explain and justify the states of the world in terms of posterior causes, which may be relegated to far-

Figure 9: The WHOLE system

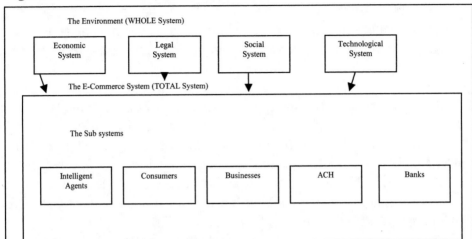

offfutures. Purposeful behavior is that which is directed toward the attainment of a goal, a final state (VanGigch, 1991). The most distinctive character of the behavior of higher organisms is its goal-directness, its apparent purposiveness. According to d'Inverno (1996), an agent is something that satisfies a goal or set of goals.

2. *S (The agent) has a measure of performance.* Agents are evaluated based on attainment of goals. In some collaborative systems based on genetic algorithms, inefficient agents are replaced, and only those agents that perform satisfactorily survive.

3. *S (The agent) has a client.* There is always a buyer or owner whose interests are served by the agent, in such a manner that the higher the measure of performance, the better the interests are served.

4. *S (The agent) has an environment.* Agents interact in an environment. The environment may include different agent communication protocols or multiple platforms.

5. *The agent has a designer.* The designer conceptualizes the nature of the agent, in such a manner that the designer's concepts potentially produce actions in the decision maker, and hence, changes in the measure of performance of the agent.

ABSTRACTION IN SYSTEMS THEORY

The agent paradigm in artificial intelligence is based upon the notion of adaptive, autonomous, internally motivated entities interacting in changing environments in which they act. The term intelligent agent has been used to describe a program that can perform tasks on behalf of its owner and can interact with the user or other agents, with system resources, in order to accomplish some goals. Agents can communicate using messages. They may also have commitments and goals.

Abstraction is an important concept in general systems theory. By using abstraction, we can extract the most important characteristics from reality and create a model of a system. We can apply abstraction to the electronic commerce field and represent interactions and transactions using abstracted terms. When we describe certain transactions performed by a software program as "Shopping Agents Finding Bargains in a Cybermall," we are indeed using an abstraction. This abstraction describes flows of information, goods, services, and values in an electronic market. The term cybermall is an abstract term that describes a single entry to a collection of electronic storefronts. It is a set of independent electronic stores that shares some electronic commerce mechanisms.

An abstraction is composed of concepts. Abstraction lets us model our images of reality through different levels of conceptualization. Whenever a domain is increasingly large and complex, we might need to appeal to a level of abstraction at which the problem and its solution can be better represented. We can use human attributes to represent agent characteristics, this is an abstraction. We could describe agents has having intentional attitudes, usually attributed to humans (Haddadi, 1996). This agent view provides just the right level of abstraction at which we envisage computational systems that are able to operate globally on the entire net (Barbuceanu, 1995). In some sense, even the word "agent" is used as a metaphor to illustrate some of the characteristics of this software entity. We use the agent concept as an abstraction to describe the unique features of a software program. According to Laufmann (1996), the agent metaphor provides an intuitive abstraction, which resembles the word of human activities, it provides a coordination model, and it offers conceptual separability of the model and its implementation. In this view, the agent takes on anthropomorphic qualities, making the approach quite intuitive to humans. The term "intelligent agent" describes a program that performs tasks for its user that can interact with other agents and the environment.

THE ENVIRONMENT

When studying open systems, such as the intelligent agents, it is important to determine system boundaries. The interactions with the environment are also critical. The electronic marketplace is a very complex place for agents to act in. The complexity of the agent depends on the number and type of relationships with other entities.

Most agent architectures are designed to only deal with a subset of the total possible electronic marketplace complexity, and act in very particular domains, such as auctioning, price comparison, etc. For example, some architectures assume that the environment is static and that the only way that the environment conditions are changed is by the agents' actions. Other electronic commerce models consider a dynamic environment but expect consistent or predictable surroundings. This type of models is overly simplistic, although useful to improve our understanding of the electronic market. A static environment consists of fixed surroundings in which an agent interacts. In this representation of the electronic market, the agent is not required to adapt to new situations, and the programmer is not concerned with the unpredictability of the electronic environment. Although this would be an ideal environment for an agent to navigate in, the real marketplace is not static, but dynamic. The conditions of the electronic market are always changing, prices fluctuate, new goods and services are offered on a daily basis, and the agent must be aware of these changes. The goal of the agent's programmer is to design an agent that can interact in several platforms. In order to create an agent that can interact in a variety of situations, it is necessary to provide the agent with the capabilities to operate in a dynamic environment. A dynamic environment is one that changes over time, independent of the actions of the agent. There are some prototype applications with a static environment, but these are artificially controlled situations. We may want to implement agent in the real world, where conditions are dynamic. Many prototype applications in e-commerce have not been commercialized, because they only operate in a simulated environment. Before an agent can be released to the public, it must have robust mechanisms to face dynamic and unpredictable circumstances in a complex environment.

Developing an agent that can interact in the electronic marketplace requires taking into account the multitude of uncertain events caused by dynamic and unpredictable situations. Certainly, an agent that operates in a simulated environment performs better and is easier to train, because the surroundings are simplified. On the other hand, using a simulated environment allows the programmer to test different hypothetical situations in a controlled setting.

An electronic commerce environment may be very complex. There may exist thousands of products and services, varied prices, and multiple agents. The agent must have a way of managing this complexity.

Agents may be complex or simple and they may work alone or in collaboration with other agents, creating a multiagent environment. Most electronic commerce applications use proprietary vendor-specific, communication protocols. It is very difficult for agents with different environments or protocols to interact. To address this issue, agents should at least adhere to a common ontology. Such ontology provides a minimal basis for interagent communication (Giroux, 1995). We can view the cooperation and collective activities in the electronic commerce environment from two different levels, the object level and the metalevel (Haddadi, 1996). The object level deals with the rationality and communication actions of a single agent. The metalevel means the collection of agents with its communication language and negotiation protocols. At the object level, we are concerned with designing an individual agent; at the metalevel, we design the interaction rules for interaction among all the agents in the electronic environment.

Kinny (1996) has found that it is very desirable to have a set of models at two levels of abstraction: the external and the internal viewpoints. We can parallel the external viewpoint with the metalevel and the internal viewpoint with the object level. The internal viewpoint contains information about the environment, the goals, and the plans to achieve the goals. From the external viewpoint, the system is fractionated into agents. Each agent is a complex object with a purpose, services to perform, and external interactions.

Each agent has knowledge about itself and about other agents. In this type of structure, it is possible to have several levels of decomposition. For example, agents having the same function (i.e., information filtering, price comparison, etc.) can be joined in the same group, which allows for two levels of images of the system: the agent's level and a global view of functions (Guichard, 1994).

CONCLUSION

This chapter was devoted to the presentation of a variety of general systems theory concepts and its applicability to the domain of intelligent agents for e-commerce. Many concepts were applied from the value of the thinking of scholars who have contributed to the writing general systems theory. The designer of intelligent agents will find the concepts of general systems theory insightful and applicable to the domain of intelligent agents. This approach can be used for further analysis. For example, Van Gigch (2000) uses the general systems approach to propose the need of a formal, control system, i.e., a metasystem to act as a metalevel controller over the activities of the virtual community. For those individuals already familiar with general systems theory, this chapter provides some insights into the relationship of the two disciplines. An important objective of this chapter was to provide for those interested in e-commerce and intelligent agent technologies, a basic presentation of general systems theory, and a range of possible applications of general systems theory to e-commerce. The consequences of using cybernetics and general systems theory as an approach to e-commerce and agent technology have been discussed.

REFERENCES

Ashby, W. R. (1960). Adaptation in the multistable environment. *Design for a brain* (second edition), 205–214. New York: John Wiley & Sons.

Barbuceanu, M. & Fox, M. S. (1995). The architecture of an agent building shell. *Intelligent agents II, agent theories, architectures and languages*, 235–250. IJCAI 1995 Workshop, Montreal, Canada.

Brenner, W., Zarnekow, R., & Wittig, H. in cooperation with Schubert, C. (1997). *Intelligent software agents: Theory and applications*. Berlin: Springer-Verlag.

Brustoloni, J. C. (1991). *Autonomous agents—Characterization and requirements. Technical report CMU-CS-91-204*, Carnegie Mellon University, Pittsburgh, School of Computer Science.

Castelfranchi, C. (1994). Guarantees for autonomy in cognitive agent architecture. *Intelligent agents, Proceedings of the ECAI-94 workshop on agent theories*, 56–70. Architectures and Languages, Amsterdam, The Netherlands.

Churchman, C. W. (1971). *The design of inquiring systems*. New York: Basic Books, Inc.

Cunnyngham, J. (1980). Cybernetic design for a strategic information system, applied systems and cybernetics. In Lasker, G. E. (Ed.), *Systems concepts, models and methodology*, 920-925.

Dent, L., Boticario, J., Mc Dermott, J., Mitchell, T., & Zabowski, D. (1992). A personal learning apprentice. *Proceedings of the National Conference on Artificial Intelligence*.

d'Inverno, M. & Luck, M. (1996). Formalising the contract net as a goal-directed system. *Agents breaking away*, 72–85. Berlin: Springer-Verlag.

Etzioni, O. & Weld, D. (1994). A softbot-based interface to the Internet. *Communications of the ACM, 37*(7), 72–76.

Franklin, S. & Graesser, A. (1996). Is it an agent or just a program?: A taxonomy for autonomous agents. *Intelligent agents III, agent theories, architectures and languages*, 21–36. Berlin: Springer-Verlag, Heidelberg.

Genesereth, M. R. & Ketchpel, S. P. (1994). Software agents. *Communications of the ACM, 37*(7), 48–53.

Gilbert, D., Aparicio, M., Atkinson, B., Brady, S., Ciccarino, J., Grosof, B., O'Connor, P., Osisek, D., Pritko, S., Spagna, R. & Wilson L. (1995). The role of intelligent agents in the information infrastructure. *IBM Report*.

Giroux, S. (1995). Open reflective agents *Intelligent agents II, agent theories, architectures and languages*, 315–330. IJCAI Workshop, Montreal, Canada.

Guha, R. V. & Lenat, D. B. (1994). Enabling agents to work together. *Communications of the ACM, 37*(7), 127–141.

Guichard, F. & Ayel, J. (1994). Logical reorganization of distributed artificial intelligence systems. *Intelligent agents, Proceedings of the ECAI-94 workshop on agent theories, architectures and languages*, 118–128. Amsterdam, The Netherlands.

Haddadi, A. (1996). *Communication and cooperation in agent systems, 1–2,* 52–53. Berlin: Springer-Verlag.

Huhns, M. N. & Singh, M. P. (1998). *Reading in agents.* San Francisco, CA: Morgan Kauffman.

Katz, D. & Kahn, R.L. (1966). Common characteristics of open systems. *Systems thinking*, 86-104. Middlesex, England: Penguin Books, Middlesex.

Kinny, D., Georgeff, M. & Rao, A. (1996). A methodology and modeling technique for systems of BDI agents. *Agents breaking away*, 56–71. Berlin: Springer-Verlag.

Koehler, W. (1938). Closed and open systems. *Systems thinking*, 59-59. Middlesex, England: Penguin Books.

Labrou, T., Finin T., & Peng, Y. (1999). Agent communication languages: The current landscape. *IEEE Intelligent Systems, 14*(2).

Lashkari, Y., Metral, M. & Maes, P. (1994). Collaborative interface agents. *Proceedings of the National Conference on Artificial Intelligence.*

Laufmann, S. (1996). The information marketplace: Achieving success in commercial applications. *Electronic commerce: Current research issues and applications*, 115–147. Berlin: Springer.

Maes, P (1995). Artificial intelligence meets entertainment: Life-like autonomous agents. *Communications of the ACM, 38*(11).

Maes, P. (1994). Agents that reduce work and information overload. *Communications of the ACM, 37*(7), 31–40.

Maes, P. & Kozierok, R. (1993). Learning interface agents. *Proceedings of the AAAI'93 Conference.* New York: MIT-Press.

Minsky, M. (1985). *Society of mind.* New York: Simon and Schuster.

Mitchell, T., Caruana, R., Freitag, D., McDermott, J. & Zabowski, D. (1994). Experience with a learning personal assistant. *Communications of the ACM, 37*(7), 81–91.

Murch, R. & Johnson, T. (1999). *Intelligent software agents.* Upper Saddle River, NJ: Prentice Hall.

Newell, A. (1990). *Unified theories of cognition.* Cambridge, MA: Harvard University Press.

Nwana, H. S. (1996). Software agents: An overview. *Knowledge Engineering Review, 11*(3), 1–40. Cambridge, MA: Cambridge University Press.

Nwana, H. S. & Ndumu, D. T. (1998). A brief introduction to software agent technology. In Jennings, N. R. & Wooldridge, M. J. (Eds.), *Agent technology, foundations, applications, and markets*, 29–48. Berlin: Springer-Verlag.

Pekelis, V. (1974). Self adapting system. *Cybernetics A to Z*, 264–269. Moscow, Russia: Mir Publishers Moscow (English Translation, 1974).

Simon, H. (1977). *The new science of management decision*, 39–81. Englewood Cliffs, NJ: Prentice Hall.

Van Gigch, J. P. (2000). Do we need to impose more regulation upon the World Wide Web? A metasystem analysis. *Informing Science*, *3*(3), 109–116.

Van Gigch, J. P. (1991). *Systems design modeling and metamodeling*. New York: Plenum Press.

Wooldridge, M. (1996). Agents as a Rorschach test: A response to Franklin and Graesser. *Intelligent agents III, agent theories, architectures and languages*, 45. Berlin: Springer-Verlag, Heidelberg.

Section IV

Information Systems' Organizational and Social Issues

Chapter VI

Information Systems as Social Systems

N. F. du Plooy
University of Pretoria, South Africa

ABSTRACT

Since the very early days of computing, information systems were regarded as "man-machine" systems. This definition is of far greater importance to the teaching of information systems as well as to the profession of information systems developers than is often recognised. The majority of teachers, and textbooks, are still caught in the paradigm that information systems development is a technical "art" rather than a field that concerns sociological, rather than technical problems. This chapter argues that the "human" or sociological side of information systems is of such importance that it should be seen as the core of the discipline, and that information systems are best understood when viewed as social systems.

Examining the nondeterministic nature of information systems and applying Ashby's Law of Requisite Variety are helpful to describe and explain these systems as social systems. The paper also refers to current thinking on systems (especially soft systems methodology) and its place in supporting information systems in a constantly changing environment.

Finally, the implications of viewing information systems as social systems are discussed with respect to teaching and research, the impact of information systems on organizations, and the shortcomings of current software engineering methodologies.

INTRODUCTION

I wish to make clear right at the onset of the chapter, that when we refer to information systems, we have in mind systems that are used in an organizational setting (typically a business or a State department), supporting transactional activities as well as managerial decision making.

In 1968, a conference was held in Europe to discuss the so-called "software crisis." During that conference, much was said about budget overruns, systems being late, systems being produced but never used, a growing backlog of applications, systems being unmanageable, etc. The conference concluded that there is an "...urgent need for techniques and methods which allowed the complexity inherent in large software systems to be controlled" (Sommerville, 1989).

This goal seems to be somewhat elusive, since more than two decades later, Ng and Yeh (1990) stated that "...the average application backlog in large development shops has increased from 19 months to 27 months in just three years." However, they confidently continue that "...a solution to this... is to automate the software development and maintenance process..."

But the quest for techniques and methods to reduce the problems of software development seems to have been less than successful, because nearly 35 years after the initial conference, the "software crisis" is clearly still with us. Kautz and Larsen (2000) state that: "...unfinished projects, project overruns, systems failures and missing functionality is still the norm (in software development)...."

A starting point in understanding the mainly technological response to software development problems and failures could be in, *inter alia*, an older paradigm of computer science, namely, that the basic question underlying all of computing is: "What can be (efficiently) automated" (Denning et al, 1989). The implication of this statement is that in order to increase the efficiency of an organization, we should automate all or part of it, and similarly, in order to increase the productivity of the systems developers, we must also automate the automation process! Such arguments are quite commonplace among the computing fraternity, being one of the driving forces behind the search for a shared information systems development methodology, a methodology that will be repeatable and that will enable us to develop systems that are efficient and effective and that are completed and used. It could also very well be that this same sentiment underlies the technological hope that a kind of "generic" information system (e.g., ERP systems) that fits all organizations could be found.

But possibly, there exists another view of this situation and that is that the actual nature of information systems is not fully understood by its developers. The fact that information systems are sociotechnical systems is often ignored. This will be the basis of the argument for information systems as social systems in this chapter. I intend to show that, if we view information systems as social systems, the process of information systems development and its associated issues can much more readily be appreciated.

TECHNOLOGICAL UTOPIANISM FUELED BY OUR MECHANISTIC HERITAGE

Many technologists, scientists, journalists, managers, etc., seem to have an ongoing romance with the intriguing and much heralded technology of computers and information systems. A likely explanation for this could be that technologists are caught up in a particular way of thinking that was inspired by the spectacular advances of science and technology in the past century. Such thinking resulted in a certain form of technological Utopianism, which holds that the best way to attack and solve problems is by applying yet more (and ever more complex) technology. The ideological foundation for this view is the belief that all problems can ultimately be defined in technical terms and are solvable with the aid of scientific knowledge and advanced technology (Dillard & Burris, 1993). In its most extreme form, technology becomes the end, not the means (Angell & Straub, 1993).

Information systems designers often hold similar technologically Utopian views. Being trained in computer technology, they know a lot about solving computational problems and tend to see a new information system as just another problem that can be reduced algorithmically (or diagrammatically) and solved in a rational manner by feeding the "correct" rules and procedures to a machine. Organizational concerns are typically not important topics of study in the computer science curriculum. Therefore, with their emphasis on efficiency and effectiveness, information technologists tend to concentrate on the software engineering aspects of their work, reducing the information system to a software problem, with little regard for the consequences (both positive and negative) that the adoption and use of their systems may have in an organizational setting (Brooke & Maguire, 1998).

In 1988, it was estimated that between 50–75% of all information systems development is never completed, or, if completed, never used (Lyytinen, 1988). It is generally agreed that most, if not all, of these failures could be attributed not to a lack of tools and techniques but to the neglect of "human factors" in the dominant systems analysis and design practices (Willcocks & Mason, 1987:70).

This situation has, if anything, become worse. "Software development projects are in chaos, and we can no longer imitate the three monkeys — hear no failures, see no failures, speak no failures." (The Standish Group, 1995).

According to this group, "… a staggering 31.1% of projects will be cancelled before they ever get completed, and … 52.7% of projects will cost 189% of their original estimates." Their report also states that while some of the information systems they researched were high-risk ventures, many were as mundane as a drivers' license database, a new accounting package, or an order entry system. On the success side, the report continues, the average is only 16.2% for software projects that are completed on time and on budget. Furthermore, 48% of the IT executives in their research sample feel that there are more failures currently than just five years ago.

Abundant research that aims to explain the social complexity and general "messiness" of information systems that often lead to failures of a nontechnical origin has been undertaken and published but seems to have gone largely unnoticed by information systems development practice (Wastell & Newman, 1996; Brooke & Maguire, 1998; Nandhakumar & Avison, 1999). The solutions sought and offered by the computer community, are still mainly technological in nature rather than sociological (Fitzgerald, 1998). [The promises (sometimes overstated) of the vendors of case tools, object orientation, data mining, etc., come to mind] Conventional systems development approaches still do not equip the developer with tools or knowledge for dealing with the social processes intrinsic to information systems development (Hirschheim & Newman, 1991).

In other spheres of society, however, changes have occurred that resulted in a shift from efficiency and effectiveness toward social acceptability and appropriateness. People are concerned about the quality of their lives – also in the workplace (Mumford, 2000). They are demanding the right to participate in anything that is likely to affect their lives and their jobs, and without a doubt, information technology affects the jobs of most people in an organization.

Western society has a long tradition of love for mechanical artifacts. This originated with the interest in and later supremacy, in a sense, of mathematics and natural philosophy as the purest expression of "science." Natural science sees the world as being filled with natural objects that can be studied and described objectively and rationally, since they follow certain rational rules and obey natural "laws."

Seduced by their successes in the natural world, scientists transferred the rational expression to the social world, aiming to understand the social world in a similar positivist manner. This resulted in a particular mechanistic worldview (Dahlbom & Mathiassen, 1993). At the very heart of the mechanistic view is the notion that we can introduce explicit rules (or techniques) that tell us how to think and how to speak, and that we can develop exact representations of situations in the world. The modern worldview is, in the main, still a positivist, rational and mechanistic one (Truex, 2001).

But, to bring these notions closer to home, it is also clear that this view underpins all of computing. Computers and information technology are probably the epitome of rational, mechanistic thinking. Mechanistic ideals continue to have strong influences on the way we develop information systems and the way we implement them. This mechanistic heritage also determines our approach to organizational and work life, with its extreme emphasis on order and control.

PROBLEMS WITH MECHANISTIC AND UTOPIAN VIEWS OF THE WORLD

When we try to bring order to an organization with algorithms and computer programs, we bring with us a view based on the premise that the organization is itself an ordered, fundamentally unchanging entity (like, for instance, a mathematical puzzle). The mechanistic view of information technology use in organizations often ignores the fact that work is socially constructed. Amongst other things, this means that the objectives of people forming work groups, organizations, or societies could be, and probably are, completely different from those of the technologists who devise information systems in organizations (Markus, 1983).

Our mechanistic heritage also affects our view of information itself. If individual or organizational information requirements can be unambiguously defined, it means that information can be managed as some kind of corporate property. It gives information something akin to a physical substance. That the definition of information is much more problematic than this, has been shown by a number of authors (e.g., Boland, 1987; Tuomi, 2000).

Furthermore, mechanistic thinking ignores the powerful forces of change that so typically occur in the modern organization. In a changing world, exact rules are difficult to formulate and even more difficult to adhere to. The typical information system developed along mechanistic lines will have difficulty in providing information that continues to be useful in a changing world.

One early reaction to the mechanistic worldview was to defend nature and everything natural against machines and everything artificial. Romantic philosophers stressed the importance of creativity and individual expression, interpreting the world rather than understanding it (Dahlbom & Mathiassen, 1993). Most information technologists would say that such worldviews are all well and good for philosophers and artists but are not of much use in the realities of information technology application, where the problems are real and immediate, with not much scope for interpretation. Others, such as Walsham (1993), will disagree and argue that this worldview is as important as the mechanistic one. Although information technologists work with mechanistic devices, the use thereof in organizations cannot be purely mechanistic since other values and elements (people, politics, culture, etc.) are at stake (Dubé & Robey, 1999). Information technology must therefore be subjectively interpreted.

THE SOCIAL ASPECTS OF INFORMATION SYSTEMS

That information systems have a social side or context has long been recognized. For instance, as early as 1974, Gordon B. Davis defined an information system as an: "...integrated man-machine system..." (Davis, 1974).

In those days, however, nobody gave much thought to what this definition in terms of its social context really meant, nor to what the implications were. Recently, more voices were raised pointing out the social context of information systems and the effect such systems have on their social environment. For instance, Boland (1987) wrote that: "Designing an information system is a moral problem because it puts one party, the system designer, in the position of imposing an order on the world of another."

The impact of information systems and information technology on individuals and organizations is more multi-varied, deeper, and radical than often assumed.

SOME CONCEPTS FUNDAMENTAL TO THE SOCIAL SIDE OF INFORMATION SYSTEMS

We now wish to introduce a few concepts that can be regarded as fundamental to the understanding of information systems as social systems.

NonDeterminism in Information Systems

What is an information system? The following simple definition (Figure 1) explains it rather well. 'Otherware' (also 'orgware', according to Bjorn-Andersen, 1988) includes:

'... the important human organization working with the hardware and software, specifically the system's goals, the owner, the users, the operational procedures, the tasks and responsibilities of the people involved, offices, etc...' (Van Steernis, 1990).

What is useful about this definition is that it identifies three subsystems, namely, the hardware and software (the "computing" subsystems) of the information system, and the "otherware."

There is an important difference between these subsystems. The first two, the hardware and software subsystems, are deterministic systems consisting of machines and coded algorithmic procedures. These two subsystems are designed to be deterministic and reliable. The higher the level of determinism achieved in the design, the more successful the computing subsystem will be. Therefore, in most cases, it can be expected (even if it can be proven only with great difficulty) that the output of a computing system is predictable, given certain inputs.

Figure 1: An information system

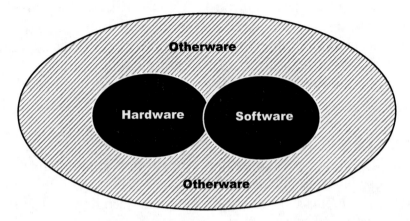

However, in the "otherware" subsystem, according to the definition, one finds systems owners, users, and support personnel, etc., with very unpredictable behaviour patterns, human failures, and shortcomings. This is not a "designed" subsystem in the same sense as the computing subsystem is designed. People may have agendas and goals that differ vastly from those of the organization (Markus, 1983; Myers & Young, 1997). This subsystem will, therefore, be non-deterministic.

The consequence of this is that the total subsystem, the information system, is also to a greater or lesser extent non-deterministic. Moreover, the environment of an information system is usually an organization of some kind, which is also non-deterministic systems, for similar reasons.

Consequences of Non-Determinism in Information Systems

- Only in very closed organizations can rules be made and exact procedures or methodologies be provided along the lines of which information systems could be developed.
- Methodologies, by their nature, tend to be deterministic, while the systems that we develop using the methodologies, are not.
- In a changing environment, the imposition of a rigid software engineering discipline cannot be expected to succeed. Such a discipline involves deliverables that are agreed upon during the initial stages of a development project and are then expected to remain unchanged over the period of development. Due to the inherently open, dynamic nature of most organizations, such expectations can only be realized over the very short term (Truex, Baskerville, & Travis, 2000).
- Introducing any kind of technology (which is deterministic) into an organization is inevitably going to interfere with the non-deterministic subsystem, the

"otherware" consisting of users, owners, etc., and the outcome of such interference is unpredictable (Orlikowski, 1991, 1992; Myers & Young, 1997).

• The more open the user environment (the organization) into which the information system delivers its information, the less will the information meet the requirements of managers. This is so because information systems are designed to operate deterministically and cannot anticipate changes in the user environment.

Ashby's Law of Requisite Variety

One of the basic notions of system control theory is the need for requisite variety to obtain and maintain control (Davis, 1974) (Figure 2). Put simply, this means that to control each possible state of the system, there must be a corresponding control state. In other words, there must be at least as many variations of control as there are ways for the system to get out of control. For example, in order to control the temperature of a room, the typical thermostat needs to sense whether the temperature is below or higher than a certain set temperature. These control states have sufficient variety to control the temperature of the room. If the thermostat loses one of its states (e.g., due to the thermostat's sensor not working), the control variety becomes insufficient for the number of systems states, and the situation cannot be adequately controlled.

Now, if systems are deterministic, they can only exhibit a finite number of possible states (as in the case of the example above, given that everything is in working order). On the other hand, if systems are non-deterministic, the number of possible states that they may achieve approaches infinity.

Organizations, being non-deterministic, will discover an infinite number of ways of reacting to outside stimuli, such as competitors, laws, client demand, etc. Furthermore, in order to survive, organizations also tend to increase their variety—

Figure 2: Ashby's law of requisite variety

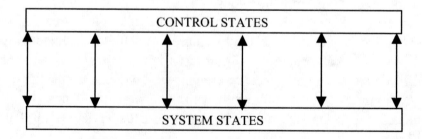

they emerge and become more complex. Organizations will then, amongst other things, look toward information from information systems to control and impose order on the complexity.

Consequences of Ashby's Law for Information Systems

- It is not possible to build information systems that would have control responses for all possible states of the organization.
- The *tidiness* of information systems methodologies (Angell & Straub, 1993) denies the variety inherent in organizations and information systems. A two-by-two matrix and a data flow diagram are simply too *tidy* to cope with the messy reality of organizations.
- An information system can therefore only partially automate the systems in an organization and only partially respond to information requirements. The search for a perfect fit between information from an information system, and information required by a manager, is in this sense, a futile one.

If one wishes to automate an office, one of the prerequisites will be to define precisely and completely all the activities in that office. Making the knowledge of an abstract system such as an office sufficiently explicit to be incorporated in a deterministic design of an information system is, in the very least, difficult and usually impossible (Dahlbom & Mathiassen, 1993).

Current Systems Thinking

General systems thinking has undergone a fundamental shift over the last few decades. In the fifties and sixties, systems thinking was based on the notion of a system as an autonomous whole. Systems were assumed to exist in the world and to be purpose-directed, striving toward a predetermined goal or set of goals (Introna, 1996).

This approach and assumption also underlie much of the traditional approach to information systems development. It is tacitly assumed that the system's objectives can be defined, and that the means of achieving them can be modelled and measured against some declared criteria. In systems terms, this is "hard systems" thinking, a type of means-end thinking, which is a product of the mechanistic worldview.

Put in the context of this chapter, hard systems thinking says that all that is required is to move an information system through its project life cycle and a successful information system will result. Organizations, according to this way of thinking, are regarded as goal-seeking machines, and information systems exist to enable the information needs associated with organizational goals to be met.

However, from the earlier discussion of non-determinism and Ashby's Law, as well as the fact that modern organizations are becoming ever more emergent (Truex, Baskerville, & Klein, 1999), it is clear that some of the assumptions of the hard systems approach are too simplistic. Firstly, organizations are not goal-seeking machines, but could just as well be regarded as cultures, tribes, political battlegrounds, networks, or whatever (Checkland & Scholes, 1990); a non-deterministic open system, in other words. Also, changes in technology make it difficult to keep to the 'project life cycle approach—in some cases, the technology goes directly to the user, bypassing the systems developer and creating all sorts of problems around so-called "end-user" computing. The latter problems are mostly ones of control, as predicted by Ashby's Law.

Thus, the change in systems thinking went from traditional hard systems thinking to soft systems thinking. Soft systems thinking realizes that any view of a particular situation or system is influenced by the background or worldview of the observer, and thus, there are many variations of "reality." Furthermore, soft systems thinking accepts that systems are not "out here in the world" but really exist only in the minds of the analysts or observers. They conceive systems only in an *abstract* sense.

Soft systems thinking is a way of dealing with a constantly changing world. It allows observers to have different perspectives of systems by having different assumptions about them. A soft system has emergent properties; that is, new properties emerge as the different levels (perspectives) of the system are uncovered. What a hard systems thinker sees as a system with definite properties, a soft systems thinker will see as only one of several perspectives to the system (Checkland & Scholes, 1990; Checkland, 1999).

THE SOFTWARE CRISIS REVISITED

The inferences in the previous paragraphs present us with a different way of looking at the software crisis mentioned earlier. It is clear that, in many ways, systems developers and software engineers have been chasing after a goal that is extremely difficult to achieve. Bigger and better boxes, newer and newer generations of software, automated systems development methodologies, etc., are not going to solve the information problems of the average organization and its managers. We have noticed earlier that advocating and using these methodologies have not done much to alleviate the failure rate of information systems. It simply has not been realized that the situation being automated is a soft and non-deterministic one; a situation that may be intractable to automation or that may even violently reject it. It appears that information systems should rather be seen as social systems that are technically implemented (Hirschheim & Klein, 1994).

THE SHORTCOMINGS OF CURRENT SOFTWARE ENGINEERING METHODOLOGIES

The deterministic view of software engineering argues that information systems development can be considered a largely rational process, undertaken with the help of various tools and techniques (methodologies), based principally on the so-called 'systems approach' taken from classical (natural) science. This leads to the prevailing view of information systems as technical systems, being technically implemented and with mainly technical consequences.

However, viewing information systems as non-deterministic (social) systems makes one aware of the inherent shortcomings of such a rational approach to information systems development. One simply cannot engineer information systems in the same way as structures or machines (which are deterministic). The fundamental concepts of non-determinism, Ashby's Law and Soft Systems Thinking, explained earlier must be incorporated in some or other way in a systems development methodology. Some methodologies have emerged that differ fundamentally in paradigm and underlying philosophy from the rational approach (Klein & Hirschheim, 1987; Hirschheim & Klein, 1992, 1994).

Perceiving information systems as social systems suggests that information systems development is, in most organizations, a never-ending process. Information systems evolve, adapt, grow, and decline as the organization goes through similar phases in its 'life' (Truex, Baskerville & Klein, 1999). The software 'engineering' paradigm (suggesting in its very name a rational project-oriented approach) is therefore inappropriate to serve information systems development. A possibly more appropriate paradigm for information systems development could be one that echoes the notion of change and evolution, namely that of bricolage or 'tinkering' (Dahlbom & Mathiassen, 1993; Ciborra, 1997). This notion suggests that information systems are 'tinkered' with by systems developers who continually strive to achieve alignment between the organization and its information systems. Tinkering is not engineering, neither is it pure "art," as systems development was so often described by computer scientists in earlier days.

However, as pointed out by Büscher et al. (1997), as more and more 'standard' software packages become available, organizations will have to go through increasingly difficult customising procedures, since very few organizational processes are actually so generic that standardized 'one-size-fits-all' software can be designed. Ciborra (1996) referred to this same issue when he discussed the shortcomings of automation in organizations - automation cannot as yet support a very prevalent and important aspect of organizational work, namely that of 'improvising' which is so often required when the standard rules of decision making or procedures are not applicable to a particularly new or novel situation.

DEFINING AND TEACHING INFORMATION SYSTEMS

The following definitions (currently in use at the Department of Informatics, University of Pretoria, South Africa) are offered here to reflect some of the social context of the information systems field:

- 'Information Systems is an interdisciplinary subject area where we study information and information systems, and the integration thereof with the organization, in order to benefit the total system (the individual, the organization, as well as society).'

The 'fundamental question' underlying the entire field of research in information systems is:

- '... how to *balance* the contribution of information systems towards the mission of the organization with the ethical responsibility to ensure their social acceptability...'

In short, these definitions recognize that:

- '... information systems are developed by people for people.'

Teaching information systems can therefore never be complete unless, apart from teaching the technical system and the method, the social (and organizational) context is taught as well. Successful information systems are not contrived in some organizational back room, but are constructed in full view of the rest of the organization. Implementing an information system may have significant impacts on individuals and structures in various areas of the organization. Information systems developers should therefore no longer be regarded as experts in the domain of information systems, but rather as expert partners of clients in other domains of the organization which use information systems (adapted from Denning, 1992).

THE NEW ROLE OF THE SYSTEMS ANALYST

What makes a systems analyst competent to decide what the impacts of information systems will be? At the very least, only if that person is well versed in organizational and social (behavioural) theory—not a typical competence amongst most systems analysts. Only if we view information systems as social systems will these competencies be given their due consideration during the training of systems analysts. If not, the danger of Tayloristic work designs fostered by the technology is very real (Friedman & Kahn, 1994).

Tayloristic work designs are often the result of a misinterpretation or misunderstanding of work itself. Suchman (1995) points out how 'distance' can influence the analyst's perception of the work of others. The further removed the analyst is from the work of others, the more simplified, even stereotyped, such work appears to the analyst. In practice, if a new information system has to be designed, this 'distance' can result in work being deterministically automated with no understanding of the social content that workers in fact put into their work. Mumford (1981) stressed the fact that the experts on operational factors such as task design *are the people who do the jobs*! These people are intimately and immediately involved in their tasks—they are not at a 'distance' from them in the way that systems analysts often are.

Grindley (1992) reports that research in the United Kingdom showed that a marked lack of appreciation of each other's skills and competence (and contribution toward the success of the organization) exists between information systems professionals and their business colleagues. He called this lack of appreciation a 'culture gap,' stressing that this gap is a key factor in limiting the successful utilization of information systems in their companies.

The major reason for the existence of this culture gap, however, is still the incorrect view that most people have of information systems. As long as these systems are seen as deterministic systems, the professionals will be trained as technologists, with no real regard for, or appreciation of, the culture in which their products are to be used (Fitzgerald & Murphy, 1994). As long as the deterministic view holds sway, information systems development methodologies will be based on hard systems thinking.

If, however, the view of information systems as social systems is accepted, the situation changes completely. Training of information systems professionals can then take cognisance of the social problems inherent in introducing information systems and information technology in organizations. Information systems professionals thus trained will probably be more appreciative of their role as agents of change, and better prepared to accept this responsibility with greater humility than is often displayed by the technically trained 'computer expert.'

How can such training be achieved? At college and university level, one answer could be to include subjects from the social sciences in the curricula of future systems analysts. *Inter alia*, topics like sociology, anthropology, and organizational behaviour come to mind. Another very useful approach is to expect of final-year students to work in small groups to develop a real information systems for a real user (which they have to find themselves). We have found that this approach exposes students to most of the conflict experienced in groups, as well as to the unpredictability of users and the lack of clarity in requirements that so often occur. Furthermore, emphasis is placed on the soft systems methodology that is used to 'understand' the issues and problematic situations, before hard analysis starts.

CONCLUSION

Tricker (1992) argued that information systems studies have tended to confuse means with ends. Concentration on the utilization of computers and other aspects of information technology and on managing data and supporting decisions with what has been called information has focused attention on the means. The end is not more data, held more accurately, made available more quickly and more widely; it is not even better informed decision-makers. The end should be a more knowledgeable organization (Zuboff, 1988). Social expertise, such as that required by information systems developers, should not be confused with technical expertise.

This chapter has argued why information systems should be regarded as social systems. In other social systems (groups, organizations, and societies) such concerns are typical and important, and therefore, must be considered as typical and important in information systems. Furthermore, with the aid of the basic concepts of Non-determinism, Ashby's Law, and Systems Thinking, the notion of information systems as social systems, as well as some of the more relevant consequences of this viewpoint, can be explained.

REFERENCES

Angell, I. O. & Straub, B. H. (1993). Though this be madness, yet there is method in. *Proceedings of the First European Conference on Information Systems*. Henley-on-Thames.

Bjorn-Andersen, N. (1988). Are "human factors" human? *The Computer Journal, 31*, 386–390

Boland, R. J. (1987). The in-formation in information system. In Boland, R. J. & Hirschheim, R. (Eds.), *Critical issues in information systems research*. New York: John Wiley & Sons.

Brooke, C. & Maguire, S. (1998). Systems development: A restrictive practice? *International Journal of Information Management, 18*, 165–180.

Büscher, M., Gill, S., Mogensen, P. & Shapiro, D. (1997). Landscapes of practice. *Draft paper, Private Communication.*

Checkland, P. (1999). Systems thinking. In Currie, W. L. & Galliers, B. (Eds.), *Rethinking management information systems*. Oxford: Oxford University Press.

Checkland, P. & Howell, S. (1998). *Information, systems and information systems: Making sense of the field.* Chicester: John Wiley & Sons.

Checkland, P. & Scholes, J. (1990). *Soft systems methodology in action.* New York: John Wiley & Sons.

Ciborra, C. U. (1996). Improvisation and information technology in organizations. In DeGross, J. I. (Eds.), *Proceedings of the Seventeenth International Conference on Information Systems*, December, Cleveland, OH.

Dahlbom, B. & Mathiassen, L. (1993). *Computers in context: The philosophy and practice of systems design.* Oxford: NCC Blackwell.

Davis, G. B. (1974). *Management Information Systems.* New York: McGraw-Hill.

Denning, P. J. (1992). Educating a new engineer. *Communications of the ACM, 35*(12), 83–97.

Denning. P. J. (1989). Computing as a discipline. *Communications of the ACM, 32*(1), 9–23.

Department of Informatics. (1991). *Unpublished Working Document*, University of Pretoria, South Africa.

Dillard, J. F. & Burris, B. H. (1993). Technocracy and management control systems. *Accounting, Management and Information Technology, 3,* 1151–1171.

Dubé, L. & Robey, D. (1999). Software stories: Three cultural perspectives on the organizational practices of software development. *Accounting, Management and Information Technologies, 9,* 223–259.

Fitzgerald, B. (1998). An empirical investigation into the adoption of systems development technologies. *Information & Management, 34,* 317-328.

Fitzgerald, B. & Murphy, C. (1994). Introducing executive information systems into organizations: Separating fact from fallacy. *Journal of Information Technology, 9,* 288–296.

Friedman, B. & Kahn, P. H. (1994). Educating computer scientists: Linking the technical and the social. *Communications of the ACM, 37,* 65–70.

Grindley, K. (1992). Information systems issues facing senior executives: The culture gap. *Journal of Strategic Information Systems, 1,* 57–62.

Hirschheim, R. A. & Klein, H. K. (1992). Paradigmatic influences on information systems development methodologies: Evolution and conceptual advances. In Yovits, M. (Ed), *Advances in computers, 34,* 293–392.

Hirschheim, R. A. & Klein, H. K. (1994). Realizing emancipatory principles in information systems development: The case for ethics. *MIS Quarterly, 18,* 83–109.

Hirschheim, R. A. & Newman, M. (1991). Symbolism and information system development: Myth, metaphor and magic. *Information Systems Research, 2,* 29–62.

Introna, L. D. (1996). Notes on ateological information systems development. *Information Technology & People, 9,* 20–39.

Kautz, K. & Larsen, E. A. (2000). Diffusion theory and practice: Dissemination quality management and software process improvement innovations. *Information Technology & People*, 13, 11–26.

Klein, H. K. & Hirschheim, R. A. (1987). Social change and the future of information systems development. In Boland, R. J. and Hirschheim, R. (Eds.), *Critical issues in information systems research*, 275–305. New York: John Wiley & Sons.

Lyytinen, K. (1988). Expectation failure concept and systems analysts' view of information systems failures. *Information and Management*, 14(1).

Markus, M. L. (1983). Power, politics and MIS implementation. *Communications of the ACM*, 26, 430–444.

Mumford, E. (1981). Participative systems design: Structure and method. *Systems, Objectives, Solutions*, 1, 5–19.

Mumford, E. (2000). Technology and freedom: A socio-technical approach. In Coakes, E., Willes, D. & Lloyd-Jones, R. (Eds.), *The new socio-tech: Graffiti on the long wall*. London: Springer-Verlag.

Myers, M. D. & Young, L. W. (1997). Hidden agendas, power and managerial assumptions in information systems development: An ethnographic study. *Information Technology & People*, 10, 224–240.

Nandhakumar, J. and Avison, D. E. (1999). The fiction of methodological development: A field study of information systems development. *Information Technology & People*, 12, 176-191.

Ng, P. G. & Yeh, R. T. (Eds.). (1990). *Modern software engineering: Foundations and current perspectives*. New York: Van Nostrand Reinhold.

Orlikowski, W. J. (1991). Integrated information environment or matrix of control? The contradictory implications of information technology. *Accounting, Management and Information Technology*, 1, 9–42.

Orlikowski, W. J. (1992). The duality of technology: Rethinking the concept of technology in organizations. *Organization Science*, 3, 398–427.

Sommerville, I. (1992). *Software engineering* (fourth edition). Reading, MA: Addison-Wesley.

Suchman, L. (1995). Making work visible. *Communications of the ACM*, 38(9), 56-64.

Tricker, R. I. (1992). The management of organizational knowledge. In Galliers, R. (Ed.), *Information systems research: Issues, methods and practical guidelines*. London: Blackwell Scientific Publications.

Truex, D. P. (2001). Three issues concerning relevance in IS research: Epistemology, audience and method. *Communications of the AIS*, 6, Article 24.

Truex, D. P., Baskerville, R. & Klein, H. (1999). Growing systems in emergent organizations. *Communications of the ACM, 42,* 117–123.

Truex, D. P., Baskerville, R, & Travis, T. (2000). Amethodological systems development: The deferred meaning of systems development methods. *Accounting, Management and Information Systems, 10,* 53-70.

Tuomi, I. (2000). Data is more than knowledge: Implications of the reversed knowledge hierarchy for knowledge management and organizational memory. *Journal of Management Information Systems;* Winter.

Van Steernis, H. (1990). *How to plan, develop & use information systems: A guide to human qualities and productivity.* New York: Dorset House Publishing.

Walsham, G. (1993). *Interpreting information systems in organizations.* New York: John Wiley & Sons.

Wastell, D. & Newman, M. (1996). Information systems design, stress and organizational change in the ambulance services: A tale of two cities. *Accounting, Management and Information Technology, 6,* 283–300.

Willcocks, L. & Mason, D. (1987). *Computerising work: People, systems design and workplace relations.* Paradigm.

Zuboff, S. (1988). *In the age of the smart machine.* New York: Basic Books.

Chapter VII

The SoSM Revisited—
A Critical Realist Perspective

Philip J. Dobson
Edith Cowan University, Western Australia

ABSTRACT

The chapter revisits the System of System Methodologies (SoSM) and suggests that use of the SoSM as a framework for defining methodological assumptions is difficult when the concerned methodologies have significantly different meanings for one axis of the framework— "system" complexity. It is suggested that the purpose of the underlying system can provide a more appropriate frame for defining system approaches—such purpose being defined as interaction or transformation (Mathiassen & Nielsen, 2000).

The chapter also uses aspects of critical realism to provide insights into the SoSM and the critical theory underpinning the framework. The SoSM helped to highlight the neglect of coercive situations and ultimately helped prompt the development of critical systems theory which is focused on three basic commitments, critical awareness, methodological pluralism, and emancipation. Maru and Woodford (2001) recently argue that the focus on emancipation has been relegated due to a concentration on pluralism. This chapter suggests that this is a logical outcome of the epistemological focus of the underlying critical theory of Habermas. The Habermas focus on the epistemological or knowledge-based aspects of the development process must necessarily relegate the importance of ontological matters such as the conditions necessary for emancipatory practice. This chapter proposes that the philosophy of critical realism has insights to offer through its highlighting of the ontological issues in more detail and in arguing for a recognition of the deep structures and mechanisms involved in social situations.

INTRODUCTION

In the systems area, probably the best-known model for structuring thinking with respect to systems methodologies is Jackson and Keys' System of System Methodologies (1984) (SoSM). This framework suggested that a mapping of system complexity against the decision-makers environment allowed a useful means of categorising systems methodologies to provide an indication as to their underlying assumptions concerning systems complexity (simple or complex) and participant situation (unitary, pluralist, or coercive). Banathy (1988) and Keys (1988) both used the SoSM to argue that an examination of problem contexts can suggest suitable methodological approaches. According to Jackson (1990), this use of the SoSM was seen to be a functionalist interpretation of the framework, and such a use for the SoSM was invalid as problem context and system's characteristics are "in the eye of the beholder."

The framework was developed as a practical tool to encourage methodological pluralism by suggesting a critical approach to the use of systems methodologies. The framework encompasses such diverse "systems approaches" as Beer's Viable System Model, Forrester's System Dynamic Modeling, Ackoff's Interactive Planning, and Checkland's Soft Systems Methodology. This paper argues that given the multiplicity of systems approaches, the practicality of such a framework is doubtful. The various "systems approaches" differ so fundamentally in their underlying assumptions regarding, for example, what "system" in fact means, that it is difficult to apply a framework that has system complexity as one of its major axis.

For example, Mingers (2000a) points out Checkland's SSM regards the concept of a "system" as being purely an epistemological device having no ontological foundation. According to Checkland, systems thinking is a "particular way of describing the world" (Checkland, 1983, p. 671). Yet a theory such as Forrester's System Dynamic Modeling provides a markedly different view of systems, giving them a far greater solidity. Forrester's concept of systems as real objects with important cybernetic interactions is more ontologically focused and would allow a far deeper *explanatory* analysis of systems and their components.

The SSM concept of a system as being entirely conceptual places systems in what a critical realist would argue as the "transitive" world. Mingers (2000a) suggests that the lack of solidity within SSM toward the concept of a system is one of the major shortcomings of SSM. "With a single blow Checkland reduces the force of systems thinking" (p. 749) by its placement of SSM solely within the conceptual world. Such a placement does not allow for an explanatory focus for the methodology. Each investigated system is seen as being a unique study, open to differing perceptions and conclusions. The possibility of deriving deep explanatory concepts that are loosely generalisable is denied.

Figure 1: The system of system methodologies with example approaches (from Flood and Jackson, 1991, p. 42)

	Problem Context		
	Unitary	Pluralist	Coercive
Simple	**Operations Research** **Systems Dynamics**	**SAST**	**Critical Systems Heuristics**
Complex	**Viable Systems Model**	**Interactive Planning** **SSM**	**??**

Problem Type (row axis label)

CRITICAL REALISM

Bhaskar's (1978, 1979, 1986, 1991) brand of realism [referred to by Searle (1995) as external realism] argues that there exists a reality totally independent of our representations of it; the reality and the "representation of reality" operating in different domains—roughly, a transitive epistemological dimension and an intransitive ontological dimension. For the realist, the most important driver for decisions on methodological approach will always be the intransitive dimension, with the target being to unearth the real mechanisms and structures underlying perceived events. Critical realism acknowledges that observation is value laden as Bhaskar points out in a recent interview: "...there is no conflict between seeing our scientific views as being about objectively given real worlds, and understanding our beliefs about them as subject to all kinds of historical and other determinations" (Norris, 1999).

The critical realist agrees that our knowledge of reality is a result of social conditioning and thus cannot be understood independently of the social actors involved in the knowledge derivation process. However, it takes issue with the belief that the reality itself is a product of this knowledge derivation process. The critical realist asserts that "real objects are subject to value laden observation;"

where the *reality* and the value laden *observation of reality* operate in two different dimensions, one intransitive and relatively enduring and the other transitive and changing.

Critical realism places a strong emphasis on the unearthing of the deep structures and mechanisms that make up the world. It is interesting to examine the SoSM in general from a perspective that specifically emphasises the importance of social structures. The SoSM maps the relationship between the problem context (unitary, pluralist, or coercive) and the problem type (simple, complex) (Figure 1). The problem context is seen to be definable dependent on the relationship between the main actors. Critical realism would view such relationships as social "structures."

For the critical realist, the SoSM framework has a limited conception of structure, with the SoSM equating organisational context with organisational "structure" (unitary, pluralist, or coercive). A critical realist perspective would suggest that the organisational context reflects a complex interplay of multiple interacting structures and mechanisms (both internal to the organization and external to the organization) that affect the agency action of "IS development and deployment" in various ways. Every organisational situation necessarily involves a plurality of structures—a structure being seen as "an internal network of social relations" (Brown, 1999). For the critical realist, a coercive situation may indicate the presence of a dominating inequitable structure that needs to be addressed. The emancipatory focus of critical realism would suggest that this inequitable structure would need to be made explicit as the first step in emancipatory action.

Given the categorisation evident within the SoSM, it can be concluded that, in general, the systems approaches considered are each placed firmly within a unitary, pluralist, or coercive "structure." Structure is therefore not considered to be a variable, and thus, it does not play a pivotal role within the various approaches. This is in conflict with a critical realist perspective which sees social structures as all important.

Critical realism has little to say concerning practical advice, as Wad (2001, p. 12) argues:

> One may get the feeling that critical realism develops a huge superstructure of ontological and epistemological insights, but when it comes to practical research we are left with the usual methodological suspects, delivered by inductivists, positivist and empirical-analytical scientists.

Examining the Soft Systems Methodology in particular from a critical realist point of view provides some methodological insights particularly highlighting the need for a greater recognition of social structure.

SSM AND SOCIAL STRUCTURES

SSM is a practical methodology. Its focus is on achieving systemically desirable and culturally feasible change. This focus on accommodation has opened the methodology to the criticism that it is ultimately overly conservative and does not encourage radical change. Tsoukas (1992) suggests that systems perspectives derivable from within an interpretivist paradigm suffer the common shortcoming of all such interpretive approaches—a neglect of wider impacting social structures and power relationships:

> ...[the systems perspective] rightly stresses the importance of open debate among actors in order to explore different points of view and arrive at a rational consensus. However, it barely addresses the societal conditions under which debate among actors is (or ought to be) conducted. In particular, the omission to deal with cases where "there is conflict between interest groups, each of which is able to mobilize different power resources" (Jackson, 1990, p. 663) results in ISP [Interpretive Systems Perspective] being unable to generate a "genuine consensus" among actors, and thus failing to realise its true potential (p. 640).

Systems approaches founded on both the interpretivist or functionalist paradigm have been criticised for "favouring regulation and the status quo rather than advocating radical social change" (Tsoukas, 1992, p. 639). Jackson (1982) makes a similar claim, as does Mingers (2000a): "SSM, in focusing exclusively on the espoused beliefs and values of individual people, thereby lost connection to the wider social and political structure that shaped such beliefs" (p. 743).

Rose (2000, p. 78) highlights the importance of interpretation within Checkland's SSM:

> The epistemological, or learning premise of his work involves the conscious movement between unstructured perceptions of the world and perceptions structured by systems principles, in order to foster debate.

He argues that Checkland's SSM does not provide a specific model on organisational change or provide a mechanism for explaining the reproduction of social structure between people:

> Though Checkland clearly adheres to the notion of a socially constructed world, the mechanisms of that social construction are less clearly specified. The closest his writings come to these understandings are in his commentary on Vickers (p. 77).

In line with Vickers (1965), Checkland and Holwell (1998, p. 48) argue that the "soft" systems movement sees organizations as "social entities which seek to manage relationships." This so-called "tribal" view sees organizations as relationship managing entities, yet the SSM in practice concentrates more on transformation than interaction (Mathiassen & Nielsen, 2000) and does not particularly emphasise such relationships, perhaps the major recognition being in the development of a rich picture to identify such relationships and their interaction. Once this interaction has been identified, however, there is little further reference within the methodology to the rich picture and identified structures.

Mathiassen and Nielsen (2000) argue that the traditional focus within SSM on transformation makes it difficult to examine systems that involve personnel "interacting" with information systems. The transformative element is exemplified within SSM by the requirement that the root definition of the system include a transformation. However, as Rose (2001) points out in discussing Mathiassen and Nielsen's argument:

> ...other aspects of their systems development work [were] poorly characterized by the idea of transformation. For instance, the investigated management practice itself (sets of activities concerned with communicating, allocating resources, performance assessment, planning and troubleshooting), does not easily fit this description. Transform what into what? They propose that these human activity systems are better characterized by the notion of interaction. They suggest that, in general, management, information and administration systems are better thought of as interaction systems.

They suggest that SSM would gain a wider application if it allowed for a clearer recognition of the interaction aspect of IS. They argue that if the primary system purpose is interaction, the root definition should identify an interaction together with the relevant domain (see Table 1).

Similarly, Rose (2000, p. 102) argues that the two primary metaphors reflected within Checkland's SSM are transformation and interaction. He suggests that traditionally, transformation has been the primary focus of SSM and action

Table 1: Two different system types (from Mathiassen and Nielsen, 2000, p. 249)

	Transformation System	**Interaction System**
Identity	A mapping from one domain (input) to another domain (output)	A domain with state and state transitions
Activity	Transformation from input to output without consideration of intermediate states	Interaction with a domain that maintains the invariance of its structure
Examples	Organisational change Systems development Design and Intervention Construction Production	Management of a domain Information provision about a domain Administration of a domain

research in general. For the action researcher, the primary aim of research intervention is transformation with emphasis on systematically desirable and culturally feasible *change*. In my view, this concentration on action and process has resulted in a neglect of underlying structures such as power relationships and external economic, social, and governmental impositions. As Mathiassen and Nielsen (2000, p. 248) argue:

> *IT organizations are concerned with the processes as well as the structural properties of IS and to accommodate for this we need to emphasize both aspects in our systems thinking. We need to include verbs as well as nouns as important elements of our basic vocabulary.*

Rose (2000) argues that later versions of SSM have concentrated more on the idea of the organization as a human activity system with the primary focus on relationship maintenance. This move toward an interaction metaphor would help address the criticism of SSM that it does not adequately reflect preexisting structural relationships. Rich pictures have always provided a mechanism for recognising such relationships, yet the structures identified through these rich pictures are not used to any great extent in the later formal modeling process. The rich picture is primarily used to define the root definition of the system, which reflects a concentration on process thinking and the transformative metaphor rather than on social structures and interaction.

From a critical realist perspective, the concentration within SSM on transformation and process misses much of the story. As Reed (1997) argues, approaches that concentrate solely on processual issues and situated social action can tend to ignore important wider impacting structural impositions that can "constrain actors' capacities to make a difference" (p. 25). Approaches that "work with 'flat' or 'horizontal' social ontologies in which the processual character of social reality totally occupies the analytical and explanatory space available" (p. 24) face the danger of ignoring important structural constraints.

The incorporation of techniques within SSM to specifically emphasise social structures and their interaction seems sensible. One example of such an approach would be Vidgen (1997), who proposes an extension of Multiview 2 to include stakeholder analysis. His method proposes that first a rich picture be developed to reflect the complex and messy situation under investigation. The rich picture is then used along with a stakeholder map to identify the concerned stakeholders. Once the concerned stakeholders are identified, the target is then to consider how the new system might impact each of their situations, thus allowing for their inclusion in the ultimate new system. Stakeholder analysis provides an opportunity to more clearly reflect the pluralism Vidgen sees as evident in all systems development situations. He feels that a pluralist perspective is invariably the norm in systems projects and rejects the "simple" category reflected within the SoSM.

It is interesting to note the close relationship between the definition of stakeholders and the critical realist conception of social structures. Vidgen (1997) quotes Mitroff and Linstone (1993, p. 141) who see stakeholders as "any individual, group, organization or institution that can affect as well as be affected by an individual's, group's, organization's or institution's policy or policies." Similarly, the Stanford Research Institute of 1963 is quoted as defining stakeholders as "those groups without whose support the organization would cease to exist." Vidgen suggests the organization be seen as a web of stakeholder relationships rather than a single entity. This perception is similar to the critical realist perception of structure as defined by Brown (1999): "For critical realism an internal network of social relations essentially constitutes a social structure."

Adopting a simplistic approach to this argument derives Figure 2, which suggests that when examining systems in which interaction is the most appropriate metaphor, social structure is particularly important. In this case, the use of a tool such as stakeholder analysis to identify such impacted structures would be particularly useful. When examining systems in which transformation is the most appropriate metaphor, the recognition of social structure is perhaps less important, and SSM can be used in the traditional manner.

CRITICAL REALISM AS "UNDERLABOURER"

While critical realism provides little practical guidance, it allows special insights into research and practice. Bhaskar (1975) sees that philosophy in general (and critical realism in particular) can play a useful role as "underlabourer" to research and practice—the term underlabouring taken from Locke (1894, p. 14) as "clearing the ground a little...removing some of the rubbish that lies in the way of knowledge."

Bhaskar suggests that philosophy can play an integral and important role in the investigation of social situations with its continuing role being contingent on the

Figure 2: A framework for suggesting a theoretical approach

		ORGANISATIONAL	
		PLURALIST	COERCIVE
SYSTEMS	INTERACTIVE	SSM + Stakeholder Analysis	??
	TRANSFORMATIVE		

ultimate success of the resultant research or practice outcomes. The practical focus of the IS area has naturally tended researchers in the field toward methodology and epistemology rather than ontology, yet philosophy can offer different and valuable insights. Critical realism, in particular, provides an opportunity to place a re-emphasis on ontology and philosophy.

The above discussion presents some methodological issues unearthed through a critical realist approach. Similarly, one can derive useful ontological insights as is indicated in the following discussion on the role of emancipation in critical systems theory in general.

CRITICAL SYSTEMS THEORY AND CRITICAL REALISM

Maru and Woodford (2001) call for a greater commitment to the development of emancipatory development methodologies. They suggest that Ulrich's critical systems heuristics is the only critical systems methodology that offers real practical tools for achieving emancipatory development, and they argue for a greater commitment to the development of new methodologies in the area. They point out that critical systems theory reflects a practitioner focus in that emphasis is very much directed toward action. They quote Schecter (1991, p. 213), who describes the commitment to critical awareness as a never-ending attempt to uncover hidden assumptions and conceptual traps of paradigms, methodologies, plans, and practices together with the conditions that give rise to them. The commitment to pluralism "is a result of the critical awareness that all systems approaches are partial and therefore have their own limitations and legitimacies" (p. 63).

In my view, the epistemological focus of critical theory, and consequently critical systems theory, forces a concentration on the knowledge gaining aspects of research and practice, and thus, necessarily neglects ontological matters such as, for example, the (structural) conditions necessary for emancipatory action. Critical systems theory was developed based around Habermas' epistemologically focused critical theory and as such, must concentrate more on the knowledge gaining aspects of the situation. Bhaskar would suggest that this represents a concentration on the *transitive* aspects of the situation; the *intransitive* relatively enduring real structures and mechanisms impacting the situation of lesser consideration.

Maru et al. (2001) argue that the necessary emancipatory focus of critical systems theory has been diverted largely due to a concentration on pluralism. They quote Jackson (1997, p. 359), who sees the commitment to emancipation and critical awareness as buttressing pluralism. The focus becomes not on emancipation but on pluralism, which, in my view, reflects the practitioner focus of the systems developer.

Flood and Jackson's TSI is an example of a systems approach based around critical theory. It rests on the assumption that the organisation has no meaning outside the mind of the participants—the underlying view behind TSI being that the only way to change social systems is by changing people's worldviews or Weltanschauung. Such a perspective makes it difficult to focus on the actualities of real organisational change. Without a clear recognition of the reality of social structures, there can be little guidance as to ways and means of changing them. Bhaskar's critical realist approach can provide a useful insight into the (ontological) preconditions for change and the need for popular, realistic change.

For the critical realist, emancipation involves the transformation of preexisting social structures by self-determining agents. Smith (1998) defines social structures as involving "relations and patterns of behaviour which have become so well established across time and space that they provide the (largely unquestioned) conditions for human action and thought." (p. 27). For the realist, emancipation is more than simply improving conditions within existing structural arrangements, emancipation implies the transformation of structures rather than "freedom enhancing ameliorations of states of affairs" (Collier, 1994, as quoted in Archer, 1998, p. 464).

Critical realism sees social structures as referring to actual forms of social organisations, as "real entities with their own powers, tendencies and potentials" (Archer, 1995, p. 106). Such structures cannot be perceived and thus cannot be identified except through examination of their effects. Social systems depend on the relations between and within a plurality of structures, such relations having their own independent causal properties. The resulting system founded on the various relations has emergent properties that may affect agents acting within the system.

Critical realism is termed "depth realism" by Collier (1994) due to its recognition of deeply stratified layers of structure. Within this brand of realism, emancipation is seen to involve deep structural change and is thus revolutionary in its intent (i.e., deep and sudden, rather than necessarily violent). Critical realism suggests that structures will not be changed through the cumulative effect of reforms in accordance with those structures, the structures themselves must be addressed.

Bhaskar provides little real guidance for progressing emancipatory practice apart from elevating the role of explanatory critique. Collier (1994, p. 171) explains the important role of explanatory critique within the critical realist conception of emancipatory practice:

> ...the production of explanations of social institutions is not only, as a general rule, a precondition of criticising and changing them; sometimes it is criticising them and beginning the work of their subversion.

An explanatory critique of unfair institutional practices and the associated unearthing of the false beliefs supporting such practices provide the necessary preconditions for emancipatory practices. In this situation, social science can generate practical emancipatory projects by "showing there to be (a) a need, (b) some obstacle preventing its satisfaction, and (c) some means of removing this obstacle" (Collier, 1994, quoted in Archer, et al. 1998, p. 455). It may also have a more direct effect in that the unearthing and exposition of false beliefs can directly undermine the imposing institution.

Much of critical realist argument is concerned with explanatory critique asking questions such as "what must be the case in order for intentional action to be possible" (Bhaskar, 1991, p.147). According to Bhaskar (1986, p. 211), emancipatory action requires that the following conditions be met:

- The results of the emancipatory action must be achievable, realistic and popular.
- The new transformed structure itself must have "knowable emergent laws."
- The emancipatory action itself must also meet the following requirements:
- The emancipatory action needs to be a direct result of agency intervention (i.e., critique). That is, the emancipatory reasons for the action must actually cause the action (otherwise, it may be just coincidence rather than emancipative practice).
- The explanatory critique must originate from within that part of society of which it is a critique.

In short, Bhaskar (1986) sees emancipation as involving the transformation of constraining structures by self-determining agents that act from within the imposing structure to produce popular realistic change that can again be structurally supported after the event. Critical systems theory in being underpinned by Habermas' critical theory has a different perspective on emancipation. Alvesson and Willmott (1992) argue the following:

> ...central to critical theory is the emancipatory potential of reason [-] to reflect critically on how the reality of the social world, including the construction of the self, is socially produced and, therefore, is open to transformation. The task of critical theory is to combine philosophy with social science to facilitate the development of change in an emancipatory direction.

They point out that this view suggests that the process of emancipation is a linear cycle of "suffering-critical reflection-emancipation" and question the negativity of this view and whether the process is so simple. The individual's power to reason and consequent self-emancipation play a major role in Habermas' critical theory. This underlying belief is reflected in various aspects of critical systems theory.

Bhaskar's approach concentrates on ontological issues, and Habermas concentrates on epistemological issues. This chapter suggests that the ontological focus of Bhaskar also has something to offer critical systems theory, in particular, through its revisiting of emancipation from the ontological view rather then the methodological and epistemological focuses of traditional critical systems theory.

CONCLUSION

Various systems approaches are based upon a range of philosophical theories. TSI is based on an individual mix of interpretivism and critical theory, whereas SSM is focused almost entirely on interpretivism. Historically, it can be argued that one of the most powerful components of SSM is its interpretive stance as Holwell (2000) suggests:

Checkland's work is recognised for adding interpretive thinking to the fields of systems, problem-solving and IS; so much so, that his argument and language have become part of the general discourse" (p. 778).

Checkland's (1981) emphasis on the problem situation rather than the problem itself provided a fresh way of looking at organisational problem-solving and allowed a deeper recognition of the problem context. In Bhaskar's terms, SSM would be considered to reside within the so-called transitive dimension. The name systems "thinking" highlights this emphasis and provides one of SSM's major strengths. Interpretivism, however, has its weaknesses, not the least of which is its concentration on individual perceptions and its neglect of wider impacting social structures.

This chapter suggests that given the underlying interpretivist perspective of SSM, SSM must suffer the same weakness. The chapter further suggests that SSM can grow further through a clearer recognition of social structures and their impact on problem situations. The inclusion of stakeholder analysis within a soft systems investigation would appear to be one way of addressing this issue, particularly in the examination of interaction systems that depend more heavily on the interaction between existing and potentially important social structures. As detailed in Figure 2, if the primary focus of the system is interaction, then a more detailed investigation of stakeholders and their concerns is essential. For a transformative system, a traditional use of SSM with its strong focus on process and transformation is sufficient.

The chapter concludes by arguing that philosophy can play a greater role as underlabourer for research and practice, providing needed ontological support. An example is provided to suggest that critical realism can offer new insights into emancipatory practice and widen the ontological support for critical systems theory in general.

REFERENCES

Alvesson, M. & Willmott, H. (1992). On the idea of emancipation in management and organization studies. *Academy of Management Review, 17*(3), July, 432–464.

Archer, M. (1995). *Realist social theory: The morphogenetic approach.* Cambridge, MA: Cambridge University Press.

Archer, M., Bhaskar, R., Collier, A. & Lawson, T. (1998). *Critical realism: Essential readings.* New York: Routledge.

Banathy, B. H. (1988). Matching design methods to systems type. *Systems Research, 5,* 27–34.

Bhaskar, R. (1978). *A realist theory of science.* Sussex: Harvester Press.

Bhaskar, R. (1979). *The possibility of naturalism.* Hemel Hempstead: Harvester Wheatsheaf.

Bhaskar, R. (1986). *Scientific realism and human emancipation.* London: Verso.

Bhaskar, R. (1989). *Reclaiming Reality: A critical introduction to contemporary philosophy.* London: Verso.

Bhaskar, R. (1991). *Philosophy and the idea of freedom.* Oxford: Blackwell.

Brown, A. (1999). *Developing realistic methodology: How new dialectics surpasses the critical realist method for social science, Economics Discussion Paper No. 66,* MiddleSex University Business School, March 1999. Retrieved January 18, 2001, from the World Wide Web: http://www.raggedclaws.com/criticalrealism/archive/abrown_drm.html.

Checkland, P. (1981). *Systems thinking, systems practice.* Chichester: John Wiley & Sons.

Checkland, P. (1983). OR and the systems movement—Mappings and conflicts. *Journal of the Operations Research Society, 34*(8), 661–675.

Checkland, P. & Holwell, S. (1998). *Information, systems and information systems—Making sense of the field.* London: John Wiley & Sons.

Collier, A. (1994). *Critical realism: An introduction to the philosophy of Roy Bhaskar.* London: Verso.

Craib, I. (1992). *Modern social theory: From Parsons to Habermas.* Hertfordshire: Harvester Wheatsheaf.

Fay, B. (1987). *Critical social science.* Cambridge, England: Polity Press.

Flood & Jackson (1991). *Creative problem solving: Total systems intervention.* Chichester: John Wiley & Sons.

Habermas, J. (1984). *The theory of communicative action: Reason and the rationalization of society, 1,* (T. McCarthy, translator). Boston, MA: Beacon Press.

Hirschheim, R. & Klein, H. K. (1994). Realizing emancipatory principles in information systems development. *MIS Quarterly, 14*(1).

Holwell, S. (2000). Soft systems methodology: Other voices. *Systemic Practice and Action Research, 13*(6), 773–797.

Jackson, M. C. (1990). Beyond a system of systems methodologies. *Journal of the Operational Research Society*, *41*(8), 657–668.

Jackson, M. C. (1997). Pluralism in systems thinking and practice. In Mingers, J. & Gill, A. (Eds.). *Multimethodology: The theory and practice of combining management science methodologies*. Chichester: John Wiley & Sons, 347–378.

Jackson, M. C. & Keys, P. (1984). Towards a system of system methodologies. *Journal of the Operational Research Society*, 35, 473–486.

Keys, P. (1988). A methodology for methodology choice. *Systems Research, 5*, 65–76.

Kuhn, T. (1970). *The structure of scientific revolutions* (second edition). Chicago, IL: The University of Chicago Press.

Maru, Y. T. & Woodford, K. (2001). Enhancing emancipatory systems methodologies for sustainable development. *Systemic Practice and Action Research, 14*(1).

Mathiassen, L. & Nielsen, P. A. (2000). Interaction and transformation in SSM. *Systems Research and Behavioral Science, 17*, 243–253.

Mingers, J. (2000a). An idea ahead of its time: The history and development of soft systems methodology. *Systemic Practice and Action Research, 13*(6), 733–755.

Mingers, J. (2000b). The contribution of critical realism as an underpinning philosophy for OR/MS and systems. *The Journal of the Operational Research Society, 51*(11), 1256–1270.

Mitroff, I. & Linstone, H. (1993), *The unbounded mind, breaking the chains of traditional business thinking*. Oxford: Oxford University Press.

Norris, C. (1999). Bhaskar interview. *The Philosophers' Magazine*, (8), Autumn, 34.

Reed, M. I. (1997). In praise of duality and dualism: Rethinking agency and structure in organisational analysis. *Organisation Studies, 18*(1), 21–42.

Rose, J. (2000). *Information systems development as action research—soft systems methodology and structuration theory*, PhD thesis, Management School, Lancaster University, England.

Schecter, D. (1991). Critical systems thinking in the 1980s: A connective summary. In Flood, R. L. & Jackson, M. C. (Eds.), *Critical systems thinking: Directed readings*, 213–226. Chichester: John Wiley & Sons.

Searle, J. R. (1995). *The construction of social reality*. New York: Free Press.

Smith, M. (1998). *Social science in question*. London: Sage Publications.

Tsoukas, H. (1992). Panoptic reason and the search for totality: A critical assessment of the critical systems perspective. *Human Relations, 45*(7).

Vickers, G. (1965). *The art of judgement*. London: Harper and Row.

Vidgen, R. (1997). Stakeholders, soft systems and technology: Separation and mediation in the analysis of information system requirements. *Information Systems Journal*, 7, 21–46.

Chapter VIII

Soft Evaluation: A Systemic Approach for Postimplementation Review

Ala Abu-Samaha
Amman University, Jordan

ABSTRACT

In this chapter, the author describes an alternative approach to evaluating Information Technology (IT) projects, which involves developing a holistic view of IT interventions. The main methodological problem in evaluating any intervention is to choose the right indicators for the measurement of success or lack of it. These indicators will obviously be linked to the aims but will also be relevant to the objectives chosen to achieve these aims. Acknowledging the difficulty of choosing appropriate measures of performance, the author proposes the use of Soft Evaluation. The approach used brings together formal work in evaluation with a qualitative process of investigation based on Soft Systems Methodology in order to allow us to make judgements about the outcomes of an implementation in a systemic manner and from a number of different viewpoints or perspectives.

INTRODUCTION

Traditionally, Information Technology (IT) evaluation, preimplementation appraisals and postimplementation reviews, has been characterised as economical, tangible, and hard in nature. The literature review on IT evaluation shows a great bias toward using economical and tangible measures that represent the management's view of what is "good" and "bad," which has been described as narrow in scope and limited in use. Smithson and Hirschheim (1998) explain that "there has been an increasing concern that narrow cost benefit studies are too limited and there is a need to develop a wider view of the impact of a new system." Ezingeard (1998) emphasises the importance of looking at the impact of IS on both the overall system and the whole organisation.

This chapter starts by looking in depth at evaluation in general, trying to identify different views and shed more light into this grey area of the systems development process. Second, Soft Evaluation will be introduced, emphasising its approach and building blocks. Third, a case study is introduced to demonstrate how this method can and may be used. Finally, a number of lessons and conclusions are identified from using soft evaluation in a real-life situation, and a refinement of the initial method is presented.

IT EVALUATION

Evaluation is not a new concept or a new property of the information age. Evaluation in Information Systems Development Process (ISDP) has existed from the early days of the "Waterfall Model" or the "Systems Development Life Cycle." The concern at this level is to measure whether the IT solution meets its technical objectives and to what extent. In such activity, instrumentation is highly appreciated and particularly chosen. These classical but widely popular models show the classical but simplistic perception of IT/IS evaluation that controlled IT/IS research for years. Product oriented, instrument-led and unitary are the main characteristics of such a perception. Mainly, evaluation was seen as a by-product of the decision-making process of information systems development and installation. Most of the evaluation tools and techniques used were economic based, geared to identifying possible alternatives, weighing the benefits against the costs, and then choosing the most appropriate alternative. Although these models have recognised the importance of evaluation and included evaluation as a separate step or a series of steps, they still did not address the need and objective of evaluation or even the "how about?."

Patton (1986) draws a parallel between evaluation and research arguing that "Research is aimed at truth. Evaluation is aimed at action." Patton goes on to argue that "program evaluation is the systematic collection of information about the activities, characteristics, and outcomes of programs for use by specific people to reduce uncertainties, improve effectiveness, and make decisions with regard to what those programs are doing and affecting." Reith (1984) explains that "the purpose of evaluation is, straightforwardly, to provide feedback." St. Leger et al. (1992) explain that evaluation is "the critical assessment, on as objective a basis as possible, of the degree to which entire services or their component parts fulfil stated goals." Rossi and Freeman (1982) advocate that "evaluation research is the systematic application of the practice of social research procedures in assessing the conceptualisation and design, implementation and utility of social intervention programs." Farhoomand and Drury (1996) by way of contrast explain that "the Oxford Dictionary defines success as 'the accomplishment of what was aimed at'. The success of an IS, then, can be defined as the extent to which the system achieves the goals for which it was designed. In other words, IS success should be evaluated on the degree to which the original objectives of a system are accomplished."

Postimplementation Review

This section will discuss the concerns raised by a number of researchers in the IS discipline and social sciences as an introductory to soft evaluation.

Postimplementation evaluation has been described by Ahituv et al. (1986) as "probably the most neglected activity along the system life cycle." Avison and Horton (1993) report that "evaluation during the development of an information system, as an integral part of the information systems development process, is even more infrequently practised." Ezingeard (1998), while reflecting on manufacturing information systems, reiterates the importance of looking at the impact of IS on both the overall system and the whole organisation. Bannister (1998) uses instinct and gut feeling, as opposed to reason, to call for the further study of the decision-making process in order to influence and improve IT investment.

Smithson and Hirschheim (1998) explain that evaluation has traditionally focused on the potential or actual costs and benefits of introducing a new system. Avison and Horton (1993) advocate that "evaluation can be viewed as a social and political process, both in itself and as part of the development and introduction of an information system." Abu-Samaha and Wood (1999a) explain that "evaluation in its broadest sense covers all those procedures which allow a judgement to be made about the success in achieving the stated aims of a project. This focus on achievement means that the evaluation process does not necessarily include an evaluation of the aims themselves."

In acknowledging all of the above concerns about the evaluation of IT interventions, the author presents in this chapter a measures identification method which aims at identifying those measures or indicators of performance which are relevant to all the stakeholders involved in such interventions.

A Conceptualisation of Systemic Postimplementation Review

Many researchers concerned with IT evaluation, mainly postimplementation reviews, have identified an urgent need to migrate from this "traditional" and economical view toward using a mixed approach to IT evaluation. Such an approach will allow IT evaluators to mix between "hard" and "soft" measures, as well as economical and noneconomical measures (Chan, 1998). Furthermore, there is a need to shift toward utilising an approach that reflects the concerns of all involved stakeholders rather than a Unitarian approach (Smithson & Hirschheim, 1998). Any systemic approach to IS evaluation must take into account two main issues regarding the collective nature of IS: choosing the relevant measures of performance and equal account for economical as well as noneconomical measures.

Choosing the Relevant Measures of Performance

Abu-Samaha and Wood (1999b) show the following:

...the main methodological problem in evaluating any project is to choose the right indicators for the measurement of success, or lack of it. These indicators will obviously be linked to the aims but will also be relevant to the objectives chosen to achieve these aims, since if the wrong objectives have been chosen for the achievement of an aim, then failure can be as much due to inappropriate objectives as to the wrong implementation of the right objectives.

Willcocks (1992), in a study of 50 organisations, gives ten basic reasons for failure in evaluation practice, and among these reasons are inappropriate measures and neglecting intangible benefits. Ezingeard (1998) shows that in manufacturing information systems "…it is difficult to decide what performance measures should be used," as it could be said about any other information system. On the other hand, a different set of indicators or measures of performance will be chosen at each level or layer of the IT intervention (product, project, and programme) which adds more to the relevance of the chosen measures.

Another important aspect of choosing indicators or measures of performance is to choose the relevant measures that add value to a particular person or group of persons. Smithson and Hirschheim (1998) explain the following:

There are different stakeholders likely to have different views about what should be the outcome of IS, and how well these outcomes are met. Who the different stakeholders are similarly need to be identified. Their goals and objectives must also be articulated. Once this is done, metrics in each of the three zones can hopefully be identified and applied.

These zones include efficiency, effectiveness, and understanding. The measures identification method proposed by the author in this chapter provides such relevance through the identification of stakeholders and the subsequent Human Activity System analysis. This is done by exploring the particular Worldview, which is unique for each stakeholder, and by identifying the relevant criteria for efficacy, efficiency, and effectiveness of each stated transformation process. Such an investigation would allow for the identification of the most relevant measures or indicators of performance for the stated stakeholder(s).

Avison and Horton (1993) explain that "many groups and individuals can be affected by a system, and the effect is unlikely to be the same for all groups…it is therefore important to have the views of all relevant parties (stakeholders) included in evaluation studies." Furthermore, Avison and Horton (1993) suggest that "there is no single best approach to evaluation but the choice needs to be made to suit specific applications and organisations."

Equal Account for Economical as well as NonEconomical Measures

Postimplementation reviews have had a tendency to concentrate on "hard," "economical," and "tangible" measures. Chan (1998) explains the importance of bridging the gap between "hard" and "soft" measures in IT evaluation, realising that "this in turn requires the examination of a variety of qualitative and quantitative measures, and the use of individual, group, process and organisation-level measures."

Smithson and Hirschheim (1998) explain that "over the years, there has been an increasing concern that narrow cost benefit studies are too limited and there is a need to develop a wider view of the impact of a new system". Avison and Horton (1993) warn against confining postimplementation reviews to monitoring cost and performance and feasibility studies on cost-justification, saying that "concentration on the economic and technical aspects of a system may cause organisational and social factors to be overlooked, yet these can have a significant impact on the effectiveness of the system." Fitzgerald (1993) suggests that a new approach to IS evaluation, which addresses efficiency and effectiveness criteria, is required.

The approach described in this chapter gives an equal account to tangible as well as intangible benefits of IT intervention by identifying efficacy and effectiveness measures along with efficiency measures. The measures identification method proposed by the author provides a better understanding of the context of evaluation which would give a better account of the content of evaluation.

SOFT EVALUATION

The approach advocated here brings together formal work in evaluation (Patton, 1986; Rossi & Freeman, 1982) with a qualitative process of investigation based on soft systems methodology (Checkland & Scholes, 1990) in order to allow us to make judgements about the outcomes of an implementation from a number of different viewpoints or perspectives. The performance measures identification method proposed in this chapter operates through three stages.

Stage One, Stakeholder Analysis

The first stage of the proposed method is to identify the intra- and interorganisational stakeholders involved in the intervention. A stakeholder, as defined by Mitroff and Linstone (1993), is any "individual, group, organisation or institution that can affect as well as be affected by an individual's, group's, organisation's, or institution's policy or policies." Mitroff and Linstone (1993) explain that "an organisation is not physical 'thing' per se but a series of social and institutional relationships between a wide series of parties. As these relationships change over time, the organisation itself changes." Mitroff and Linstone's view of an organisation is synonymous to Checkland and Howell's (1997), which negates the hard goal-seeking machine organisation.

Stakeholder analysis can be seen as a useful tool to shed some light on the subjective process of identifying relevant measures of performance for evaluation. A number of questions can be asked at this stage such as "where to start?" and "whom to include and whom to leave out?" Checkland and Scholes (1990) explain that "no human activity system is intrinsically relevant to any problem situation, the choice is always subjective. We have to make some choices, see where the logical implications of those choices takes us, and so learn our way to truly relevant systems." The value of the investigation will be of greater importance if all relevant stakeholders are identified and included in the evaluation effort. It is obvious at this stage that some stakeholders will be of greater importance than others because of the power base that they operate from, and such stakeholders are to be acknowledged. At the same time, however, other relevant stakeholders should not be undermined for lack of such power.

While Mitroff and Linstone (1993) do not describe the process through which stakeholders may be identified, they recommend the use of a Stakeholder Map, see Figure 1. Mitroff and Linstone (1993) explain that "a double line of influence extends from each stakeholder to the organisation's policy or policies and back again—an organisation is the entire set of relationships it has with itself and its stakeholders." On the other hand, Vidgen (1994) recommends the use of a rich picture, being a pictorial representation of the current status, to support this activity.

Stage Two, Human Activity Systems Analysis

The second stage of the proposed method constitutes the systemic organisational analysis of the problem situation, or subject of evaluation. Soft Systems Methodology (SSM) is based upon systems theory and provides an antidote to more conventional, "reductionist" scientific enquiry. Systems approaches attempt to study the wider picture: the relation of component parts to each other, and to the whole of which they are a part (holism) (Avison & Wood-Harper, 1990; Checkland, 1981; Checkland & Scholes, 1990; Lewis, 1994; Wilson, 1990). SSM uses systems not as representations of the real world, but as epistemological devices to provoke thinking about the real world. ("They all featured human beings in social roles trying to take purposeful action ... all revealed people immersed in

Figure 1: Generic stakeholder map, adopted from Mitroff and Linstone (1993, p.141)

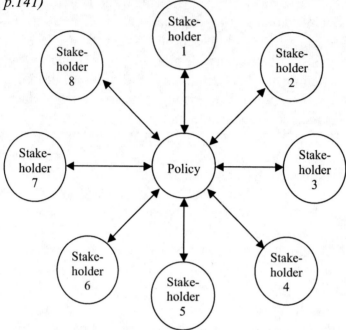

complex action which they were trying to make purposeful rather than instinctive or merely random ... Why not then take a set of activities connected together in such a way that the connected set makes a purposeful whole," (Checkland & Scholes, 1990). SSM is not an information systems development methodology. It is rather a general problem-solving tool that provides us with the ability to cope with multiple, possibly conflicting, viewpoints.

Within this stage the aim is to determine a root definition for each stakeholder, which includes their "worldview," a transformation process, together with the definition of the criteria for the efficacy, efficiency, and effectiveness of each stated transformation process (Wood-Harper et al., 1996). A root definition is a short textual definition of the aims and means of the relevant system to be modeled, defined by Checkland and Scholes (1990) as "the expression of the core purpose of the purposeful activity system. The core purpose is expressed as a transformation process in which some entity 'input' is changed or transformed into some new form of that same entity 'output'." Besides identifying the world-view and the transformation process, there are the three E's to consider as well (Checkland & Scholes, 1990), these being:

- E1: Efficacy—does the system work—is the transformation achieved?
- E2: Efficiency—a comparison of the value of the output of the system and the resources needed to achieve the output— in other words, is the system worthwhile?

- E3: Effectiveness—does the system achieve its longer-term goals?

As well as the three Es outlined above, Checkland and Scholes (1990) explain that "they (3Es) can be supplemented with other considerations of a broader nature if it seems appropriate in a particular field. For example, considerations of ethicality and elegance would bring in ethics and aesthetics, incidentally making the '3Es' into '5Es'."

Stage Three, Measures of Performance Identification

According to Checkland's Formal Systems Model, every human activity system must have some ways of evaluating its performance and ways of regulating itself when the desired performance is not being achieved. This final stage aims at identifying appropriate measures of performance related to the criteria identified in the earlier stage. For each criterion of the three Es identified in the earlier stage, it is important to identify the measure of performance that would allow us to judge the extent to which the system has achieved its objectives.

Figure 2 provides a diagrammatic representation of the generic process of soft evaluation, which shows the relationship between the different tools used to investigate the success/failure of an IT intervention. This generic model was used in an action case study to evaluate the impact of EDI (Electronic Data Interchange) links between General Practices and Hospital Trusts in the UK to exchange laboratory test results. The following sections describe the context of the case study as well as discuss the findings and major conclusions from that action case study and the learning cycle.

CASE STUDY

As part of the British government's commitment toward reducing the burden of bureaucracy on public services and enabling service providers to concentrate on their primary function, the government had introduced a number of policies into General Practice (GP) to aid general practitioners in spending more time with their patients than on paperwork, called "Patients not Papers." With over 90% of patients contacts with the National Health Services (NHS) conducted through General Practices, the NHS's Information Management & Technology (IM&T) strategy has been designed to explore the benefits of using information technology and information systems for the purpose of information gathering, storage, and transmission tasks that General Practices routinely undertake (NHS, Executive 1995, 1996a).

The IM&T strategy focuses on the creation and delivery of a wide variety of infrastructure projects designed to deliver basic standards and facilities across the whole NHS. These standards will provide consistency and enable data to be

Figure 2: The generic process of soft evaluation

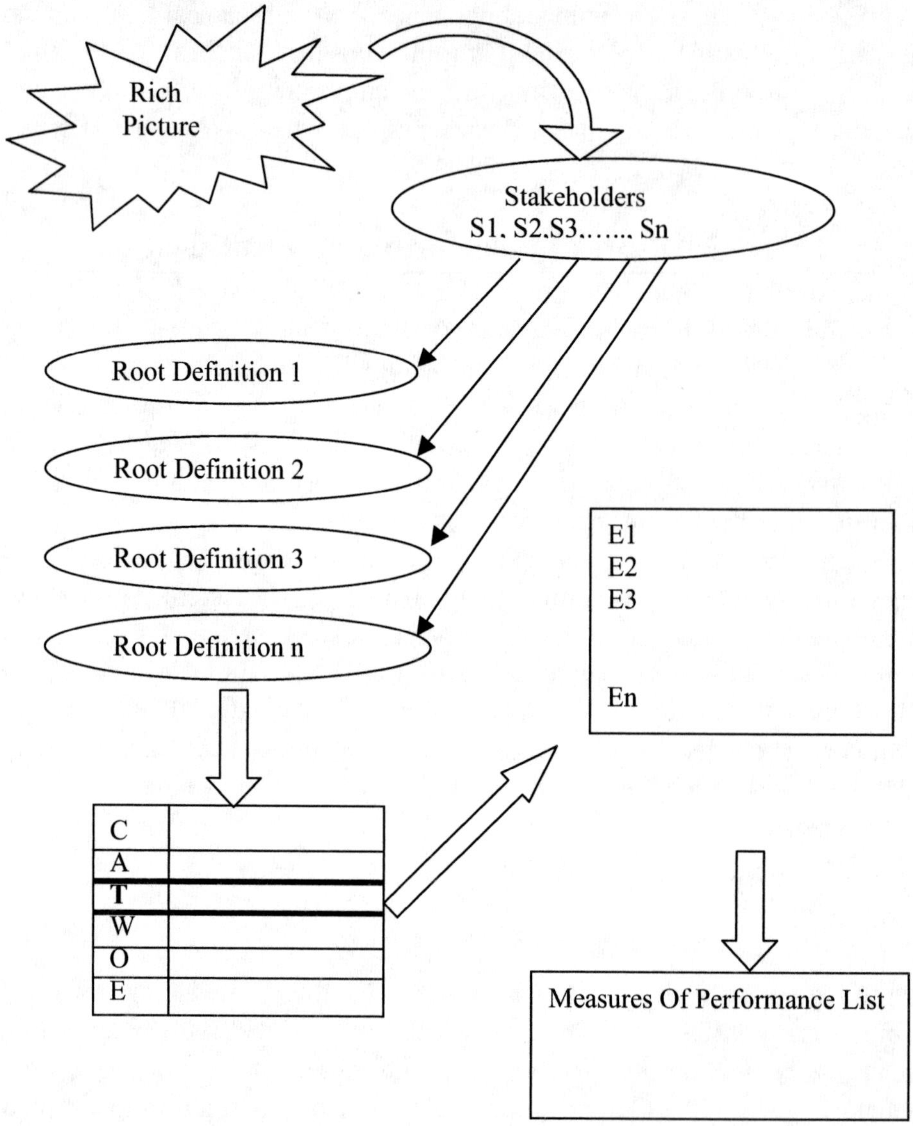

exchanged and aggregated by all agencies in the NHS for the purpose of contracting resource management, clinical audit, and clinical outcomes (NHS Executive, 1995, 1996a).

For the objectives explained above, the NHS has introduced two main initiatives for the exchange of information within the NHS. First, GP Administrative Links were introduced, which involve linking General Practice computers with Family Health Services Authority (FHSA) computers to replace paper-based processes for patient registration and items of service with an EDI system. Second,

GP Clinical Links were introduced which involve the development of national standard messages for the electronic transfer of pathology, radiology, discharge and other laboratory requests and reports (NHS Executive 1995, 1996).

The GP Clinical Links are believed to deliver potential improvements in the areas of patient care and professional satisfaction. These links have faced a number of problems, mainly operational and legal. On the legal level, General Practices are obliged by their terms of service to maintain adequate paper-based records on their patients. On the operational level, not all general practitioners are convinced that there is an urgent need for linking electronically their systems with the hospital's. Some of their concerns are related to confidentiality, quality, and security of the clinical data sent over telephone lines. Since 1992, the NHS Executive has been managing a range of projects to turn the NHS's strategy for IM&T into reality. The infrastructure for IM&T is believed to provide more efficient communication and information processing.

The main objective of the IM&T strategy is the deployment of sophisticated information technology for the purpose of automating many of the practices' routinely carried tasks to make general practitioners concentrate more on their patients than on their paper records. The NHS Trailblazers were designed to automate the receiving and processing of the laboratory reports to allow General Practices to concentrate on their core processes, which involve providing a medical service for the practice's population.

Avon Trailblazer

The Avon Trailblazer is one of two projects initiated to address the transfer of medical data from the appropriate hospital to the General Practice via an electronic medium as a practical application for the IM&T Strategy. The other trailblazer project is based in Nuneaton and involves one trust and a number of General Practices, practices where discharge letters are being implemented at the moment. The Avon Trailblazer consists of three hospitals, SouthMead, UBHT, and Frenchay trusts, and a number of General Practices. The GPs use a number of system suppliers, EMIS, VAMP, AAH Midetel, and many more. On the other hand, the hospital trusts use three different laboratory systems, one supplied by EDS, one an in-house system, and the third a system built around a proprietary system which had been extensively modified in-house. The target was to have all three pathology departments in the three trusts sending reports to 30 General Practices before the end of 1997.

The Avon Trailblazer committee had found that previous attempts to realise benefits from installing the EDI-Link have failed, because most of the time freed up is used for other tasks, and the cost of installing the software are is not paid back. The committee felt that more benefits would be realised if an holistic approach was taken to the realisation of benefits, so that both ends of the link work together to free up the maximum level of benefits. In order to assess what the current situation is and how the pilot scheme is actually working, the Trailblazer committee agreed to get external bodies to evaluate the pilot scheme. The evaluation process is to be performed in a two-stage approach. The initial analysis/evaluation is to be carried out so that once all the nominated General Practice sites have been linked, the full evaluation will have a better understanding of the situation and also what to expect from the different sites. The preliminary evaluation looks at a relatively few sites, which cover a large geographic area with differing software, hardware, size, information systems, practices, and communication processes. The aim of this phase is to identify the measures of performance that are going to be used in the second phase of this investigation to assess the success or failure of the Trailblazer initiative.

The Evaluation Effort

The evaluation effort using the soft evaluation method described earlier was carried out in two phases. The first phase of the evaluation scheme measures of performance is the identification phase, aimed at identifying measures of performance for each stakeholder involved in the Avon Trailblazer from three criteria (efficacy, efficiency, and effectiveness). Phase two aimed at using these measures of performance as guidelines to judge the success or failure of the Avon Trailblazer initiative. Seven practices were visited in the first wave of interviews over an extended period of time, four of which had been linked electronically to their associated hospitals. Another seven practices were visited in the second phase of evaluation to measure to what extent the identified measures of performance have been met by the participating practices. Figure 3 shows the stakeholder web for Avon Health Authority Trailblazer.

Here is an example of a root definition identified for practice population as well as the 3Es:

> *A system owned and operated by the doctor(s) and their assistants for the provision of medical assistance of the patients and their families. This provides a service for people with health problems to diagnose, prescribe and treat the patient's ill-health through either preventive care, referring to secondary care, or by normal treatment methods to reduce and eliminate the patient's illness.*

- Patient with health problem—transformed into—healthy person.
- Efficacy: Meeting the needs of the practice population. That is to cure the person.
- Efficiency: Time. That is how long it takes to cure the patient.
- Effectiveness: Maintaining and improving the health of the patient; that is, not to come back for the same health problem.

Figure 3: Stakeholder Web for Avon Trailblazer project

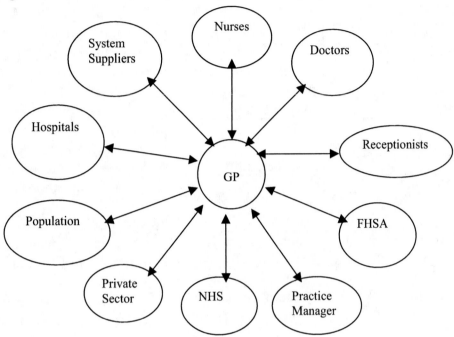

Results

Technically, all the visited practices have the infrastructure to communicate with their hospitals electronically. The practices are technically versed and quite knowledgeable about the computer technology available. Also, all visited practices have already installed and operated an EDI-Link to the FHSA (Family Health Service Authority) for the purpose of patient registration and items of service. The information provided by hospitals through the EDI-Link was thought to give the practices the ability to perform tasks required by the general practitioner more efficiently, or at least that was the perception of the whole practice, but in actual fact, this was a misnomer. What the practices performed originally was a combination of manual and automation through a person(s) inputting relevant data onto the computer. Most of the practices that utilise the EDI-Link have either used both the information received via the link and the paper results received via the internal post to perform their normal procedures or have stopped using the information received via the EDI-Link. As a result of the interviews carried out at each practice, the evaluation team has made the following assessment of the progress achieved so far with respect to the claimed benefits of implementing EDI links:

- Improvements in the accuracy of the information and the reduction of errors: Unknown. The evaluation team was provided with a lot of hearsay evidence,

Table 1: Summary of measures of performance table for Avon Trailblazer

Stakeholder	Measure
Practice Population	Time Health outcome Patient Satisfaction Confidentiality
Doctors	Patient care Time Confidentiality
Hospitals	Cost Security Time
Family Health Services Authority (FHSA)	Value for money Promoting Health Resource management
Government/National Health Services (NHS)	Resource management Population satisfaction Health of the nation
Receptionists	Time and Effort Pressure Satisfaction
Practice Manager	Resource management Satisfaction
Systems Providers	Cost Security Satisfaction
Private Sector	Competitiveness Relations with partners Better health service Customer/patient satisfaction Better health service

and some practices had undertaken limited forms of checking, but there has been no systematic logging of test results both in and out of the practices.

• A reduction in the amount of data entry: Not yet achieved. The number of keystrokes required at the GP end to initially assimilate data into the practice systems and to refer to it later remains significant.

• Increase in the speed of delivery: Achieved. In some practices, however, this faster turn around time has not led to any gain because the results are still dealt with in the same time-frame as before by the GP.

• A reduction in the levels of paperwork used: Not achieved. Most of the practices visited are still running parallel paper system, and the net effect therefore has been to double the amount of work for those GPs involved.

• Value for money: Unknown. There have been higher than predicted capital costs, and the system suppliers at both ends and in the middle see the project as a means to open up and exploit another long-term revenue stream.

• Standardisation: Not achieved. Messages remain system specific and are constructed simply to "get them through." Coding schemes remain contingent on practice and provider habits.

- Improvement in the quality of patient care: Unknown. These may be realised in the longer term but could well be highly dependent upon other factors such as improvements in the quality of the practice computer systems.

Lessons

Three Ps: Programme, Project, and Product Evaluation
The literature survey, the interviews, and the subsequent analysis have revealed three levels of IS/IT intervention evaluation, these being:

- Product Evaluation: The emphasis at this level is on the technical product, software, IT solution, or information system. The concern at this level is to measure to what extent the IT solution meets its technical objectives. The emphasis here is on efficacy: "does the chosen tool work?", "does it deliver?"
- Project Evaluation: The emphasis at this level is on the project, which represents the chosen objective(s) to achieve the aims of the programme. The concern at this level is to measure whether the project meets these objectives and to what extent it matches user expectations. The emphasis here is on efficiency. Does the project meet its objectives using minimal resources?
- Programme Evaluation: The emphasis at this level is on the programme and its aims. The concern at this level is to measure whether the programme aims have been met and whether the correct aims have been identified. The emphasis here is on effectiveness, in other words, is the use of IT going to aid general practitioners in providing a more effective service to their patients?

It is clear from this classification that any programme commissioned would have to choose the appropriate tools or project(s) to bring the programme's aims to life. The most elusive aspect of such a classification is to choose the most relevant

Figure 4: Product, project, and programme layers of IT evaluation

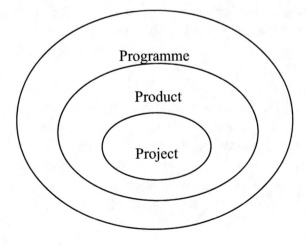

and appropriate measures/indicators of performance. Measures would differ at each level of analysis, prompting a different tool or process of evaluation. Evaluation could be conducted at each level of the above framework without exploring the other levels, such as investigating the credibility of an IT solution without exploring the project objectives or even the programme aims. On the other hand, evaluating one level could lead to the evaluation of the other, going from product to project to programme, or the other way around.

Choosing the Relevant Measures of Performance

The main methodological problem in evaluating any project is to choose the right indicators for the measurement of success, or lack of it. Ezingeard (1998) has shown that in manufacturing information systems "...it is difficult to decide what performance measures should be used," although this could be said about any other kind of information system. Such indicators must obviously be linked to programme aims but must also be relevant to those project or product objectives chosen to achieve these aims, because if the wrong objectives are chosen for the achievement of an aim, then any failure can be as much due to inappropriate objectives as to the wrong implementation of the right objectives. On the other hand, the earlier classification of product, project, and programme evaluation shows that a different set of indicators or measures of performance will be chosen at each level or layer of the IT intervention which adds more to the relevance of the chosen measures.

Concerning IT evaluation, a large number of stakeholders are involved. This number of stakeholders will rise even more in the case of ICT (Information and Communication Technology)-based information systems. These stakeholders may have different, possibly conflicting, interests and views regarding IS evaluation and development. Such views should be taken into account, and where possible, conflicts should be accommodated. The author calls for a subjective approach to IT evaluation that provides such relevance through the identification of stakeholders and the subsequent Human Activity System analysis. Such investigation would allow for the identification of the most relevant measures or indicators of performance for the stated stakeholder(s).

The measures identification method proposed by the author provides such relevance through the identification of stakeholders and the subsequent Human Activity System analysis. This is done by exploring the particular worldviews, which are unique for each stakeholder, together with identifying the relevant criteria for the efficacy, efficiency, and effectiveness of each stated transformation process. Such an investigation allows for the identification of the most relevant measures or indicators of performance for the stated stakeholder(s).

Equal Treatment of Economic as well as Noneconomic Measures

The proposed approach gives equal consideration to the tangible as well as the intangible benefits of IT intervention by identifying efficacy and effectiveness measures along with efficiency measures. Furthermore, the method can be used as a front-end for any postimplementation evaluation schemes for information technology interventions. The output of such a method can be used as an input to the second step of an evaluation scheme, i.e., the "how to measure" step.

The method proposed provides a better understanding of the context of evaluation and in turn gives a better account of the content of evaluation. In such a context, the benefits of technology interventions are not directed simply to the main user, in our case, General Practices, but primarily to the observing body, local health authority. For this reason, using efficiency-oriented methods proved to be meaningless. Instead, the performance measure identification method presented in this chapter was used and proved to be more insightful for our research.

PROPOSED FRAMEWORK

Figure 5 provides a diagrammatic representation for the proposed interventions IT evaluation, named the soft evaluation framework. The framework makes use of the three layers of IT intervention, which allow IT evaluators to identify measures of performance that are relevant to a particular layer as well as to a prospective stakeholder. This distinction between these three layers allows IT evaluators to pay equal attention to technical as well as political and organisational issues concerning IT interventions. The framework shows that evaluators must identify different instruments to measure different indicators of performance based on their nature. Furthermore, the framework pays attention to the political process that underpins any IT evaluation effort. It is evident that success or lack of it could be attributed to one of these three factors: choosing inappropriate measures of performance, choosing inappropriate instruments, or existence or lack of evidence for an improved situation.

Figure 6 provides a diagrammatic representation of the soft evaluation method, where the three layers of IT intervention, product, project, and programme, have been included in the evaluation process.

CONCLUSION

This proposed IT evaluation framework is refined from an earlier work by Abu-Samaha and Wood (1999) to reflect the layered nature of IT interventions. The approach advocated here is founded on the interpretive paradigm (Burrell &

Figure 5: Soft evaluation framework in use

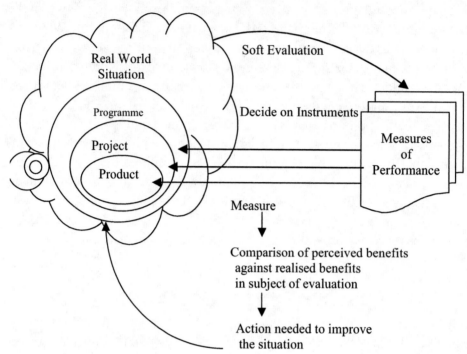

Morgan, 1979) and brings together formal work in evaluation (Patton 1986; Rossi & Freeman, 1982) with a qualitative process of investigation based on soft systems methodology (Checkland & Scholes, 1990) in order to allow us to make judgements about the outcomes of an implementation from a number of different viewpoints or perspectives. The performance measures identification method proposed in this chapter operates through three stages:

- *Stage One*: Stakeholder Analysis (based on Mitroff and Linstone, 1993) aims at identifying the intra- and interorganisational stakeholders involved in an IT intervention.
- *Stage Two*: Human Activity Systems analysis uses the tools of Soft Systems Methodology to determine a root definition for each stakeholder, which includes the definition of a transformation process (Wood-Harper et al 1996).
- *Stage Three*: Measures of Performance Identification, are used to identify appropriate measures of performance related to the criteria identified at the earlier stage. This approach gives equal weight to the tangible as well as the intangible benefits of an IT intervention.

Following is a summary of the most significant findings that arose from the fieldwork carried out for the Avon Health Authority Trailblazer.

- *Participation is instrumental for the success of ICT (Information and Communication Technologies)*: The participation of trading partners, Gen-

Figure 6: Soft evaluation method in use

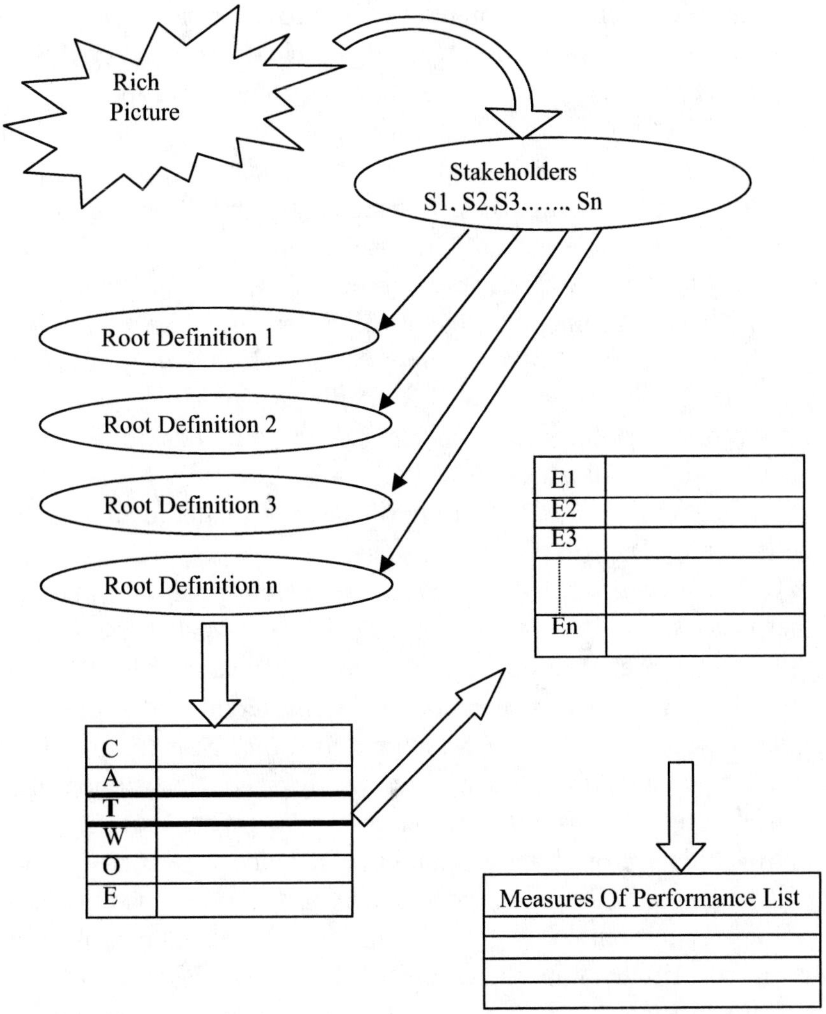

eral Practices in this case, is vital to the realisation of benefits for the hub organisation, Hospital Trust. It could be described as a network of stakeholders, some of which are recipients and others are providers.

- *Benefits of ICT (Information and Communication Technologies) Are Elusive:* In this particular case study, the most important area appeared to be the impact of the changes in the way General Practices dealt with test results, and the translation of these changes into tangible benefits. Sending a message from A to B via an electronic medium is a straightforward action, but integrating such a message with all the changes it encompasses is not an easy task.
- *Integration is a technical as well as an organisational concern:* The

integration of the received messages within the information systems and the working procedures of the practices have proven to be problematic. Some practices have changed their working procedures, and even the roles of employees, to make such an integration as successful as possible. This is because EDI is not simply about technology, it extends it to the organisational and personal specifications needed to accommodate such a technology, plus its emphasis on structuredness, standardisation, and electronic transfer.

- *Job description and role changes are inevitable in the case of ICT*: Each visited practice had a different set of procedures for dealing with traditional paper-based lab results, and although the differences were often quite minor in nature, they seemed to have an important influence on the way in which the new arrangements were viewed. Switching to a paperless practice meant certain job descriptions had to be changed to accommodate changes brought about by the introduction of ICT.

- *Paperless or paper less*: The importance of the paper result resides in its content as well as in its physical existence.

- *3Ps: Programme, Project, and Product evaluation*: The literature survey, the interviews, and the subsequent analysis have revealed three levels of IS/IT intervention evaluation. Measures would differ at each level of analysis, prompting a different instrument as well as a different process of evaluation.

- *Relevance is of paramount importance for IT and IS evaluation*: The main methodological problem in evaluating any project is to choose the right indicators for the measurement of success, or lack of it. The earlier classification of product, project, and programme evaluation shows that a different set of indicators or measures of performance will be chosen at each level or layer of the IT intervention, which adds more to the relevance of the chosen measures. Another important aspect of choosing indicators or measures of performance is to choose the relevant measures that add value to a particular person or group of persons.

- *Noneconomic as well as economic measures are of equal importance*: The proposed approach gives an equal consideration to the tangible as well as the intangible benefits of IT intervention by identifying efficacy and effectiveness measures along with efficiency measures.

- *Immediacy is interpreted differently by different stakeholders*: One of the most perceived improvements that switching to electronic messaging has brought is reducing receiving and (administrative) processing time of the lab results, this has meant a major time saving for the practices. On the other hand, Switching from paper medium to electronic medium had meant a lot of problems to the doctors. Many of these problems have been associated either with the format of the screen or the interaction between the users and their systems or both.

- *The existence of a champion is crucial for IS success*: The existence of a champion or an enthusiast had a positive effect toward the acceptability as well as the usability of the system.
- *Security and reliability issues are not as important issues as originally thought it:* In certain cases, there have been laps in the security environment, which has resulted in data being transferred to practices where information should not have been transferred. Although the information did not provide any suitable use for the practice, this piece of information could be accessed, read, and even printed. In theory, at least, these types of errors can be costly.
- *Training will always make a difference*: There have been certain reservations among medical professionals in the visited practices toward training. Most have described it as inadequate and short in terms of time.

REFERENCES

Abu-Samaha, A. & Wood, J. R. G. (1998). Evaluating inter-organisational systems the case of (EDI) in general practice. *Proceedings of the 11th Bled Electronic Commerce Conference*, 174–190. Bled, Slovenia, June 7th–9th.

Abu-Samaha, A. & Wood, J. R. G (1999a). GP/Provider links: Who benefits? *Healthcare Computing Conference*, 114–120. Harrogate UK, March 6th–9th.

Abu-Samaha, A. & Wood, J. R. G. (1999b). Soft evaluation: A performance measures identification method for post-implementation reviews. *Proceeding of the 6th European Conference on Information Technology Evaluation*, 221-228. Brunel University, Uxbridge, London UK, November, 4th–5th.

Ahituv, N., Even-Tsur, D., & Sadan, B. (1986). Procedures and practices for conducting post-evaluation of information systems. *Journal of Information Systems Management, 3*(2).

Avison, D. E. & Horton, J. (1993). Evaluation and information systems development. In Arduini, R. (Ed.), *Investimenti in information technology nel settore bancario*, 248–279. Milan: Franco Angeli.

Avison, D. E. & Wood-Harper, A. T. (1990). *Multiview: An exploration in information systems development.* Oxford: Blackwell Scientific Publications.

Bannister, F. (1998). In defence of instinct: IT value and investment decisions. *5th European Conference on The Evaluation of Information Technology, Reading University Management Unit, Reading, U.K.*

Bergvin, L. Johansson, B., & Borjesson, U. (1993). Distribution of laboratory test results to primary health care centres with EDIFACT standard. *Clinica*

Chimica Acta, 222, 141–145.

Bingham, D. (1997). GP-Provider links: Experiences, opportunities and benefits: The trust perspective. *Exchanged Healthcare Informatics Conference,* Manchester, U.K.

Branger, P. J. & Duisterhout, J. S. (1995). Communication in health care. *Methods of Information in Medicine, 34*(3), 244–252.

Branger, P. J., van der Wouden, J. C., Schudle, B. R., Verboog, E., Duisterhout, J. S., van der Lei, J., & van Bemmel, J. H. (1992). Electronic communication between providers of primary and secondary care. *British Medical Journal, 305,* 1068–1070.

Burrell, G. & Morgan, G. (1979). *Sociological paradigms and organisational analysis.* London: Heinemann.

Chan, Y. E. (1998). IT value—the great divide between qualitative and quantitative, and individual and organisational, measures. *5th European Conference on The Evaluation of Information Technology,* Reading University Management Unit, Reading, U.K.

Checkland, P. (1981). *Systems thinking, systems practice.* Chichester: John Wiley & Sons.

Checkland, P. & Howell, S. (1997). *Information, systems and information systems: Making sense of the field.* Chicheter: John Wiley & Sons.

Checkland, P. & Scholes, J. (1990). *Soft systems methodology in action.* Chichester: John Wiley & Sons.

Collier, P. & Spaul, B. (1991/1992). An introduction to EDI. *Accounts Digest 276,* 1–9. The Institute of Chartered Accountants.

Cox, B. & Ghoneim, S. (1996). Drivers and barriers to adopting EDI: A sector analysis of UK industry. *European Journal of Information Systems, 5,* 24–33.

Emmelhainz, M. A. (1990). *Electronic data interchange: A total management guide.* New York: Van Nostrand Reinhold.

Ezingeard, J.-N. (1998). Towards performance measurement process for manufacturing information systems. *5th European Conference on The Evaluation of Information Technology,* Reading University Management Unit, Reading, U.K.

Farhoomand, A. F. & Drury, D. H. (1996). Factors influencing electronic data interchange success. *Data Base Advances, 27*(1), 45–57.

Howles, J. & Wood, M. (1995). Diffusion and management of electronic data interchange: Barriers and opportunities in the UK pharmaceutical and healthcare industries. *Technology Analysis and Strategic Management, 7*(4), 371–386.

Kimberley, P. (1991). *Electronic data interchange.* New York: McGraw Hill.

Lewis, P. (1994). *Information systems development.* New York: Pitman.

Massaro, T. A. (1993). Introducing physician order entry at a major academic medical centre: II. Impact on medical education. *Academic Medicine, 68*(1), 25–30.

Mitroff, I. I. & Linstone, H. A. (1993). *Unbounded mind: Breaking the chains of traditional business thinking.* Oxford: Oxford University Press.

NHS Executive. (1995). Patients not paper. Report of the efficiency scrutiny into bureaucracy in general practice.

NHS Executive. (1996a). Patients not paper. Summary of the efficiency scrutiny into bureaucracy in general practice.

NHS Executive. (1996b). The impact on the NHS. Implementing the infrastructure for information management and technology in the NHS.

Parfett, M. (1992). *What is EDI: A guide to electronic data interchange* (second edition). New York: NCC Blackwell.

Patton, M. Q. (1986). *Utilisation-Focused Evaluation* (second edition). Thousand Oaks, CA: Sage.

Rossi, P. H. & Freeman, H. E. (1982). *Evaluation: A systematic approach* (second edition). Thousand Oaks, CA: Sage.

Sarich, A. (1990). *Electronic data interchange and paperless trade: The implementation guide* (third edition). Blenheim Online Publication.

Smithson S. & Hirschheim R. (1998). Analysing information systems evaluation: Another look at an old problem. *European Journal of Information Systems, 7*(3), 158–174.

St. Leger, A. S., Schnieden, H., & Walsworth-Bell, J. P. (1992). *Evaluating health services effectiveness.* Open University Press.

Swatman P. M. & Swatman P. A. (1992). EDI systems integration: A definition and literature survey. *Information Society, 8*(3), 169–205.

Symons, V. J. (1991). A review of information systems evaluation: Content, context and process. *European Journal of Information Systems, 1*(3), 205–212.

Vidgen, R. (1994). Research in progress: Using stakeholder analysis to test primary task conceptual models in information systems development. *Proceeding of the 2nd International Conference of the British Computer Society Information Systems Methodologies Specialist Group*, Heriot-Watt University, Edinburgh UK, 31st August–2nd September.

Willcocks, L. (1992). Evaluating information technology investments: Research findings and reappraisal. *Journal of Information Systems, 2*(4).

Wilson, B. (1990). *Systems: Concepts, methodologies and applications.* Chichester: John Wiley & Sons.

Wood-Harper, A. T., Corder, S., Wood, J. R. G., & Watson, H. (1996). How we profess: The ethical systems analyst. *Communication of the ACM, 39*(3), 69–77.

Section V

Information Systems Incorporation: Case Studies

Chapter IX

Addressing Organisational and Societal Concerns: An Application of Critical Systems Thinking to Information Systems Planning in Colombia

Rodrigo Córdoba and Gerald Midgley
University of Hull, UK

ABSTRACT

Most current information systems (IS) planning methodologies are focused on achieving 'successful' plans, i.e., plans that provide competitive advantage, can be implemented in a given period of time, and that solve the problems of information needs by taking advantage of the latest technologies available. Concerns are technology and business driven and focus on how to get the maximum profit for organisations from investing in information systems. However, this relatively narrow focus can be problematic, especially in developing countries, where the social contexts of IS implementation may require a different primary focus. This chapter presents a methodology for IS planning based on critical systems thinking—an approach that encourages the critical analysis of stakeholder understandings of social contexts prior to the selection and/or design of planning methods. The methodology presented in this chapter uses a combination of the systems theories of autopoiesis and boundary critique, which deepen our understanding of what it means to reflect on participation, values, and social concerns during IS planning. In the course of applying the methodology in a project in Colombia, an issue arose of the ethics of the practitioner. To address this issue, following completion of the project, we sought to enhance critical systems thinking with Foucault's notions of power and ethics, which offer interesting alternatives for practitioner self-reflection. Implications for IS planning are derived from this perspective on ethics and power.

INTRODUCTION

In the development of the world-wide information society, information systems (IS)[1] play an essential role: they provide access to opportunities for exchanging information. For nation states, the use of information systems is seen as a condition for survival in a global economy characterised by the management of knowledge as information (Toffler, 1992). For organisations, they provide support for achieving task efficiencies and dramatic reductions in service delivery time and/or costs (Hammer and Champy, 1995). Hence, the process of IS planning becomes important at all levels—international, national, and organisational. Any investment in information systems or technology should be made carefully in order to achieve success in terms of the stated goals of a plan (Andreu et al., 1996). A key aspect in the process of IS planning is the definition of an initiative from a strategic point of view, i.e., considering the possibilities that an information system presents in giving some players advantages over others (García, 1993).

For third world countries, information systems and information technologies have been seen as the means by which they can catch up with the economic development of the first world (Economist, 1996). A new type of society, the information society, can be created to achieve better conditions of life, education, higher employment, and the enhancement of democracy (Information I, 1996; Gore, 1998). However, practical results suggest the need to consider what assumptions are being made when people enter IS planning processes, particularly the relationship that is assumed between information systems and improved quality of life (Friis, 1997; Wickham, 1997).

Most existing IS planning methodologies focus on reformulating corporate strategy with the use of information systems in such a way that competitive advantage is provided for an organisation (Ward et al., 1990; García, 1993; Walsham, 1993; Galvis, 1995, 1998). These methodologies emphasise two aspects:

1. Defining information needs in relation to performance and the control of tasks
2. Analysing the potential offered by information systems to create new business or service opportunities (Andreu et al., 1996)

The main concern here seems to be the achievement of economic benefits for an organisation through the implementation of information systems (Ward et al., 1990). This concern is reflected in the discourse of IS planning as focused on "computer based information systems" (Walsham, 1993) or the "orderly provision of data and information within an organisation using IS" (Checkland & Holwell, 1998).

In this chapter, we challenge the assumptions of the majority of IS planning methodologies by proposing a critical approach in which different concerns expressed in the *way of life* of people can be brought into debate. We argue that traditional IS planning methodologies generally fail to account for a sufficiently diverse set of concerns, and thereby lose opportunities to define information systems in ways that can play more meaningful roles in the group contexts where they are going to be used. We argue that our application of a critical approach to IS planning in a Colombian organisation (Javeriana University) resulted in identifying concerns that are often excluded from planning but actually contribute to improving some of the aspects of life in Colombia, as well as the use of information systems. Also, this application brought forth the issue of the ethics of the IS practitioner. To address this issue after our application was over, we conducted further research on ethics and power. In particular, we focused on the work of Michel Foucault, which we suggest offers interesting alternatives for the self-reflection of practitioners during interventions. Implications for the practice of IS planning are then derived from the synergy of Foucault's ideas with our own methodological thinking.

The chapter is structured as follows. First, a description of IS planning methodologies in the information society is presented, bearing in mind some of the consequences that their use has brought for organisations and societies. Our reflections on IS planning have led us to propose an alternative approach, drawing upon 'critical systems thinking' (a set of methodological ideas mostly found in the management systems and operational research literatures), which is presented next. A methodology to support the implementation of the approach is defined, as well as some reflections on its application in an IS planning exercise at Javeriana University (Colombia). From there, the idea of enriching the approach with Foucault's understanding of ethics and power is proposed. This brings interesting possibilities for the practice of IS planning. Most importantly, it encourages awareness in practitioners of the issue of ethical self-development.

IS PLANNING METHODOLOGIES IN THE INFORMATION SOCIETY

In the past few years, new information and communication technologies (ICTs) have been developed, principally integrated with computers.[2] This creates opportunities for enhancing the performance of business processes with ICTs (Keen, 1991; Galvis, 1995). In first world, countries the development of economies in which products and services enable the exchange of knowledge in the form of electronic data has been complemented with a political concept called the 'information society' (Information I, 1996; Commission of the European Community, 1997; Gore, 1998). In the information society, it is said that almost every aspect of daily life will require information (Information I, 1996). Also, just about anyone can create information-based products and exchange them because the main capital invested is intellectual knowledge rather than money (Toffler, 1992). The information society can therefore enhance democracy and empowerment (Rogerson, 1996). UNESCO (1992) goes so far as to claim that third world countries should view ICTs as an opportunity to foster the development of their economies within the new information society, allowing them to catch up with first world nations.

IS planning methodologies are often used when people propose the adoption of ICT-supported information systems in organisations. These methodologies usually link thinking about information systems with the corporate strategic planning process in such a way that information systems are primarily seen as providing competitive advantage (Ward et al., 1990; Walsham, 1993). Nevertheless, it is often said that IS planning can empower people and give them greater autonomy (Hammer & Champy, 1995). The potential 'users' of the technology need to be involved, because they are the ones who know best how information systems can be employed to support business processes or practices. Their commitment is essential (Ginzberg, 1978, 1981; Ward et al, 1990). However, it is generally taken for granted that (i) individuals at different levels have the same concerns as the businesses they work for, and (ii) they actually do want greater autonomy (Currie, 1994; Willmott, 1995). There is arguably a contradiction embodied in the supposedly participatory practice of IS planning: people are given a degree of autonomy in decision making, but at the same time, are expected to make more of a commitment to dominant organisational purposes (Willmott, 1995). Organisations are still viewed as unitary systems with coherent purposes and goals rather than as collections of people with many (sometimes conflicting) concerns (Clarke & Lehaney, 1997a,b).[3]

For society in general, it is assumed that the main reason for using information systems is to gain economic benefits that can help to improve people's quality of life. The premise for thinking that information systems will help in this way is that existing marginalised groups can be included in the economic sphere, perhaps for the first time. A well-researched example is disabled people who can take advantage of new technologies to do jobs that were largely inaccessible to them previously (Floyd, 1993). Marginalised groups, including those in developing countries, can have access to information and create, maintain, or sell information-based products (IBM, 1997; DTI, 1998). The new economy is more accessible for all: "More accurately, as the super symbolic (information) economy unfolds, the proletariat becomes a cognitariat" (Toffler, 1992, p.75). New technology is adopted and used in different sectors like commerce and education as a way of catching up with development (UNESCO, 1992). It is said that the sooner ICTs are adopted, the smaller the gap will be between the first, second, and third worlds, and the more economic benefits will be reaped by all (IDC Colombia, 1999).

Nevertheless, research on the results of the development of the information society suggests that the anticipated improvements to quality of life should perhaps be subject to some skeptical questioning. For instance, there is no evidence that the development of an information society has helped to foster better relationships between people (Wickham, 1997). In countries like Denmark, where a national ICT initiative has been running since the beginning of the 1990s, it is said that ICTs inhibit the promotion of certain democratic values that were, until then, important for the society (Friis, 1997). In the Republic of Ireland, one of the key problems to overcome seems to be a lack of awareness amongst people of the social consequences of having an information based economy (Information I, 1996). In South Africa, there is a significant division between groups of people according to their ability to access ICT services, adding to existing pressures in an already divided society (Wresch, 1996).

Although the above involve wider issues than just the implementation of information technology, reflecting on what has happened has led us to re-consider what is being done in the name of IS planning. It appears as if, in most planning processes, there is no clear means to address social concerns promoted by groups with interests that extend beyond competitive advantage. Within less developed economies, even business-related issues like job security, ergonomics, and working conditions have not been considered as primary concerns in IS planning (Chepaitis, 1997). Also, although the involvement of key employees in defining information requirements, maintaining information systems, and fostering information cultures' is considered an essential element for the success of IS planning in organisations, wider forms of participation have been neglected (Clarke & Lehaney, 1997a; Earl, 1998; Lyytinen & Robey, 1999). Despite a seemingly *superficial* concern with participation, IS planning methodologies have tended to favour forms of user involvement that do not lead to any questioning of dominant organisational purposes.

ISSUES IN COLOMBIA

In Colombia, IS planning at the national level has resulted in the launch of numerous initiatives (e.g., PNT, 1997; PNI, 1997; Agenda Conectividad, 2000a,b). Plans to develop and use information systems have been formulated and implemented in areas like education, infrastructure development, promoting community awareness, community information provision, and support for software companies (PNI, 1997). Two imperatives that inform the implementation of information technology in Colombian society are:

1.   The need for an 'information culture'—a set of shared values and norms which allow information to be considered important (Earl, 1998);
2.   The need to build the communications infrastructure in order to facilitate access for different economic sectors of the population and overcome a gap between groups of 'information-haves' and 'information have-nots' (Wresch, 1996).

Planning exercises have involved participants from government and other sectors (PNI, 1997). The results reveal the complexity of the situation and the importance of addressing a variety of different aspects when defining the scope and purposes of ICT, taking into account the needs and desires of all sectors of the population. Nevertheless, the dominant focus still seems to be establishing an information culture for economic purposes. This is evidenced by the different levels of success achieved in implementing aspects of the National Plan for Information Technology, designed to bring the information society into being in Colombia. Significant advances have been made in the development of the telecommunications infrastructure, the deregulation of telecommunications, the establishment of Community Information Technology Centres,[4] and the enhancement of conditions for developing software industries and mobile telephony (PNT, 1997; IDC Colombia, 1999; Agenda Conectividad, 2000a). Nevertheless, there are still major problems with making IS services more accessible to the general population (Foro, 1999; Agenda Conectividad, 2000b). Vast rural areas remain isolated from the rest of the country. Initiatives to widen participation often lack the full commitment of the authorities responsible for their implementation. Plans to use information systems *massively* in education, but within existing resource constraints, are meeting resistance from teachers and educational institutions (ElTiempo, 1999).[5]

At the organisational level in Colombia, the traditional model of IS planning linked to corporate strategy has been adopted, and with it, the myth that better technology will inevitably help solve practical problems (Lyytinen & Robey, 1999). Technology seems to be a powerful driver for businesses. It is expected that technology will strongly steer the design of organisational processes, policies, and hierarchical structures (García, 1993; Galvis, 1995, 1998; Fundacion Social, 1999). Currently, a vast number of organisations fail to implement IS plans on time, and therefore, struggle to keep competitive and to bring economic benefits amid the existing recession which brings with it a 20% level of unemployment (ElTiempo, 1999; Agenda Conectividad, 2000a). A huge amount of time and money has been invested by organisations to implement initiatives stemming from IS planning. The difficulties that have arisen lead some writers to critically reflect on the whole idea that the information society will bring with it improvements in quality of life (Murray-Lasso, 1992).

Given all the above, we argue that it is both necessary and timely to review the assumptions being made by most IS planning methodologies. We need to look again at what it means to enable a better society to emerge through the use of information systems and information technologies. It also seems important to explore how the participation of people in defining IS plans has been framed, and how it could be improved to allow people to include their *own* multiple concerns in planning processes (not just the already-expressed concerns of their organisations).

These (and other) issues of values, social purpose and participation have been addressed in the literature on critical systems thinking (CST). However, only a minority of CST writers have engaged in applications of information systems and most focus on planning and management more generally, both within organisations and more widely across organisational boundaries when dealing with social issues like older people's housing, services for homeless children, disaster planning, health service quality, etc. We have based our own approach on some ideas derived from the continuous dialogue among CST practitioners. More specifically, we combine the theories of *boundary critique* and *autopoiesis*, which have been interrelated on a previous occasion by Córdoba et al. (2000). CST and these two theories are summarised below.[6]

CRITICAL SYSTEMS THINKING (CST)

The above issues of values, the importance of the context in which planning is conducted, and the need to debate with people about the consequences of plans have been core concerns of critical systems thinkers for a number of years. CST practitioners are primarily interested in the development of *intervention methodology* and the *design of social system*, which is why it is a relevant source of ideas for IS planning.

The purpose of an intervention, from a CST point of view, is to bring about an *improvement*. The notion of improvement is important because practitioners are restricted in the number of interventions they can undertake, and must therefore make decisions about what they should and should not do. The extent to which various interventions look like they may or may not bring about improvements, or may bring about improvements that have greater or lesser priority, is a useful criterion for making these decisions.[7]

However, it is important not to be naïve when talking about improvement. "Improvements" need to be understood temporarily and locally. The word "local" does not necessarily imply that the understanding is confined to an organisation or small group (although this may be the case), a local understanding may be very wide spread, even to the extent of providing the foundations for legal statutes and international agreements. However, the terms "local" and "temporary" remind us that it can be dangerous to assume that an "improvement" will be universally regarded as such. As different people may use different boundary judgements defining what is to be included in analyses and whose views have credibility, what looks like an improvement through one pair of eyes may look like the very opposite through another (Churchman, 1970). Also, even if there is widespread agreement between all those directly affected by an intervention that it constitutes an improvement, this agreement may not stretch to future generations. The temporary nature of all improvements makes the concept of *sustainable* improvement particularly important, while even sustainable improvements cannot last forever, gearing improvement to long-term stability is essential if future generations are to be accounted for. We can say that an *improvement* has been made when a desired consequence has been realised through intervention. In contrast, a *sustainable* improvement has been achieved when this seems like it will last into the indefinite future without the appearance of undesired consequences (or a redefinition of the original consequences as undesirable). Of course, whether an improvement is sustainable or not is a matter of judgement (and judgements are inevitably temporary and local, even if they are widely accepted): the limitations of human understanding mean that what may appear to be sustainable at one moment may seem less so at the next. Therefore, in aiming for sustainable improvement, people involved in IS (and other) planning need to periodically review the criteria of sustainability that they are using.

The *boundary* concept follows from this understanding of improvement. We can talk about boundaries defining who is included, excluded, or marginalised in debate around a set of plans. Boundaries also define the issues that are seen as relevant, are marginalised or are ignored from particular points of view. It is important to be aware that boundaries concerning who is involved and what is considered relevant to IS (and other) planning initiatives will always be present, even if the participants are unaware of them. Therefore, explicit reflection on boundaries, and conscious choice between alternatives, enables interventions to be undertaken in a spirit of social awareness, allowing understandings of improvement to be subject to critical analysis. These ideas have been developed by a number of authors[8] and are essential to the theory of *boundary critique* (to be presented shortly).

Another issue of importance to many CST practitioners is *theoretical and methodological pluralism*. These have meaning in terms of the focus on boundary judgements mentioned above. If understandings can be bounded in many different ways, then each of these boundaries may suggest the use of a different theory. The use of multiple boundaries, therefore, legitimises the use of multiple theoretical perspectives.[9] *Methodological* pluralism then also becomes meaningful because methods and methodologies embody different theoretical assumptions. Choices between boundaries and theories suggest which methods might be most appropriate. The principle reason for embracing methodological pluralism is that, in principle, no one method yet devised can deal adequately with all the contingencies we might be faced with during an intervention. A more flexible and responsive practice can be developed by drawing upon methods from a variety of methodological sources and mixing them creatively in response to our understandings of the contingencies of the local situation. Many writings on this have been published in the CST literature.[10]

In this chapter, we focus, in particular, on issues surrounding the inclusion of different categories of people in IS planning, the phenomenon of marginalisation, and the use of different methods to address specific concerns that might emerge during the planning process. These are all matters that the theory of boundary critique addresses, so this is discussed below. Afterwards, we move on to detail the theory of autopoiesis which introduces some additional concerns that we see as relevant.

BOUNDARY CRITIQUE

Our review of the theory of boundary critique will start with the work of Churchman (1968a,b, 1970, 1971, 1979), who has been widely acknowledged as a major contributor to the development of systems thinking. It will then move on to examine the writings of Ulrich (1983, 1986, 1988, 1990, 1993, 1994, 1996a,b), Midgley (1992a, 1994, 2000), and Yolles (2001), who have built upon the foundations laid by Churchman.

Prior to the work of Churchman, many people assumed that the boundaries of a system are "given" by the structure of reality. In contrast, Churchman made it clear that boundaries are social or personal constructs that define the limits of the knowledge that is to be taken as pertinent in an analysis. There is also another important element of Churchman's understanding of system. When it comes to human systems, pushing out the boundaries of analysis may also involve pushing out the boundaries of who may legitimately be considered a decision maker (Churchman, 1970). Thus, the business of setting boundaries defines both the knowledge to be considered pertinent *and* the people who generate that knowledge (and who also have a stake in the results of any attempts to improve the system). This means that there are no experts in Churchman's systems approach, at least in the traditional sense of expertise, where all relevant knowledge is seen as emanating from just one group or class of people wide spread stakeholder involvement is required, sweeping in a variety of relevant perspectives.

Churchman (1979) also discusses critique. In examining how improvement should be defined, he follows Hegel (1807), who stresses the need for rigorous self-reflection, exposing our most cherished assumptions to the possibility of overthrow. To be as sure as we can that we are defining improvement adequately, we should, in the words of Churchman (1979), pursue a "dialectical process": this involves seeking out the strongest possible "enemies" of our ideas and entering into a process of rational argumentation with them. Only if we listen closely to their views and our arguments survive should we pursue the improvement.

Churchman produced a great deal of highly influential work in the 1960s and 1970s, and in the 1980s, several other authors began to build upon it in significant new ways. One of these authors was Werner Ulrich. Ulrich (1983) agrees that Churchman's desire to sweep the maximum amount of information into understandings of improvement is *theoretically* sound, but also acknowledges that the need to take practical action will inevitably limit the sweep in process. He therefore poses the question, how can people rationally justify the boundaries they use? His answer is to develop a methodology, critical systems heuristics, which can be used to explore and justify boundaries through debate between stakeholders. In producing his methodology, Ulrich draws upon the later writings of Jürgen Habermas (1976, 1984a,b) concerning the nature of rationality. Habermas regards rationality as dialogical—and the tool of dialogue is language, which allows us to question. The basis of dialogue is, therefore, open and free questioning between human beings. However, Habermas does not take a naïve line concerning dialogue. He acknowledges that it may be distorted through the effects of power. This may happen directly, when one participant coerces another, or indirectly, when participants make unquestioned assumptions about the absolute necessity for, or inevitable future existence of, particular social systems. To overcome these effects of power, we need to establish what Habermas calls an "ideal speech situation": a situation where any assumption can be questioned and all viewpoints can be heard.

However, while Ulrich (1983) accepts the *principle* of Habermas's understanding of critique, he nevertheless criticises him for being utopian. For all viewpoints to be heard, the ideal speech situation would have to extend debate to every citizen of the world, both present and future. This is quite simply impossible. Ulrich sees his task as the *pragmatisation* of the ideal speech situation, and a marriage between critical and systems thinking is the means by which this can be achieved. Truly rational inquiry is said to be *critical*, in that no assumption held by participants in inquiry should be beyond question. It is also *systemic*, however, in that boundaries always have to be established within which critique can be conducted. Indeed, Ulrich claims that both ideas are inadequate without the other. Critical thinking without system boundaries will inevitably fall into the trap of continual expansion and eventual loss of meaning (as everything can be seen to have a context with which it interacts, questioning becomes infinite). However, systems thinking without the critical idea may result in a "hardening of the boundaries," where destructive assumptions remain unquestioned because the system boundaries are regarded as absolute.

An important aspect of Ulrich's (1983) thinking about boundaries is that boundary judgements and value judgements are intimately linked. The values adopted will direct the drawing of boundaries that define the knowledge accepted as pertinent. Similarly, the inevitable process of drawing boundaries constrains the ethical stance taken and the values pursued. Debating boundaries is, therefore, an ethical process, and a priority for Ulrich is to evolve practical guidelines that can help people steer the process of critical reflection on the ethics of drawing system boundaries. For this purpose, Ulrich (1983) developed a list of 12 questions that can be used heuristically to question what the system currently is and what it ought to be. It is important to note that some of these questions relate to who should participate in discussing boundary judgements in the first place, meaning that there is always the possibility for people to enter or leave discussions.

There is a key guiding ideal embedded in this work. According to Ulrich, if rationality is dialogical, plans for improvement should, in principle, be normatively acceptable to all those participating in a given dialogue. In practice, this means (if at all possible) securing agreement between those designing an improvement and those affected by it (of course, judging who or what is actually involved and/or affected already involves making a boundary judgement). When agreement is not secured, citizens who disagree with implementing the improvement, and who are affected by it, may legitimately use Ulrich's 12 questions in a "polemical" mode. This means building an argument with which to embarrass planners in future public debate by exposing the limited nature of the expertise they lay claim to.

We have now seen how Ulrich has built on and developed the work of Churchman. In a similar fashion, Midgley (1992a) has extended the work of Ulrich. For both Churchman and Ulrich, the question of what system boundaries are to be used in an analysis is essentially an ethical question, because value and boundary judgements are intimately related. Midgley (1992a) uses this insight as a starting point to ask what happens when there is a conflict between different groups of people who have different ethics (values in action) relating to the same issue, and thereby make different boundary judgements.

If one group makes a narrow boundary judgement and another makes a wider one, there will be a *marginal* area between the two boundaries. This marginal area will contain elements that are excluded by the group making the narrow boundary judgement, but are included in the wider analysis undertaken by the second group. We can call the two boundaries the *primary* and *secondary* boundaries (the primary boundary being the narrower one). This is represented visually in Figure 1.

Midgley argues that when two ethical boundary judgements come into conflict, the situation tends to be stabilised by the imposition of either a *sacred* or a *profane* status on marginal elements. The words "sacred" and "profane" mean valued and devalued, respectively. This terminology has been borrowed from the tradition of anthropology, exemplified by the work of Douglas (1966), and it should be stressed that they are not meant in an exclusively religious sense but refer to the special status of a marginalised element. The imposition of either a sacred or profane status on marginal elements stabilises a conflictual situation in the following manner. When marginal elements become profane, the primary boundary and its associated ethic are focused upon and reinforced as the main reference for decision making. People or issues relegated to the margins are disparaged, allowing the secondary boundary to be ignored. Conversely, when marginal elements are made sacred (and thereby assume a special importance), the secondary boundary and its associated ethic is focused upon and reinforced.

However, this is not the end of the story. Not only do ethical tensions give rise to sacredness and profanity, but this whole process comes to be overlaid with social ritual. Midgley (1992a) defines ritual as "behaviour, in whatever context, that contains certain stereotypical elements that involve the symbolic expression of wider social concerns." (See Douglas, 1966, and Leach, 1976, for further thoughts on the relationship between ritual, sacredness and profanity) An observation of the

Figure 1: Marginalisation

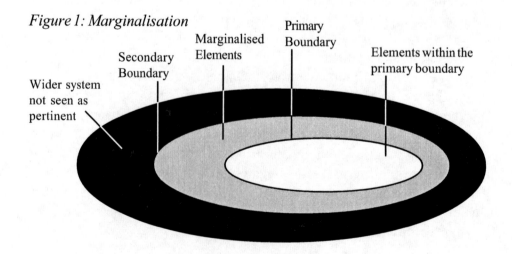

presence of ritual can tell us where sacredness and profanity might lie, and hence, where ethical conflicts related to marginalisation might be found. In order to make this clearer, the whole process has been represented diagrammatically in Figure 2.

In Figure 2, we see one ethic arising from within the primary boundary and another from within the secondary. These come into conflict—a conflict that can only be dealt with by making one or other of the two boundaries dominant. This dominance is achieved by making elements in the margin (between the primary and secondary boundaries) either sacred or profane. The whole process is symbolically expressed in ritual, which, in turn, helps to support the total system.

While Figure 2 shows the secondary boundary *containing* the primary boundary, creating a marginal area between the two, a similar situation of marginalisation also arises when two boundaries *overlap*. The common area may be subject to dispute and can become either sacred or profane in the same manner. See Yolles (2001) for an illustration.

Of course, the system represented in Figure 2 is a model, and like all models, it does not fully express the complexity of the many value and boundary judgements that interact dynamically in social situations. A discussion of this complexity, and practical examples that clarify the process further, can be found in Midgley (1992a, 1994, 2000) and Midgley et al. (1998) One particularly important point about the complexity lying beyond the model should be borne in mind, however, this kind of "system" does not exist in isolation—it is "held in place," or granted integrity, by virtue of the fact that it expresses wider struggles between competing discourses.[11]

Figure 2: Margins, ethics, sacredness, profanity, and ritual

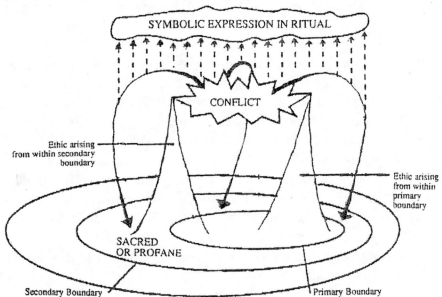

From the theory of boundary critique, we can derive some questions that can be asked during IS planning:

- What people and/or issues are being privileged?[12] What *should* be privileged?
- Do different people have different views about what is, or should be, privileged? If so, what does this tell us about our own and other people's concerns and values?
- What people and/or issues are being negatively marginalised? Should they be?
- Do different people have different views about what is or should be negatively marginalised? If so, what does this tell us about our own and other people's concerns and values?
- Are there people and/or issues that some people value highly and others devalue? If so, what does this tell us about our own and other people's concerns and values?
- When answering these questions, have you considered people and things that might be affected in the wider system as well as those in the immediate environment?
- Are there people and/or issues that are currently excluded from analysis (not just marginalised) that should be included, because they have a significant impact on what you are observing?
- Are there recurring activities, interactions, conversations, ways of dressing, etc., which might be seen as expressions of our own and/or other people's concerns and values? If so, what do these tell us about them? Are they problematic, and from whose point of view?
- What are the possible consequences of the privileging and/or negative marginalisation of people and/or issues? Are they problematic, and from whose point of view?
- What are the possible consequences of the existence of the different concerns and values identified? Are they problematic, and from whose point of view?
- Are there significant interactions between the possible consequences identified (e.g., note that local and wider consequences can sometimes interact)? Are they problematic, and from whose point of view?
- What might be the wider implications for society if these plans are implemented, both in the short term and for future generations? Are they problematic, and from whose point of view? What *should* the wider implications be?
- Who is being given the opportunity to answer these questions? Who *should* be given this opportunity?
- Who is hearing the answers? Are they hearing all or only some of the answers? Who *should* be hearing them?

Earlier, we discussed problematic issues of social inclusion in the information society. Some writers have naïvely assumed that the mass introduction of ICTs will automatically result in the empowerment of individuals and nations within the global information economy. Because boundary critique helps us focus on issues of marginalisation and exclusion, it enables us to begin to explore these issues in a more critical manner.

Boundary critique also indicates the value of a deeper form of participation in IS planning than the one usually practised. Genuine participation cannot be established on the basis of a pre-set organisational agenda (Gregory et al., 1994). People also need to be free to sweep in wider concerns, including how to improve the society in which they are living (which may, of course, have important implications for the role of the organisation). Ideally, the process of boundary critique should be continuous. As new boundaries are identified over time, the understandings of participants should evolve, and so should IS plans.

The focus of IS planning is, therefore, shifted from concerns that primarily reside within the organisational boundaries (e.g., efficiency, productivity, control) to more people-oriented concerns that might not be directly related to the use of information or technology but are still important to surface. This does not mean the wholesale abandonment of narrower organisational concerns (we certainly do not want efficiency and effectiveness to be forgotten), but it does mean seeing them in a wider context. In so doing, the goals (even the whole mission) of the organisation may be reviewed to the benefit of the organisation itself, the individuals within it, the wider community and future generations.

Having presented boundary critique, we now move on to discuss the theory of autopoiesis, which introduces another set of concerns that we believe are relevant to IS planning.

THE THEORY OF AUTOPOIESIS

While boundary critique is essentially a *social* theory, autopoiesis provides a *biological* explanation of how human beings interact as living systems.[13] A full description of this theory is beyond the scope of this chapter, but more detailed accounts can be found in Maturana (1988), Maturana and Varela (1992,) and Mingers (1995).

The word "autopoiesis" can roughly be defined as "self-producing" (Mingers, 1995). An autopoietic system is one that seeks to maintain itself, and, when it interacts with its environment, it takes actions that are determined by its current structure. The structure of a system is its arrangement of components in such a way that its organisation (that which gives it identity) is maintained. The structure of a system changes over time, but within limits laid down by its organisation. This cannot change without the system losing its identity as a self-producing entity—in other words, without it dying. Of course, the structure of an autopoietic system changes over time due to the flow of its interactions with its environment.

What this tells us about human beings is that we seek to maintain ourselves as living beings through our interactions with our environment, but that at any single moment, our actions are limited by our knowledge and understanding. However, our knowledge and understanding changes over time. We are capable of learning. This is arguably non-controversial. However, an important further insight that derives from the theory of autopoiesis is that, because a human being's actions at any moment are determined by his/her structure, the environment can only trigger changes, *it cannot cause them*. Causation is always from inside a person, and even a 'trigger' will only have an effect if the person is already predisposed to react to it. Maturana and Varela (1992) therefore say we are able to "see what we see, and what we do not see does not exist" (p. 242).[14]

Also, Maturana (1988) explicitly considers the role of language. As social animals, human beings not only *act*, we also strive to *co-ordinate* our actions. Language helps in this process: it allows us to *co-ordinate our co-ordinations of actions*. We act in co-ordination with others, and language supports the co-ordination of these co-ordinations.

Interestingly, when Maturana and Varela talk about co-ordinations of actions, they have something very specific in mind. A person can only react to outside forces on the basis of his/her current structure (maintained by, and maintaining, her organisation, or identity as a system). Nevertheless, s/he is organisationally predisposed to identify recurrent patterns of interaction and adapt his/her structure accordingly, thereby giving rise to habitual responses. When a person and an aspect of his/her environment (which may or may not be another person) have a recurrent relationship, sufficient habitual responses are set up to allow us to describe the relationship between the person and the aspect of her environment as *structurally coupled*. Structural coupling, when taking place amongst a group of people, allows the working out of co-ordinations of actions in ways that are of mutual benefit to all those concerned. Of course, language may facilitate and strengthen this process.

Language also forms "rational domains" in which people participate. Over time, a particular use of language to co-ordinate co-ordinations of actions may become more and more elaborated, allowing people to exist in very subtle, well-coordinated, structurally coupled relationships. Thereby, whole human activity systems, or domains of action, are created. People may actually participate in a variety of domains of action, but the movement of individuals from one to another – and hence from the use of one form of language to another – crucially depends on the invocation of emotion. According to Maturana (1988), emotions make individuals switch from one rationality to another. All rational arguments are "braided" with emotion (in other words, forms of language come to be associated with emotional states within individuals), so when a particular emotion is experienced, this triggers a switch to the appropriate, associated rational domain (or elaborated system of language). This is why an appeal to the emotions can have such a powerful effect in terms of changing peoples' ways of thinking (Bilson, 1996, 1997). Indeed, the relationship between rational domains (forms of language) and emotion is two-way: the use of a particular 'language game' associated with an emotion will give rise to that emotion, altering the set of rational domains that become available to participating individuals at that moment.

Human beings, then, are self-producing organisms who co-construct their realities through language. It is because of the role of language in the co-ordination of co-ordinations of actions that *conversation* is so important. Individuals flow through different domains of action by moving between different networks of conversations, guided by their emotions (Maturana, 1988). Conversations end when the emotional commitment to remain engaged in them ends.

In Maturana's view, people share a common emotion: love, or mutual respect for the 'other' as an equally valid human being. However, love is not universally extended to all people at all times. In conversations, the braiding of emotion and reason helps to specify who is the 'other' to be concerned about at any particular time, and what actions should be taken towards him or her. These concerns and/ or actions may be loving, instrumental, exclusionary or even violent. However, a true *social* system, as defined by Maturana, is indeed based on love (mutual respect) for others.

Now, the theory of autopoiesis is descriptive (concerning the nature of human beings), but it also has a normative dimension: it is *pre*scriptive about the right course of action for human beings to follow. Because it is love that enables mutual understanding during conversations, Maturana argues that we have an ethical responsibility when we engage in conversations to do so with an attitude of love— listening to the 'other' as an equally valid person. To do anything less is to negate the value of the 'other' as a fellow human being.

TOWARDS A CRITICAL APPROACH FOR IS PLANNING

Bearing in mind the above ideas of autopoiesis and boundary critique, an approach can be defined to support inquiry into IS planning processes. This approach combines both of these theories and promotes openness towards the inclusion of different people and issues, focusing on the way of life of individuals, groups, organisations, and societies (with or without the support of information technology). The main tenets of this approach follow (more details can be found in Córdoba, 2002).

It can be said that human beings flow in language with others. In each domain of interaction there are certain concerns – sets of distinctions (co-ordinations of co-ordinations of actions) which are created and re-created by each individual in interaction with others. Maturana and Varela (1992) argue that distinctions emerge from the *way of life* of individuals. Some of these distinctions can be considered *concerns for action*, which people create and re-create. Hence, there could be as many concerns for action as domains of interaction through which individuals flow. It is the sweeping in of a diversity of people and their concerns that lies at the heart of our approach.

This is motivated by the ideal of love, or mutual respect. All concerns should, in principle, be considered equally legitimate, because they come from people taking part in different domains of action, and no one domain is intrinsically superior to another. However, this does not mean that people's concerns, and the actions that may follow from them, are all equally desirable. We need to take the concerns of fellow human beings seriously, but concerns are always relative to the local and temporary interactions that individuals find themselves in. People's understandings are therefore limited, and individuals can learn about some of the limitations of their concerns through dialogue. So, the ideal situation involves listening to others; taking account of their concerns; developing a shared understanding of how their concerns may or may not fit with ours; exploring the possible strengths and weaknesses of different concerns; looking for synergies; and working towards action in partnership.

However, this is very much an *ideal*. Because we inevitably have to choose who we are going to involve in discussions at any moment, and what concerns will be central and what will be peripheral, we need boundary critique. This recognises that limits to the inclusion of people and issues are imposed through value judgements. So, if limits are inevitable, but we still want to act in a spirit of mutual respect, we have an obligation to think carefully and critically about the consequences of the different boundary judgements (both locally and more widely) that frame people's concerns. Boundary critique also allows us to transcend a limited set of concerns by exposing new possibilities for the inclusion of people and issues that might not have previously occurred to any of the participants involved in debate.

The identification of initial concerns in IS planning can lead to explorations of who should be involved, what other concerns might be legitimate, and how these explorations should be pursued in practice. We call this approach 'critical' because it emphasises the importance of both self-awareness and reflection by participants on issues of concern emerging during the IS planning process (Clarke & Lehaney, 1997a,b; Warren, 2000; Córdoba et al., 2000). Also, because local conditions of marginalisation tend to mirror wider discourses in society (many of which can be viewed as ideological), *ideology critique* is important (Gregory, 1992, 1994, 2000). Finally, our approach is critical, because it encourages the application of boundary critique to the choice and/or design of *methods* for IS planning. Sweeping in a variety of concerns, and understanding their contexts in different ways, provides a starting point for considering which methods might be most appropriate to structure a way forward (see also Midgley et al., 1998; Midgley, 2000). The approach aims at fostering a communication process in IS planning, allowing an on-going enactment of meaning between participants (Walsham, 1993). However, the concerns to be included as legitimate go beyond those usually entering IS planning processes – essentially, those that are directly connected to the application of computer information systems. In principle, debate may stray into any territory. In practice, however, limitations will emerge through the use of boundary critique – but the point is that these limitations are not pre-determined.

Having said this, treating others with mutual respect involves valuing their starting points in debate. Some people's starting points *will* primarily be concerned with information systems – especially those commissioning an IS planning exercise, otherwise it would not be labelled as such. In most contexts, it is also the case that IS planners are not working with a blank canvass: there are current and/or potential information systems initiatives already in place. Therefore, a task that is open to practitioners is to support people in building a bridge between what currently exists and what is going to be needed to address the wider set of concerns being swept in. To achieve this, different forms of communication between people can be promoted in ways that enable the avoidance of duplication. It is also important, where possible, for those responsible for existing initiatives to evaluate new concerns in dialogue with others rather than have these imposed without debate. Mutual respect involves valuing what people are currently committed to as well as the new concerns being introduced.

The idea is to create an *ongoing* IS planning process which meaningfully interrelates concerns about information systems with surrounding issues – and which can depart from IS planning altogether when appropriate. After identifying an initial set of concerns using boundary critique, it may be valuable to draw upon some of the existing planning methods from the IS literature to define specific initiatives for action (see Midgley, 2000, for details of how methods may be chosen and creatively mixed in practice). Further boundary critique can then enhance the scope of the initiatives as they are developed. *Iteration* between boundary critique and planning is encouraged.

It is not mandatory to address all concerns (including IS-based concerns) if, through boundary critique, people deprioritise them. It is usually the case that more concerns are initially swept in than can be dealt with through the construction of specific initiatives. The point is to *consider* the widest possible range of concerns before choosing paths for action. This calls for avoiding the imposition of a single point of view or single set of concerns – including the concerns of practitioners and/ or IS-experts—that may prematurely narrow the IS planning process.

METHODOLOGY

Having made a general case for a critical perspective on IS planning, we now present the specific methodology we have developed. A methodology, as we understand the term (following Checkland, 1981; Midgley, 2000; and Jackson, 2000), is the set of theoretical ideas that justifies a particular approach and/or the use of a particular method or methods. A method is a technique, or set of techniques, designed to achieve a specific purpose.

Our methodology is composed of two main phases:

- *Distinction*, in which different participants and their multiple concerns are identified.
- *Improvement*, in which the concerns identified are presented to participants to see if some of them can be transformed into concrete action, with or without information systems, in order to improve the way of life of people (those directly involved, and those potentially affected in the wider community).

These two phases are iterative. New concerns identified in the distinction phase might have an impact on what the improvement is going to be. Also, reflections on potential improvements might raise issues that take us back to distinguishing new participants and/or concerns. These phases are essentially two "lenses" through which a situation can be appreciated – they are not phases to be enacted one after the other in a linear fashion. They emphasise either identifying concerns (distinction) or structuring debate in the interests of action (improvement), and each will have implications for the other.

During both phases, an on-going *boundary critique* needs to be conducted to address issues of inclusion, exclusion, and marginalisation of people and issues. This should affect the *content* of debates, *who* is involved, and *how* debate is structured (the choices of methods).[15]

Inevitably, in any actual IS planning situation, there are practical constraints (institutional, financial, cultural, personal, etc.) that limit boundary explorations and the plans that can be considered feasible. When these constraints are encountered, boundary critique (linked into more traditional planning methods) can be particularly useful, because it enables people to do two things. First, to explore whether the constraints might, in fact, be overcome despite initial impressions (by shifting the boundaries of analysis, problems sometimes begin to dissolve). Second, if it seems that certain constraints do have to be accepted, it gives people reasons for this that can then be communicated to others who might need convincing.

Our methodology can be summarised in Figure 3.

Figure 3 represents IS planning as an on-going, iterative process allowing people to move between distinction and improvement, drawing upon boundary critique for both. The methodology also allows the mixing of methods to address the identified concerns in a flexible and responsive manner: whole methods, parts

Figure 3: A critical methodology for IS planning (from Córdoba et al., 2000)

Figure 3: A critical methodology for IS planning (from Córdoba et al., 2000)

Different concerns and values

Distinction

Boundaries

Boundary Critique

Concerns

Boundaries

Improvement

Action plans (including IS-based initiatives)

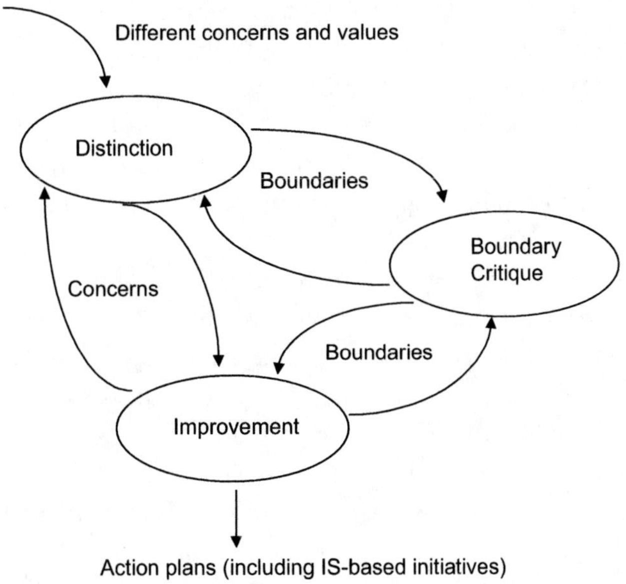

of methods, or sets of methods can be chosen and/or designed through dialogue between the facilitator and those involved (Midgley, 1990, 1997b, 2000).

APPLYING THE METHODOLOGY AT JAVERIANA UNIVERSITY

Having described our methodology, we now go on to present its application in an IS planning project at Javeriana University, Colombia. This is inevitably a highly abbreviated presentation–for more details, see Córdoba (2002). After we set out what happened in the project (from our point of view), we reflect back on the methodology and its application. This reflection gives rise to some issues of concern and some ideas for addressing them. In the account below, the names of participants have been disguised to preserve confidentiality.

The initial proposal for the project was negotiated between Javeriana University (Colombia) and the University of Hull (UK). One of the authors (José Córdoba) spent a year at Javeriana, supported at a distance by the other author (Gerald Midgley). José facilitated the IS planning in partnership with an established academic staff member at Javeriana who had specific knowledge of both IS issues and systems methodology. They were also given some administrative support by the organisation. A document specifying the proposed methodology (including the phases of distinction and improvement and the value of boundary critique) was circulated to the senior management of the University, and this was approved before the project commenced. We should note that the document was explicit about methodological issues of social inclusion, saying that we wanted to talk with a wide variety of stakeholders, and we related this to the mission of the University to contribute to the improvement of Colombian society. Our document discussed some theoretical issues too: how new concerns emerge from the interactions between individuals, and how boundaries are established that privilege some people and issues over others during planning. The idea of starting with a wide set of concerns was given prominence.

Soon after the project, began we realised that, although our methodology had already received senior management approval, the language we had used in our document constituted a barrier to effective communication with many of the people interested in taking part in the project. For practical purposes, "boundaries" was replaced by "what is being taken into account" and "limits for action," and "way of life" was rephrased as "sets of actions in a particular context."[16] We found it necessary to regularly emphasise to participants that concerns about their way of life need not necessarily be related to the use of information technology, and they did not have to be able to offer an "expert" opinion to make a useful contribution. People tended to assume that the focus was going to be information systems in the narrow sense, and that their "ordinary" point of view would be less important than 'expert' testimony. Simply countering these assumptions in an introductory letter was insufficient: we had to explain the rationale of the project in some detail before people realised why their wider concerns were going to be of value.

The Distinction Phase: Interviews and Workshops about People's Concerns

In developing the distinction phase, we decided to conduct personal interviews and group workshops to identify concerns. These two activities allowed researchers to converse directly with individuals both within Javeriana and outside it. A person's concerns could be related not only to his/her job or main activity in life, but also to his/her participation in different "scenarios" or domains of action. Our starting point was that all concerns should be considered as equally legitimate: it would be the task of everybody involved to prioritise them later in the project. Having said this, however, we did not shy away from our part in the process. We did not claim neutrality. We presented ourselves as participants *in* the situation, rather than observers *of* it. This gave us two explicit roles: (i) to take responsibility for designing the sweep-in process, ensuring that marginalised voices were included; and (ii) to contribute (but *not* privilege) our own concerns. Given an expectation laid upon us by some participants that we would act as expert consultants rather than facilitators, it was never going to be easy to introduce our concerns without privileging them. However, we believe that reflecting on the issue helped us deal with it more effectively than if we had pretended to some form of neutrality (also see Gregory & Romm, 2001, for further thoughts on non-neutral "critical facilitation").

Three people were usually present in an interview: the interviewee; the interviewer; and a "critical friend." The critical friend was either a second member of the research team or a member of the clerical support staff. His/her role was to take notes and also, when the interview was complete, to facilitate a critical evaluation of it. S/he would attempt to identify moments when the interviewer might have imposed his/her own agenda, and raise any concerns s/he felt had been left out of the discussion. In this way, the interviewers received continuous feedback on their performance in managing the boundaries of the debate.

Within each interview, in order to create a friendly atmosphere and to support interviewees in connecting with their own way of life, a selection of pictures (from of newspapers and magazines) was spread out.[17] These represented a variety of personal, community, national, and international issues that might be of potential concern. The idea was that these would remind interviewees of issues that might not otherwise be remembered in an interview (the interview situation is, after all, relatively detached from wider social concerns). Each interviewee was asked to select pictures that were meaningful for his/her way of life.[18] After a selection was made, a dialogue was initiated. This was structured around particular questions:

- Why do these pictures matter to you?
- What do they represent in terms of your own concerns or desires?
- What personal values do you see reflected in the pictures?
- Are there any ethical conflicts that could be identified from the pictures?
- What about [related concern]? Do you think it is important?

These questions were intended to tease out concerns and the ethical issues they could raise for the interviewees and for others. In dialogue, the boundaries of the identified concerns were explored with the idea of finding "blind spots" – people and issues that could be considered relevant but had not yet been identified. We also used the dialogue to explore whether there might be primary and secondary boundaries (and conflicting values) in play, indicating the possible existence of issues and people so far marginalised from mainstream discourses in Javeriana and in Colombian society more widely.

Reflection on the boundaries of our methodology was also encouraged. For instance, some people expressed disagreement with the use of pictures, and others disliked having a discussion that was not based on expert knowledge. In response to this feedback, the research team decided to make the use of the pictures optional. However, we continued to promote an open discussion about people's concerns, treating "expert" and "non-expert" testimony equally, as to have sought only 'expert' knowledge would have resulted in some significant exclusions and

marginalisations. We were conscious that this meant privileging our own methodological concern over others, and this is an issue that we will take up later in the
chapter when we discuss the ethics of the practitioner.

In total, 20 personal interviews were conducted during the distinction phase.
The first eleven (six administrators, three academic staff, and two project leaders)
were suggested by our contacts in the University. This list was then extended in
consultation with the first 11 interviewees (we added six more administrators, one
member of the Jesuit community working at Javeriana, and two more academics).
In this way, the research team rolled out the boundaries of participation (following
the method recommended by Midgley & Milne, 1995).

In addition to the 20 individual interviews, six workshops were also held.
These basically used the same format as the interviews (choosing pictures,
identifying concerns, and discussing them using the trigger questions). The idea of
these workshops was to significantly widen the boundaries of participation in the
distinction phase, especially to stakeholders outside the University. We held
workshops with students, business people in the community, and citizens more
generally (the citizens' workshop drew in people from a variety of sources—see
Córdoba, 2002, for more details).

For the workshops, the format of the individual interview (described above)
was adapted. The participants were divided into subgroups of three people, and
they rotated the roles of interviewee, interviewer, and critical friend. After everybody had been interviewed, the participants presented the outputs to the group as a
whole. The researchers then summarised the main findings and also facilitated challenges
to some of the assumptions being made regarding the way of life that people either
already had, or wanted to attain, both at Javeriana and in the wider Colombian society.

At the end of the interviews and workshops, the majority of participants
expressed their willingness to continue with the project. Having defined a series of
concerns, values, boundaries and potential actions to improve the way of life of a
diverse variety of stakeholders, the improvement phase was started.

The Improvement Phase: IS Planning to Enhance
the Way of Life at Javeriana

In practice, we called this the "design phase" because "design" seemed more
intuitively appealing to stakeholders than "improvement." The research team
devised a strategy to involve people in considering different forms of action. We
took into account the willingness (or otherwise) of different people to participate in
this phase, and also their current engagements and commitments. People at
Javeriana were already taking part in relevant conversations and actions. The
strategy involved developing two paths of intervention that we called design
exercises and critical engagements. These are explained below.

The Design Exercises

The design exercises used systems methods (holistic planning and problem solving methods) to support participants in defining a series of proposals for action to improve the situation at Javeriana. These exercises also aimed at surfacing possible implications of adopting particular boundaries and privileging certain people and issues when deciding on actions to be taken. We sought to promote a critical attitude concerning potential marginalisations that could follow from the implementation of plans.

Because most of the design work was to be undertaken by groups in workshops, bringing together diverse sets of stakeholders, we anticipated that significant synergies could be gained through the sharing and collective critique of concerns. Also, if people wanted to include new concerns, not derived from the initial distinction phase, we made it clear that they were perfectly at liberty to do so—they could return to working on distinctions at any time. Iteration between distinction and improvement was therefore encouraged. All those who took part in the first phase were invited to participate in this new phase.

In the design exercises, we proposed that participants should select, from all the concerns, values, and beliefs identified previously (some of which were about what currently is, and others about what ought to be the way of life at Javeriana), a set of three or four particularly pertinent issues. We then drew upon some of the methods from soft systems methodology (Checkland, 1981; Checkland & Scholes, 1990), which have been applied to IS planning on previous occasions (e.g., Lewis, 1994; Checkland & Holwell, 1998). First, some *relevant systems* to address the pertinent issues were defined by participants. The term *relevant system* refers to a coherent set of purposeful human activities that people believe might contribute to the improvement of a situation (Checkland, 1981). Participants were then encouraged to develop their understandings of these relevant systems by discussing possible root definitions of them. A root definition is a concise description of the core purpose of a relevant system (Checkland, 1981). The components of the *root definition* can be expressed in the mnemonic CATWOE, as follows:

Customers:	Beneficiaries and those who might be harmed by the proposed activities
Actors:	Those involved in making the system work
Transformation process:	The identification of inputs to be transformed into outputs (e.g., people not acting in solidarity to be transformed into people acting in solidarity)
Worldview:	The set of concerns, including values, that make a transformation meaningful
Owners:	Those who can stop the transformation from

happening (these are not necessarily owners in the financial sense of the term)

Environmental constraints: Things that have to be taken as given, because they cannot, or should not, be under the control of the actors

Based on the root definitions, more detailed proposals for human activity systems were developed in two ways.[19] The first way, used in some of the workshops, was to develop conceptual models (Checkland & Scholes, 1990): sets of human activities linked by arrows to show their logical connections. The second way, used in other workshops, drew upon some of the ideas in Ackoff's (1981) methodology of interactive planning. Ackoff talks about defining the ideal properties of a system. This means thinking about what a system should ideally be like, given only three constraints:

1.   Technological feasibility (no impossible technology should be proposed)
2.   Operational viability (the system should be sustainable in relation to its environment)
3.   Adaptability (the system should be able to respond to changing circumstances)

In addition to these three constraints, we also proposed that any system should promote the general values of co-operation and continuous improvement. These values are explicitly enshrined in the mission and philosophy of Javeriana University, and we found that all the stakeholders shared them.

When elaborating root definitions and conceptual models or defining ideal properties for human activity systems, the research team played a critical role by encouraging reflection on the boundaries that emerged. We asked questions like:

•   Who else should be included?
•   What else should be considered as important?
•   What about [issues or people] that you have said are not important? Why is this? Is there another point of view, and should you listen to it? If not, why not?
•   Who and what will be directly or indirectly affected by doing things this way? What does your answer suggest you should do?
•   What kind of information technology support could help in achieving the desired outcomes?

With the above questions new issues arose as marginalised elements were considered, taking people back to their work on making distinctions. This work then fed forward to changes in the set of relevant systems and agendas for action defined by participants.

Critical Engagements

The design exercises represented just one of the two paths for intervention taken in the improvement phase. The other path involved critical engagements.

These consisted of a series of conversations about IS planning projects that were already taking place at Javeriana, and whose purposes seemed to be relevant to the concerns identified in the distinction phase of our work. The research team was invited to participate in meetings about the following initiatives that were already underway:

1. Implementing internet access to library services
2. Designing and implementing a new digital library system, allowing the continual exchange and updating of information
3. Designing a new 'Information Technology in Architectural Design' education program
4. Re-designing the curriculum for the "Computer Science and Systems Engineering" programme

The research team took the explicit role of 'critical friend' in these meetings: we adopted an attitude of listening, facilitating and challenging as well as directly contributing. We started by gaining an understanding of the current concerns that people had when taking part in each initiative. We then began to introduce other concerns coming from the interviews and workshops. This was a way of challenging taken-for-granted values and boundaries while still respecting the concerns of others, and it enabled wider understandings of what it might mean to improve the situation at Javeriana to develop. Some of the questions that guided our interventions were:

*   Why is this concern or issue so important?
*   Have you considered other issues or alternatives for action (whether or not related to the use of information technology)?
*   What about the concerns and groups of people that do not seem to be represented in your plans? Have you considered them? Should you do so?
*   What additional actions would be suggested by including certain concerns in your plans?
*   What might be the implications for people directly or indirectly affected by the actions you have defined?

In total, the research team took part in six meetings about these initiatives (one meeting per initiative, plus two additional meetings on two of the initiatives). After the first round of meetings, it became apparent that the participation of the research team was having some effects. The people working on two of the initiatives said that we had made a valuable contribution and invited us back for another session. In contrast, the leaders of the other two initiatives decided we should not return. In the latter two cases, despite the expressed intention of the research team to promote improvement, co-ordination, and mutual understanding as well as challenges to taken-for-granted boundaries, there was a situation in which the issues we introduced did not sit easily with the existing conversations, and people resisted contemplating changes. A view was also expressed by people in one group that we should be acting as IS experts, making a summative report with recommendations rather than listening to a variety of views. Was it that our concern with ethics was not fully shared by other people? What should we have done? Should we have allowed the dominant conversations to flow unchallenged in the name (following Maturana, 1988) of respect for the others present? Or were we right to continue with the role of "critical friend" *also* out of respect for others—this time those excluded from participation? These are essentially ethical questions that gave rise to a new branch of research on power and ethics following completion of the project. However, before we address these questions in more detail, we present the final stage of the project.

Presenting the Findings

As the end of the improvement phase approached, the research team decided to gather together the different findings of the project and proposals for action. The idea was to simultaneously (i) make a record of the outputs for all the participants to draw upon after we had left and (ii) present a final report to the senior management of the University (backed up with a meeting to discuss it). Both were a result of what we saw as our ethical commitment to those who had participated in generating the plans. By writing up the material for the partici-pants, we were handing back the plans as a resource for them to use. The information we had gathered might also be important for particular departments in the University (e.g., Computer Science, Research Supervision, and Library Services). By presenting a report to the senior management (and meeting with them to discuss it), we were facilitating implementation by ensuring that the results of the IS planning were read by those with the highest level of decision-making power. In common with many other Jesuit institutions, Javeriana University is a strongly hierarchical organisation.

It is worth noting that when the research team met with the senior management, they were strongly supportive of the work we had done. Indeed, they wanted the team to stay together for longer to facilitate movement toward implementation. This again raised an ethical issue because we noticed a sense of dependence on us, despite the fact that we had emphasised throughout the project that the plans belonged to the participants who generated them—they were not our own. We argued that if the implementation was going to be sustainable, people at Javeriana needed to take the lead and assume responsibility for it, and the fact that one member of our research team was a lecturer in the University would make the transition relatively easy. This was an ethical, issue because we could have been flattered by the invitation to stay on, accepted it, and thereby deepened the dependence on us. Explaining this to the senior management, we brought the project to a close.

REFLECTIONS

In this section, we present some reflections on the project, leading (shortly) to some further thoughts about ethics and power. We should note that these are *our* reflections and do not necessarily represent the views of people at Javeriana.[20] We focus on three aspects: our methodology, the surfacing of ethical issues, and critical systems thinking.

On the Methodology

We believe it is reasonable for us to claim that our methodology and methods allowed the emergence of issues not often addressed by traditional approaches to IS planning. It helped people identify a *variety* of concerns, including some from stakeholders (such as external business people and citizens more generally) who might not normally be consulted. Particularly, it supported people in exploring the assumptions (boundaries and values) that flowed into their improvement initiatives, including those related to the use of information systems. Explicitly refusing to base participation on IS expertise was *partially* successful in establishing the principle that people should be listened to and respected as human beings equally concerned within the social context. The majority of the participants came to value this stance, but a minority withdrew from participation because of it.

In addition, the methodology supported people in translating their diverse concerns into meaningful paths for action. New initiatives were defined, existing ones were broadened, and people looked at issues of co-ordination across the whole network of initiatives. Importantly, some participants found that their existing information systems could help to address concerns without an expensive investment in new technology or even a detailed analysis of information needs – there was a consensus across stakeholders that they were adequate for their purpose. This is vital in the context of a University in a developing country that has to function with fewer resources than most comparable institutions in the developed world. In the case of these "good enough" information systems, future IS planning will need to be more of an exercise of co-ordination of actions and interactions than decision making on technology (at least in the short-to-medium term). This finding suggests that our methodology did not channel people down an unnecessary path of technological change, which in the context of IS planning in developing countries is, we believe, crucial.

On Ethics

However, during the application of our methodology, we encountered several situations where our own ethics clashed with the ethics of the participants (particularly the administrators). For example, some of the workshops gave rise to proposals for improving the evaluation of the social impacts of plans, and co-ordination between plans emerging from different functional units of the University. These were not seen as relevant by administrators, despite the concerns expressed by other participants about current problems with planning processes. We were trying to facilitate an improvement by facilitating the inclusion of issues that senior managers saw as difficult to address due to the fact that they were already fully committed to dealing with their existing concerns. It seems that all the debate and definitions of changes created a conflict between different ethical views about what to do. We should note that the administrators also saw this as an ethical issue: they did not confine themselves to the language of resources and feasibility. They argued that their own views should be supported for the good of themselves, the institution, and Colombian society.

The situation can be characterised as a continuous tension between different ethical views expressed in both the stages of distinction and improvement. By concentrating on ethical issues (linked with boundary judgements), our methodology made this tension an explicit focus for the participants. In our view, this was a good thing: it gave the participants opportunities to review their own assumptions in the light of ideas being proposed by others. Arguably, in most organisational scenarios, the assumptions of planners are not subject to much scrutiny from "outside." As a result, many ethical conflicts remain invisible or obscure to planners (if not to those disagreeing with them), and decisions are taken by those with the authority to do so with little explicit reflection.

However, dealing with ethical tensions is not easy. One of the facilitators actually felt the need to withdraw from participation in a workshop because of the unwillingness of the participants to even contemplate hearing the views of other people. This was a situation where no amount of discussion about the principles of our methodology would have helped: they were clearly and explicitly opposed to them. It fell to the facilitator to make an ethical decision about whether he should respect their disrespect for others (this disrespect could be seen as a legitimate concern of theirs), or decide that the principles of the methodology should be privileged over these unreflective concerns. He decided to take the latter course of action on the grounds that a wider set of concerns could be addressed, giving rise to better IS plans, if he remained faithful to the methodology in the face of this challenge to it.

This observation, that the facilitators found themselves embroiled in difficult and sometimes intractable ethical dilemmas, confirms that researchers, facilitators, interveners and practitioners (however they are labelled) are themselves ethical subjects. An ethical subject may be an individual or a group of people. While a methodology can give participants opportunities for listening to others and transcending narrow concerns, and people can point to the gains that may come from this, it would be naïve to think that this alone is always going to be sufficient to enable debate and meaningful change. There will sometimes be situations where people, for reasons they can justify to themselves, choose not to engage with others. In such situations, the facilitator (and other participants) may be placed in a position where they have to choose a path for ethical action that (temporarily) breaks with continuing communications.

On Critical Systems Thinking

The issue of ethics is, of course, not new to critical systems thinkers. The theory of boundary critique talks about the close relationship between ethical and boundary judgements (see earlier in this chapter). Also, the need for the practitioner to play a pivotal role in facilitating ethical debate because of issues surrounding the exercise of power has been discussed over a series of writings by one of the authors of this chapter (Midgley, 1990, 1997a,c, 2000). Indeed, Midgley (1997c) argues that systemic intervention needs to include options for political action and campaigning to address scenarios where one stakeholder group is blocking any consideration of the concerns of others. Direct communication is not always enough, and the intervener needs to make an ethical judgement about how to proceed. Likewise, Flood and Romm (1996b) talk about the importance of researchers explicitly addressing ethical dilemmas and choosing methods that take account of power relations blocking communications, between stakeholders.

However, reflection on the project reported in this chapter has made us realise that critical systems thinking (CST) practitioners might need to think more deeply about what it means to be an ethical subject. The importance of the issue has been realised during the last 12 years of writings on CST, but further theoretical reflections may enable the production of better methodological guidelines to support interventions (including IS planning interventions). To make a start on this, we reviewed the literature on ethics and power after our project was finished and ultimately decided to concentrate our attention on the work of Michel Foucault (1977, 1982, 1984a,b,c,d, 1985).[21] Foucault's ideas offer a detailed critical appreciation of the appearance of different ethical discourses in society, and the tensions that are continually played out amongst them. His thinking also offers the possibility of developing a form of self-critique (and a critique of the ethical concerns of others) that is relevant to the role of the IS planning practitioner.[22]

FOUCAULT ON ETHICS AND POWER

In Foucault's writings, the search for a universal ethics (one with rules that are applicable to all people in all situations)[23] is abandoned in favour of a more local and strategic engagement in discourses about ethics. For Foucault, there are multiple ethical discourses in modernity that constitute what we are as subjects. These discourses are entangled in processes of knowledge production. Moreover, they are deployed (to use one of Foucault's terms) via *power* relations. Ethics, knowledge and power are closely interrelated.

The concept of power, in particular, is essential in analysing how an ethical subject (whether an individual or a collective) has become what it is. In the works of Foucault one finds various definitions of power. These are related to the analyses that Foucault makes of different social phenomena (prisons, hospitals, human sexuality, etc.). The concept of power is an analytical tool, and in Foucault's view our understandings of tools can never be neutral, therefore, the meaning of the word itself can change according to the contexts in which it is deployed. Nevertheless, it is possible to make some general comments about its meaning by talking about the characteristics of power that seem to have remained relatively stable across all Foucault's writings. Power is primarily identified in relations between selves or subjects. It can be seen as a grid of relations that allows some people to act on the actions of others (Foucault, 1977, 1982; Dreyfus & Rabinow, 1982). It is the operation of the political technologies throughout the social body. Power produces non-egalitarian but also mobile relations. It can be distinguished in a network of relationships characterised by asymmetry and inequality and by unforeseen consequences of decisions taken in the network. The operation of power is spatially and temporally localised: no single grand theory can explain all power relations. Power is dynamic, as relations between individuals change through time. Hence, "power is a general matrix of force relations at a given time, in a given society" (Dreyfus and Rabinow, 1982, p. 186).

The operation of power is manifested at different levels: either targeting individuals, or guiding the conduct of groups and even societies. By the influence of power, subjects become normalised in their actions: i.e., their possibilities for action are constrained by what is considered normal or acceptable by others. Nevertheless, there is still a degree of freedom for individuals: Foucault is most interested in the many situations where people have the possibility of taking particular paths for action, however difficult, but choose not to do so because of the actions of others. In these situations, questions of power and freedom are interdependent (Foucault, 1982). However, within power there is also *resistance* as well as acceptance. Resistance can be employed at different nodes in the network, and is manifested as both conflict and forms of *individualisation* – the creation by subjects of new aspects to their identities and ways of being. Individualisation can be normalising, making the subject conform to a given set of expectations, or it can be about preserving possibilities for resistance.

For Foucault, ethical (and other) discourses contribute to the production and/ or reproduction of power relations. Ethical discourses can influence one another but can also be held in tension. Each one has its own rationale. This makes any conflict between ethical discourses (exhibited by individuals and/or groups) better understood as a game of power characterised by struggle and a striving for dominance (Foucault, 1984b,c; Vega-Romero, 1999).

On the mutual influence of power and ethics, Foucault has proposed that an ethical subject should be critical of those forms of individualisation that normalise or prescribe its ways of being and acting. He says:

"...maybe the target nowadays is not to discover what we are, but to refuse what we are...we have to imagine and to build up what we could be to get rid of this kind of political "double bind" which is the simultaneous individualisation and totalisation of modern power structures (Foucault, 1982, p. 216).

The critical action and self-construction of a subject has to consider the effects of power. Power is not a negative concept, only constraining action. Power can be used in a *positive* way to bring about change that the subject, and others it is engaged with, value. Individuals can still exert their judgement and utilise whatever is at their disposal to achieve specific ends. However, to do this critically, they should engage in self-reflection to make themselves more aware of how they are immersed in power relations, and how they use their own ethical rationales – linked into wider ethical discourses—for ends that are important to themselves (Vega-Romero, 1999). Foucault (1984d) offers some basic questions that can help individuals and groups to grasp the type of critique that could be developed around power, knowledge, and ethics:

- How are we constituted as subjects of our own knowledge?
- How are we constituted as subjects that exercise or submit to power relations?
- How are we constituted as moral subjects of our own actions?

Individuals or groups that want to engage in action with others towards the achievement of some collective ends could also make use of these questions. Of course, there will inevitably be tensions between individual and collective forms of the exercise of power, which subjects need to be aware of and address (Vega-Romero, 1999; Córdoba, 2002).

In the last two sections of this chapter, we offer some final thoughts on the implications of Foucault's understanding of ethics and power. First, we look again briefly at the theory of autopoiesis because Foucault's work has at least two important implications for it. Then, we come back to the main focus of this chapter—IS planning.

IMPLICATIONS FOR THE
THEORY OF AUTOPOIESIS

Foucault's notion of power raises the possibility of a new interpretation of Maturana and Varela's (1992) argument for individuals to promote co-existence. In our view, it is more than an observation that love, or mutual respect, is given to human beings in our biological make-up, so we should make use of it – it is a call to ethical action. By backing up their call with a biological discourse, Maturana and Varela are using power in a positive manner: they are drawing upon a source of knowledge (science) that is given strong crediblity in many circles, thereby enhancing their ethical argument for changes in human relations. Of course, the dark side of biological and other scientific discourses is that they often require normative or ethical injunctions to be hidden behind a veil of claims to scientific truth (Darier, 1999), and it is to the credit of Maturana and Varela that they refuse to "play the game" in this way.

However, a major implication of our analysis for the theory of autopoiesis is that co-existence and collaboration are indeed important but are not always easy or harmonious. Simply advocating openness to others is not enough: the advocacy of openness will often be in competition with other ethical discourses in local contexts. A more critical form of openness to others requires some awareness of the fact that the discourse of openness is itself a player in the power relations negotiated by ethical subjects. This issue has already been raised in a different way earlier in the chapter, when we talked about how boundary critique can support people in establishing some locally acceptable limits to openness. However, introducing the insights from Foucault helps us gain a deeper appreciation of how interactions between human beings are characterised by tensions around power relations. Co-existence always acquires a local character depending on the power relations between people. Openness to others may be valued and promoted, but advocates of openness are not able to escape the conflicts that they will inevitably get into if this advocacy successfully begins to have an effect on the networks of power relations they are a part of.[24]

IMPLICATIONS FOR IS PLANNING

In the context of the emerging information society, Foucault's ideas should be useful for enhancing awareness of the forms of identity' that are being promoted through practices that incorporate information technology into the lives of individuals (see also Munro, 2001). Furthermore, they can cast new light on IS-related discourses and help us reflect on how metaphors embodied in language can privilege some understandings over others. An example given by Munro (2001) is the "virus" metaphor which connotes illness and danger. Therefore, when a person designs a virus and infects other people's computers, it appears to be an unconscionable act. However, for some people, spreading viruses is more than malicious vandalism—it is an act of resistance against a network of power relations that they wish to undermine. Of course, the language of "viruses" and "infections" hides these political motivations.

Moving on to IS planning, the account of ethics presented earlier suggests that power is an important concept for the analysis of interactions between people. The ethical concerns that are swept into IS planning, with or without the support of a methodology like the one described earlier in this paper, can now be understood as arising from interactions between individuals and/or collectives as subjects who are immersed in power relations. These power relations would seem to be inevitable, but subjects can still reflect on their relationships with others and define positive possibilities for action. There will be tensions between different ethical concerns – even between individuals belonging to the same group. Also, tensions can be encountered *within* individuals. This is because, in modern societies, most of us interact in multiple, sometimes conflicting domains of action (Córdoba et al, 2000). For ethical subjects, these tensions can be clarified during the planning process by using methods that support stakeholder groups in surfacing their views of what is the case and "what ought to happen" in relation to issues of concern (Vega-Romero, 1999). This kind of comparison can produce possibilities for action, not only in relation to planning the future of an organisation or social system, but also in relation to the self-understanding and way of being of the ethical subject him/herself.

In the case of the project at Javeriana University, the notions of power and ethics explored in this chapter help us clarify our view of what was happening. Our research team was immersed in a web of power relations characterised by dynamism, tension, and struggle between discourses relating to what it means to achieve improvement, with or without the use of information technology. We had *our own* discourse of improvement, phrased in terms of the processes of inclusion, exclusion, and marginalisation, which we used in association with our status as researchers and IS practitioners to alter the existing balance of power relations at Javeriana and outside it. This was an exercise of power. As discourses, embodied in their human advocates (including ourselves), met with one another, there were continuous attempts to subjugate, complement, and cancel each other out (see also Foucault, 1977). There was intentionality in our research team's strategies to involve different groups of people, and these strategies produced intended consequences and also unintended ones (like having our relationships with two of the planning groups terminated by their leaders and being asked to continue with the project by the senior management of the University, even though we were due to leave).

Our participation with others in different conversational domains can be seen in terms of a variety of subjects taking part in different sets of power relations. These subjects could attempt to freeze the power relations (by invoking the support of the hierarchy at Javeriana, for example), or they could resist established relations (e.g., by using the legitimating power of our methodology to push new concerns onto the agenda). However, whatever interactions unfolded, none of the subjects (including ourselves) could escape from the influence of power – both when dealing with constraints on their actions and when exerting influence.

The research team can be seen as ethical subjects dealing continuously with tensions with others when developing their own ethical concerns. This makes sense of the ethical dilemma we faced (described under the heading "critical engagements") concerning our interactions with a stakeholder group which refused to even listen to the views of others. We decided, on ethical grounds, to disengage from participation with them. This was a result of a clash of ethical discourses, one of which was embedded in our own methodology. It is therefore not possible to describe our methodology or any IS planning methodology for that matter as neutral in relation to issues of power and ethics.[25] In advocating social inclusion, we were taking an explicit stance that would be perceived as dangerous or disagreeable by some of the stakeholders. Whatever methodology we might have chosen, it would not have been neutral: even the most instrumental methodology, taking account of only the narrowest of organisational agendas, has ethical implications – for example, that participation is best restricted to experts, and the profit motive should be of primary concern. The difference between ours and this kind of instrumental methodology is that the language of ethics is usually absent in the latter, and participation is determined by a pre-set organisational agenda, so the chances of any rethinking of ethics and concerns is minimal. While unforseen resistances can be encountered when instrumental methodologies are employed (and it is their relative naïvité about power issues that makes some of these resistances unforseen), our own methodology makes a virtue of engagement in power networks and participation in constructive collaborative/competitive struggles around definitions of improvement.[26]

Having reflected once again on our project with Javeriana University, we should also say that the understanding of power and ethics presented in this chapter suggests that there are projects, other than the usual type that employees, consultants, or researchers are commissioned to carry out, that IS planners should be aware of. These are the ethical projects pursued by individuals and groups. Midgley and Ochoa-Arias (2001) call them "life projects," because they are about the trajectories and ethical learning of people across their lifetimes in interaction with others. Life projects may develop and change over time but are seen as coherent, because they are part of the story (told, revised, and retold) of a particular person or group. However, in the context of the discussion in this chapter, such projects need not always be seen as life-long. The implication is that any IS planning project cuts across and interacts with many other projects, both organisational and non-organisational. Some of these projects may potentially be in tension with the one that has been commissioned and the ethical project of the practitioner may come into conflict with a commissioned project too. So these tensions need to be worked with constructively as part of IS planning. They provide opportunities for learning and action, both within the commissioned project and in the various "life projects" the practitioner and others participate in.

CONCLUSION

In this chapter, we have presented an IS planning methodology based on critical systems thinking and the theories of autopoiesis and boundary critique. We have also discussed a practical application of our methodology in a project at Javeriana University, Colombia. Based on this project, we argued that our methodology allows the emergence of issues not often addressed by traditional approaches to IS planning. It can help people identify a variety of concerns, including some from stakeholders who might not normally be consulted, and it can also support people in exploring the boundaries of their assumptions and the values that flow into their understandings of improvement. In addition, the methodology can assist people in translating their diverse concerns into meaningful paths for action.

However, our experience at Javeriana University also raised some ethical concerns. On several occasions, we found that our desire for the IS planning to be open to different stakeholder views came into conflict with the desires of some of the participants to continue with "business as usual." Therefore, an ethical question or dilemma was generated. Should we continue to promote respect for the views of a wide range of stakeholders, which effectively meant disrespecting those unwilling to listen, or should we simply accept the fact that some people might not want to open themselves to the perspectives of others? Having to deal with this question led us to conduct further research on power and ethics once the project had ended.

This research focused on the work of Michel Foucault, who talks about interactions between ethical discourses and networks of power relations, and several implications for IS planning can be derived from it. There is a need to think critically about the kinds of individual and group identities being promoted in the emerging information society. Also, power can be an important concept for the analysis of interactions between people in IS planning. The ethical concerns that are swept into IS planning can be understood as arising from interactions between individuals and collectives as subjects who are immersed in power relations. While power relations would seem to be inevitable, subjects can still reflect on their relationships with others and define positive alternatives for action.

Of course, we, as IS planning practitioners, are just as much subjects participating in networks of power as the stakeholders in our projects, so our methodologies can never be neutral. We therefore have a responsibility to reflect on the ethical assumptions embedded in our methodologies and consider their possible impacts on both IS planning projects and the various other types of project that people may be pursuing. By understanding our roles in networks of power, we may ultimately become more critical about our own ethical identities and our own ways of being, both as IS practitioners and as people sharing our lives with others.

ACKNOWLEDGMENT

We would like to thank all the people at Javeriana University who were involved in the project—particularly, Diego Torres (our co-facilitator) and the other members of the staff in the Computer Science and Systems Engineering Department who provided us with so much support.

ENDNOTES

1   For the purposes of this chapter, this term also embraces the information and communication technologies (ICTs) necessary to operate information systems.

2   This phenomenon seems to have started with (i) the emergence in the United States and Asian countries of important centres of hardware manufacturing for personal computing and (ii) more computing power becoming available as standard in PCs (Senker, 1992).

3   Viewing organisations as collections of people with concerns does not imply a denial of the existence of purposes at the organisational level – it simply enables us to acknowledge that these purposes are emergent properties of complex interactions structured through networks of power, knowledge and identity. Dominant purposes (and a variety of other purposes) can still be ascribed to an organisation, but these inevitably stem from processes of legitimation within and beyond the organisation that lead to action being taken in the organisation's name (Midgley, 2000).

4   One example is the Maloka Project in Bogota, an interactive centre set up in 1997 whose mission is to contribute to the appropriation of science and

technology by the Colombian people (Maloka, 2000). The Maloka Project aims to foster the creation of a knowledge-based culture in which technology is part of people's daily lives, taking into account sustainable development considerations (Maloka, 2000).

5   In order to massively expand the provision of information systems to schools, it was said in 1999 that all the schools in important cities should have at least two computers with Internet access (ElTiempo, 1999; PNE, 1999). However, this has not been achieved due to the provision of insufficient financial resources and the setting of unrealistic goals (Agenda Conectividad, 2000a,b).

6   There is an extensive literature on CST, so we can only give a flavour of the ideas here. For more in-depth presentations, see, for instance, Flood and Romm (1996a), Midgley (2000) and Jackson (2000). It is also important for us to acknowledge that the CST perspective we present here is our own interpretation, and this may be different from the interpretations made by others. There is a healthy diversity of views within the CST research community. (See Midgley, 2000, for a discussion of this.)

7   Of course, we should say why we have used the term "improvement" rather than, say, the creation of beauty, pleasure, knowledge, understanding, emancipation or spiritual enlightenment. The answer is that, if we value any of these things, the creation of these *represents* an improvement. The term "improvement" is therefore general enough to have meaning in relation to almost any value system, it simply indicates the purposeful action of an agent to create a change for the better (Midgley, 1996, 2000).

8   For example, see Churchman (1970, 1979), Ulrich (1983, 1994), Midgley (1992a, 2000), Midgley et al. (1998), Vega-Romero (1999), Córdoba et al. (2000), and Yolles (2001).

9   Of course, this then raises the issue of dealing with theoretical contradictions, which is beyond the scope of the present chapter. See Gregory (1996) and Midgley (2000) for two different views on how CST practitioners might understand and deal with theoretical contradictions.

10   For example, see Jackson and Keys (1984), Jackson (1987a,b, 1990, 1991, 1999, 2000), Keys (1988, 1991), Oliga (1988), Flood (1990, 1995a,b), Midgley (1990, 1992b, 1997a,b, 2000), Flood and Jackson (1991a,b), Gregory (1992, 1996, 2000), Flood and Romm (1996a,b), Mingers and Gill (1997), Taket and White (2000), and Clarke and Lehaney (2000).

11   An example is the marginalised position of people who are unemployed. There is a conflict between the liberal discourse of citizenship, where all people have equal value because of their status as rational beings, and the capitalist discourse of good employment practice that limits the responsibility of organisations to their employees alone. This conflict is not stabilised by either

the inclusion *or* the exclusion of the unemployed, but by their marginalisation. If unemployed people were to be fully included along with employees in the primary boundary of industrial organisation, then "good employment practice" (indeed, the whole capitalist system of organisation) would become untenable. However, if they were fully excluded, the liberal ideal of equal citizenship would become untenable instead. Both the liberal and capitalist discourses have long histories in the West and have come to be institutionalised throughout the economic and legal systems of our societies. While on the whole the two discourses are mutually supportive (Booth Fowler, 1991; Midgley and Ochoa-Arias, 1999), there are still significant tensions, and the phenomenon of unemployment points to one of them. The key to understanding the status of the unemployed is to realise that it is only possible to maintain the dual commitment to liberalism and capitalism if people who are unemployed are neither fully included nor excluded. People who are unemployed, therefore, become marginalised, but the conflict is finally stabilised when a sacred or profane status is imposed on them. When they are regarded as profane, it justifies thinking in terms of narrow organisational boundaries. When they are regarded as sacred, this justifies programmes to support social inclusion. There is rarely a consensus on whether a marginal group or issue should be viewed as sacred or profane, but there are dominant patterns of social action which come to be solidified in rituals. In the case of the unemployed, a typical example in developed nations that provide welfare payments is "signing on" (signing a register of availability to work), which many people view as an exercise in ritual humiliation.

12   When something is being privileged, it can be the result of either inclusion within a primary boundary (with other things marginalised and made profane) or a sacred status being ascribed to a marginalised element. Which of these is the case in any local situation requires some context-specific interpretation in the light of answers to some of the other questions.

13   Midgley (2000) argues that we should not regard any theory, including the theory of autopoiesis, as foundational (an absolute truth from which everything else flows). There is a tendency for some writers to treat biological theories in this way (Darier, 1999). We can be pluralistic about theories, drawing upon them when they are appropriate for the circumstances. This is the spirit in which we use the theory of autopoiesis.

14   This is, of course, a controversial assertion that some proponents of the theory of autopoiesis distance themselves from (e.g., Mingers, 1995). For Mingers, not being able to see a phenomenon (not being triggered by it) does not mean it is literally absent, but that as far as the autopoietic system is concerned, it *might as well* not exist.

15   Earlier (in the section on boundary critique), we discussed the work of Ulrich (1983) who developed a list of 12 questions that can be used heuristically to explore what any system of interest currently *is* and what it *ought* to be. Because this list includes questions about the likely effects of plans, who should participate in deciding on purposes, etc., we have found it useful in a variety of projects for operationalising boundary critique (e.g., Cohen & Midgley, 1994; Midgley et al., 1998; Boyd et al., 1999; Midgley, 2000). We would certainly not recommend restricting boundary critique to a mechanical use of the 12 questions, as if it were just a matter of ticking boxes as they are answered. Nevertheless, they are a useful starting point for considering the kinds of issues that need to be addressed when seeking to explore the boundaries of IS plans. The full list of 12 questions was first published in Ulrich (1983) and has since been reprinted in Ulrich (1986) and Midgley (1997c, 2000).

16   We did not see adapting our language for the practical purposes of communicating with non-IS practitioners as generating a problem for our methodology. On the contrary, for us to respect the rational domains of others and develop new rational domains in partnership with them (as suggested by the theory of autopoiesis), this kind of adaptation is necessary. It also fits with Zhu's (2002) observation that new languages of participation, developed as part of methodological debates in academic and practitioner communities, can actually *obstruct* participation if imposed unilaterally on users of information systems.

17   This technique was adapted from a similar one used by Weil (1998).

18   A potential criticism of this method is that by using pictures from the mass media, we were colluding in the privileging of concerns that grab media attention over other, less well-publicised concerns. This is arguably the case, but three points should be made here. First, we used a wide range of images, covering personal as well as political issues, and these were selected by three people to prevent any single view from dominating. Second, whatever we decided to use as trigger material would have promoted particular concerns. The important thing is that using this material *widened* the set of concerns beyond those that might have occurred spontaneously to interviewees, and of course, spontaneous concerns were not suppressed. Third, with regard to the specific charge of mass media influence, research evidence suggests that the media *already* shapes the issues that are considered important by the public but not what stance individuals will take on these issues (Cohen, 1963; Liebl, 2002).

19   Two ways were developed, partly because different groups seemed to be comfortable with different approaches and partly because the facilitators had

different ideas about what to do next. To make our approach as responsive as possible, we set out two paths for intervention that the facilitators and participants could choose between, depending on the contingencies of the situation.

20   There is a case for saying that, out of respect for other participants in the project, we should facilitate the publication of their reflections too (Adams & McCullough, 2002). While we accept the logic of this, there is insufficient space in the present chapter to include more than our own reflections – and in any case it is these that have led to our further thinking about power and ethics (Córdoba, 2002, and in this chapter). Hopefully, we will be able to surface wider reflections in future research.

21   We also drew on some of the secondary literature, such as Dreyfus and Rabinow (1982).

22   We should note that several previous CST writers (and others in dialogue with them) have drawn upon Foucault's work, but mostly in different ways from ours. See, for example, Flood (1990), Brocklesby and Cummings (1996), Valero-Silva (1996, 1998), Mingers (1997), Munro (1999, 2001), Vega-Romero (1999), Vélez (1999), and Taket and White (2000).

23   The idea of a universal ethics was a holy grail for philosophers for several centuries – in particular, see the tradition of practical philosophy (moral philosophy) stemming from Kant (1788).

24   Also see Vélez (1999) for some further thoughts on the implications of Foucault's ideas for the theory of autopoiesis.

25   This is a point of view we have heard several times in verbal discussions between critical systems thinkers, but in writings about CST, there is often more of a focus on the non-neutrality of the *intervener* rather than the methodological discourse s/he is advocating (see, for example, Midgley, 2000).

26   It seems to us that relatively few methodologies talk explicitly about positive uses of power, although two notable exceptions are Vega-Romero (1999) and Taket and White (2000).

REFERENCES

Ackoff, R. L. (1981). *Creating the corporate future*. New York: John Wiley & Sons.

Adams, R. & McCullough, A. (2002). The urban practitioner and participation in research within a streetwork context. *Community, Work and Family, 5*, (in press).

Agenda Conectividad. (2000a). *Agenda de Conectividad: El Salto a Internet,* (Document of the national Colombian plan called "Connectivity Agenda") Documento Conpes 3072. Departamento Nacional de Planeación: Bogotá,

Colombia. Retrieved March 2000 from the World Wide Web: http://www.dnp.gov.co.

Agenda Conectividad. (2000b). *Agenda de Conectividad: El Salto a Internet, Informe de avance al Consejo Nacional de Ciencia y Tecnología CONPES, Departamento Nacional de Planeación: Bogotá, Colombia. Retrieved August 2001 from the World Wide Web: http://www.dnp.gov.co/ArchivosWeb/ Direccion_Infraestructura_Energia/Telecomunicaciones/Documentos/ Informe_Avance_CONPES_%20Agenda.PDF.

Andreu, R., Ricart, J. & Valor, J. (1996). *Estrategia y sistemas de información.* Bogotá, Colombia: McGraw Hill.

Bilson, A. (1996). *Bringing forth organisational realities: Guidelines for a constructivist approach to the management of change in human services. PhD thesis,* Lancaster University.

Bilson, A. (1997). Guidelines for a constructivist approach: Steps toward the adaptation of ideas from family therapy for use in organizations. *Systems Practice, 10,* 153–177.

Booth Fowler, R. (1991). *The dance with community: The contemporary debate in American political thought.* Kansas, AR: University Press of Kansas, Lawrence.

Boyd, A., Brown, M. & Midgley, G. (1999). *Home and away: Developing services with young people missing from home or care.* Hull: Centre for Systems Studies.

Brocklesby, J. & Cummings, S. (1996). Foucault plays Habermas: An alternative philosophical underpinning for critical systems thinking. *Journal of the Operational Research Society, 47*(6), 741–754.

Checkland, P. (1981). *Systems thinking, systems practice.* Chichester: John Wiley & Sons.

Checkland, P. & Holwell, S. (1998). *Information, systems and information systems: Making sense of the field.* Chichester: John Wiley & Sons.

Checkland, P. & Scholes, J. (1990). *Soft systems methodology in action.* Chichester: John Wiley & Sons.

Chepaitis, C. (1997). Information ethics across information cultures. *European Review, 6*(4), 195–200.

Churchman, C. W. (1968a). *Challenge to reason.* New York: McGraw Hill.

Churchman, C. W. (1968b). *The systems approach.* New York: Dell.

Churchman, C. W. (1970). Operations research as a profession. *Management Science, 17,* B37–53.

Churchman, C. W. (1971). *The design of inquiring systems.* New York: Basic Books.

Churchman, C. W. (1979) *The Systems Approach and its Enemies.* New York:

Basic Books.

Clarke, S. & Lehaney, B. (1997a). Critical approaches to information systems development: Some practical implications. In Stowell, F., Ison, R., Holloway, R., Jackson, S. & McRobb, S., (Eds.), *Systems for sustainability: People, organisations and environments*, 333–337. New York: Plenum.

Clarke, S. & Lehaney, B. (1997b). Critical approaches to information systems development: A theoretical perspective. In Stowell, F., Ison, R., Holloway, R., Jackson, S. & McRobb, S. (Eds.), *Systems for sustainability: People, organisations and environments*, 555–560. New York: Plenum.

Clarke, S. & Lehaney, B. (2000). Mixing methodologies for information systems development and strategy: A higher education case study. *Journal of the Operational Research Society, 51,* 542–566.

Cohen, B.C. (1963). *The press and foreign policy*. Princeton, NJ: Princeton University Press.

Cohen, C. & Midgley, G. (1994). *The North Humberside Diversion from Custody Project for mentally disordered offenders: Research report*. Hull: Centre for Systems Studies.

Commission of the European Community. (1997). *Green paper on the convergence of the telecommunications, media and information technology sectors, and the implications for regulation: Towards an information society approach*. Brussels: Commission of the European Community.

Córdoba, J., Midgley, G. & Torres, D. (2000). Rethinking stakeholder involvement: An application of the theories of autopoiesis and boundary critique to IS planning. In Clarke, S. & Lehaney, B. (Eds.), *Human centred methods in information systems*, 195–230. Hershey, PA: Idea Group Publishing.

Córdoba, J. (2002). *A critical systems thinking approach for the planning of information technology in the information society, PhD thesis*, University of Hull.

Currie, W. (1994). The strategic management of a large scale IT project in the financial services sector. *New Technology, Work and Employment, 9*(1), 19–29.

Darier, É. (Ed.). (1999). *Discourses of the environment*. Oxford: Blackwell.

Douglas, M. (1966). *Purity and danger: An analysis of the concepts of pollution and taboo*. London: Ark.

Dreyfus, H. & Rabinow, P. (1982). *Michel Foucault: Beyond structuralism and hermeneutics*. Brighton: Harvester Press.

DTI. (1998). *Converging technologies: Consequences for the new knowledge driven economy*. Department of Trade and Industry: U.K. Retrieved March 2000 from the World Wide Web: http://www.dti.gov.uk.

Earl, M. (1998). Strategy making in the information age. In Currie, W. & Galliers, R. (Eds.), *Rethinking management information systems: An interdisci-*

plinary perspective, 161–174. Oxford: Oxford University Press.

Economist. (1996). A survey of the world economy, *340*(7985), 1–50.

El Tiempo. (1999). Colombian newspaper, various news on computers and education sections. Casa Editorial El Tiempo: Bogotá, Colombia. Retrieved February through August 1999 from the World Wide Web: http://www.eltiempo.com.co.

Flood, R. L. (1990). *Liberating systems theory*. New York: Plenum Press.

Flood, R. L. (1995a). *Solving problem solving*. Chichester: John Wiley & Sons.

Flood, R. L. (1995b). Total systems intervention (TSI): A reconstitution. *Journal of the Operational Research Society, 46*, 174–191.

Flood, R. L. & Jackson, M. C. (Eds.). (1991a). *Critical systems thinking: Directed readings*. Chichester: John Wiley & Sons.

Flood, R. L. & Jackson, M. C. (1991b). *Creative problem solving: Total systems intervention*. Chichester: John Wiley & Sons.

Flood, R. L. & Romm, N. R. A. (Eds.). (1996a). *Critical Systems Thinking: Current Research and Practice*. New York: Plenum.

Flood, R. L and Romm, N. R. A. (1996b). *Diversity management: Triple loop learning*. Chichester: John Wiley & Sons.

Floyd, M. (Ed.). (1993). *Information technology training for people with disabilities*. London: Jessica Kingsley Publishers.

Foro. (1999). *Plan Nacional de Informática (PNI)*, Notas de discusiones. Bogotá, Colombia: Foro de Alta Tecnología.

Foucault, M. (1977). *The history of sexuality, volume one: The will to knowledge*. London: Penguin.

Foucault, M. (1982). Afterword: The subject and power. In Dreyfus, H. & Rabinow, P. (Eds.), *Michel Foucault: Beyond structuralism and hermeneutics*, 208–226. Brighton: Harvester Press.

Foucault, M. (1984a). *The history of sexuality, volume two: The use of pleasure*. London: Penguin.

Foucault, M. (1984b). What is enlightenment? In Rabinow, P. (Ed.), *The Foucault Reader: An Introduction to Foucault's Thought*, 32-50. London: Penguin.

Foucault, M. (1984c). Truth and power. In Rabinow, P. (Ed.), *The Foucault reader: An introduction to foucault's thought*, 51–75. London: Penguin.

Foucault, M. (1984d). On the genealogy of ethics: An overview of work in progress. In Rabinow, P. (Ed.), *The foucault reader: An introduction to Foucault's Thought*, 340–372. London: Penguin.

Foucault, M. (1985). *The history of sexuality, volume three: The care of the self*. London: Penguin.

Friis, C. (1997). A critical evaluation of the Danish ICT strategy. *The Economic and Social Review, 28*(3), 261–276.

Fundacion Social. (1999). Metodologia para la Planeación Estratégica de Informática. Córdoba, J. (Ed.). Bogotá, Colombia: Fundación Social y sus Empresas.

Galvis, A. (1995). *Planeación Estratégica de Informática: Elementos Conceptuales*, Memo de Investigación Proyecto Delfos. Bogotá, Colombia: Universidad de los Andes, Departamento de Ingeniería de Sistemas y Computación.

Galvis, A. (1998). Educación para el siglo XXI apoyada en ambientes educativos interactivos, lúdicos, creativos y colaborativos. *Informática Educativa, 11*(2), 169–192.

García, A. (1993). *Sistemas de Información: Planeamiento Estratégico y Análisis*. Bogotá, Colombia: Universidad de los Andes, Facultad de Ingeniería.

Ginzberg, M. (1978). Steps towards more effective implementation of MS and MIS. *Interfaces, 8*(3), 57–63.

Ginzberg, M. (1981). Early diagnosis of MIS implementation failure: Promising results and unanswered questions. *Management Science, 27*(4), 459–479.

Gore, A. (1998). Viewpoint: HPCC policy champion foresees networked nation. *Communications of the ACM, 31*(11), 15–16.

Gregory, W. J. (1992). *Critical systems thinking and pluralism: A new constellation. PhD thesis*, City University: London.

Gregory, W. J. (1996). Discordant pluralism: A new strategy for critical systems thinking? *Systems Practice, 9*, 605–625.

Gregory, W. J. (2000). Transforming self and society: A "critical appreciation" model. *Systemic Practice and Action Research, 13*, 475–501.

Gregory, W. J. & Romm, N. R. A. (2001). Critical facilitation: Learning through intervention in group processes. *Management Learning, 32*(4), 453–467.

Gregory, W. J., Romm, N. R. A. and Walsh, M. P. (1994). *The Trent quality initiative: A multi-agency evaluation of quality standards in the national health service*. Hull: Centre for Systems Studies.

Habermas, J. (1976). *Communication and the Evolution of Society* (English edition, 1979). London: Heinemann.

Habermas, J. (1984a). *The Theory of Communicative Action, Volume One: Reason and the Rationalisation of Society*. Cambridge: Polity Press.

Habermas, J. (1984b). *The theory of communicative action, volume two: The critique of functionalist reason*. Cambridge: Polity Press.

Hammer, M. & Champy, J. (1995). *Re-engineering the corporation: a manifesto for business revolution*. London: Nicholas Brealey.

Hegel, G. W. F. (1807). *The phenomenology of mind*. (second english edition, 1931). London: George Allen and Unwin.

IBM. (1997) *The net result: Social inclusion in the information society*, Community Development Foundation and IBM: London. Retrieved March

2000 from the World Wide Web: http://www.uk.ibm.com/comm/commu-
nity/uk117.html.

IDC Colombia. (1999). The impact of e-commerce in Colombia. *IDC Conference (by Carlos Villate)*, Foro de Alta Tecnología: Bogotá, Colombia, June.

Information I. (1996). *Information society Ireland: Strategy for action*. Dublin:
Information Society Commission.

Jackson, M. C. (1987a). Present positions and future prospects in management
science. *Omega, 15*, 455–466.

Jackson, M. C. (1987b). New directions in management science. In Jackson, M.
C. & Keys, P. (Eds.), *New Directions in Management Science*. Aldershot:
Gower.

Jackson, M. C. (1990). Beyond a system of systems methodologies. *Journal of
the Operational Research Society, 41*, 657–668.

Jackson, M. C. (1991). *Systems Methodology for the Management Sciences*.
New York: Plenum.

Jackson, M. C. (1999). Towards coherent pluralism in management science.
Journal of the Operational Research Society, 50, 12-22.

Jackson, M. C. (2000). *Systems approaches to management*. New York:
Kluwer Academic/Plenum Publishers.

Jackson, M.C. & Keys, P. (1984). Towards a system of systems methodologies.
Journal of the Operational Research Society, 35, 473–486.

Kant, I. (1788). *Critique of practical reason and other writings in moral
philosophy*. L. Beck (Translation and Editing). 1949 edition. Chicago, IL:
University of Chicago Press.

Keen, P. (1991). *Shaping the future: Business design through information
technology*. Boston, MA: Harvard Business School Press.

Keys, P. (1988). A methodology for methodology choice. *Systems Research, 5*,
65-76.

Keys, P. (1991). *Operational research and systems: The systemic nature of
operational research*. New York: Plenum.

Leach, E. (1976). *Culture and communication: The logic by which symbols are
connected*. Cambridge: Cambridge University Press.

Lewis, P. J. (1994). *Information-systems development*. London: Pitman.

Liebl, F. (2002). The anatomy of complex societal problems and its implications
for OR. *Journal of the Operational Research Society, 53*(2), 161–184.

Lyytinen, K. & Robey, D. (1999). Learning failure in information systems
development. *Information Systems Journal, 9*, 85–101.

Maloka (2000). *Maloka: Centro Interactivo,* home web page, Centro Interactivo
Maloka: Bogotá, Colombia. Retrieved January 2001 deom the World Wide
Web: http://www.maloka.org/centro.

Maturana, H. (1988). Reality: The search for objectivity or the quest for a compelling argument. *Irish Journal of Psychology, 9*, 25–82.

Maturana, H. & Varela, F. (1992). *The tree of knowledge: The biological roots of human understanding*. Boston, MA: Shambhala.

Midgley, G. (1990). Creative methodology design. *Systemist, 12*, 108–113.

Midgley, G. (1992a). The sacred and profane in critical systems thinking. *Systems Practice, 5*(1), 5–16.

Midgley, G. (1992b). Pluralism and the legitimation of systems science. *Systems Practice, 5*(2), 147–172.

Midgley, G. (1994). Ecology and the poverty of humanism: A critical systems perspective. *Systems Research, 11*, 67–76.

Midgley, G. (1996). What is this thing called critical systems thinking? In Flood, R. L. and Romm, N. R. A. (Eds.), *Critical Systems Thinking: Current Research and Practice*. New York: Plenum Press.

Midgley, G. (1997a). Mixing methods: Developing systemic intervention. In Mingers, J. and Gill, A. (Eds.), *Multimethodology: Towards Theory and Practice for Mixing Management Science Methodologies*, 249–290. Chichester: John Wiley & Sons.

Midgley, G. (1997b). Developing the methodology of TSI: From the oblique use of methods to creative design. *Systems Practice, 10*, 305–319.

Midgley G. (1997c). Dealing with coercion: Critical systems heuristics and beyond. *Systems Practice, 10*, 37–57.

Midgley, G. (2000). *Systemic Intervention: Philosophy, Methodology, and Practice*. New York: Kluwer Academic/Plenum Publishers.

Midgley, G. & Milne, A. (1995). Creating employment opportunities for people with mental health problems: A feasibility study for new initiatives. *Journal of the Operational Research Society, 46*, 35–42.

Midgley, G. & Ochoa-Arias, A. E. (1999). Visions of community for community OR. *Omega, 27*, 259–274.

Midgley, G. & Ochoa-Arias, A. E. (2001). Unfolding a theory of systemic intervention. *Systemic Practice and Action Research, 14*, 615–649.

Midgley, G., Munlo, I. & Brown, M. (1998). The theory and practice of boundary critique: Developing housing services for older people. *Journal of the Operational Research Society, 49*, 467–478.

Mingers, J. C. (1995). *Self-producing systems: Implications and applications of autopoiesis*. New York: Plenum.

Mingers, J. (1997). Towards critical pluralism. In Mingers, J. and Gill A. (Eds.), *Multimethodology: The theory and practice of combining management science methodologies*, 407–440. Chichester: John Wiley & Sons.

Mingers, J. & Gill, A. (Eds.). (1997). *Multimethodology: The theory and practice of combining management science methodologies.* Chichester: John Wiley & Sons.

Munro, I. (1999). Man-machine systems: People and technology in OR. *Systemic Practice and Action Research, 12,* 513-532.

Munro, I. (2001). Informated identities and the spread of the word virus. *Ephemera, 1*(2), 149–162, Retrieved Jen 2001 from the World Wide Web: http://www.ephemeraweb.org.

Murray-Lasso, M. (1992). Latin America. *Education and informatics worldwide: The state of the art and beyond,* UNESCO: Paris, 210–220.

Negroponte, N. (1995). *Being digital.* Boston, MA: MIT Press.

Oliga, J. C. (1988). Methodological foundations of systems methodologies. *Systems Practice, 1,* 87–112.

PNE. (1999). *Plan Nacional de Educación del Gobierno Colombiano,* Casa Editorial El Tiempo: Bogotá, Colombia. Retrieved March 1999 from the World Wide Web, http://www.eltiempo.com.co.

PNI. (1997). *Bases Para Una Política Nacional de Informática.* Bogotá, Colombia: Ministerio de Comunicaciones.

PNT. (1997). *Plan Nacional de Telecomunicaciones 1997–2007.* Bogotá, Colombia: Ministerio de Comunicaciones.

Rogerson, S. (1996). Computers and human values, Centre for Computer and Social Responsibility: De Monfort University, UK. Retrieved March 2000 from the World Wide Web, http://www.ccsr.cse.dmu.ac.uk.

Senker, P. (1992). Technological change and the future of work: An approach to an analysis. *Futures, 2*(4), 351–363.

Taket, A. & White, L. (2000). *Partnership and participation: Decision-making in the multi-agency setting.* Chichester: John Wiley & Sons.

Toffler, A. (1992). *Power Shift: Knowledge, Wealth and Violence at the Edge of the 21St Century.* London: Bantam Books.

Ulrich, W. (1983). *Critical heuristics of social planning: A new approach to practical philosophy.* Berne: Haupt.

Ulrich, W. (1986). *Critical heuristics of social systems design. Working paper #10.* Hull: Department of Management Systems and Sciences, University of Hull.

Ulrich, W. (1988). Systems thinking, systems practice and practical philosophy: A program of research. *Systems Practice, 1,* 137–163.

Ulrich, W. (1990). Critical systems thinking and ethics: The role of contemporary practical philosophy for developing an "ethics of whole systems." In Banathy, B. H. & Banathy, B. A. (Eds.), *Toward a just society for future generations. volume I: Systems design.* Pomona, CA: International Society for the Systems Sciences.

Ulrich, W. (1993). Some difficulties of ecological thinking, considered from a critical systems perspective: A plea for critical holism. *Systems Practice, 6,* 583–611.

Ulrich, W. (1994). Can we secure future-responsive management through systems thinking and design? *Interfaces, 24,* 26–37.

Ulrich, W. (1996a). *A primer to critical systems heuristics for action researchers.* Hull: Centre for Systems Studies, University of Hull.

Ulrich, W. (1996b). *Critical systems thinking for citizens: A research proposal.* Centre for Systems Studies Research Memorandum #10. Hull: Centre for Systems Studies, University of Hull.

UNESCO. (1992). *Science and technology in developing countries: Strategies for the 1990s.* Paris: UNESCO.

Valero-Silva, N. (1996). Towards a critique of critical systems thinking within a Foucauldian framework: A "demystification process" or an "instrumental use" of critical theory. *Systems Practice, 9,* 539–546.

Valero-Silva, N. (1998). *A critical history of critical systems thinking, PhD thesis,* University of Hull.

Vega-Romero, R. (1999). *Health care and social justice evaluation: A critical and pluralist approach, PhD thesis,* University of Hull.

Vélez, J.I. (1999). *Autopoiesis and power, MA dissertation,* University of Hull.

Walsham, G. (1993) *Interpreting information systems in organisations.* Chichester: John Wiley & Sons.

Ward, J., Griffiths, P. & Whitmae, P. (1990). *Strategic planning for information systems.* Chichester: John Wiley & Sons.

Warren, L. (2000). Critical thinking and human centered methods in IS. In Clarke, S. & Lehaney, B. (Eds.), *Human centered methods in information systems: Current research and practice,* 175–194. Hershey, PA: Idea Group Publishing.

Weil, S. (1998). Our concerns as researchers, workshop with research students held at the School of Management, University of Hull, May 15, 1998.

Wickham, J. (1997). Where is Ireland in the global information society? *The Economic and Social Review, 28*(3), 277–294.

Willmott, H. (1995). The odd couple: Reengineering businesses; managing human relations. *New Technology, Work and Employment, 10*(2), 89–98.

Wresch, W. (1996). *Disconnected: Haves and have-nots in the information age.* New Brunswick, NJ: Rutgers University Press.

Yolles, M. (2001). Viable boundary critique. *Journal of the Operational Research Society, 52,* 35–47.

Zhu, Z. (2002). Towards user-friendly OR: A Chinese experience. *Journal of the Operational Research Society, 53*(2), 137–148.

Chapter X

The Information System Within the Organization: A Case Study

Bruce R. Campbell
University of Technology, Sydney, Australia

G. Mike McGrath
Victoria University, Australia

ABSTRACT

There is considerable evidence that many information systems (IS) projects fail because of organizational, "softer" or "people-related" issues. Considerable effort has been expended in efforts to design improved development methodologies that incorporate these softer aspects. Less attention, however, has been directed towards approaches that increase our understanding of the interaction of the implemented IS with the wider organizational environment. Our thesis is that system dynamics (SD) has much to offer here and, in this chapter, we illustrate the utility of the SD approach in this context through presentation of a field study.

INTRODUCTION

The information system (IS) literature is littered with reports of poorly performing or canceled IS projects that have cost the sponsoring organizations considerable amounts of money. In an attempt to solve many of these problems, different methodologies and techniques have been advocated. These include structured systems analysis and design (SSADM), an increased emphasis on requirements engineering, joint application development (JAD), computer aided software engineering (CASE), and method convergence.

These have not, however, had much impact on the situation. Other writers have attributed this to the reliance on the "hard" aspects of software development by these methods to the detriment of the softer, sociotechnical, aspects. In effect, we are ignoring the organization, or environment, into which a technical system will be placed. This environment is often messy, with many interrelated causal loops where cause and effect can be separated by either time and/or space. Understanding this type of situation is difficult and requires techniques not normally used within the IS discipline.

This chapter introduces a case study, where a particular technique was used to gain some understanding of a messy organizational situation that was, it was suspected, impacting the performance of the IS. The technique, using causal loop diagrams (CLDs), is described and then applied to the case study. Limitations of the technique are discussed, and directions for further research are suggested.

BACKGROUND

There is ample evidence in the literature that the effectiveness of IS development is little changed from the early years. In 1982, it was claimed that 15% of all software development projects failed completely and that overruns of 100–200% were common (DeMarco, 1982). In 1995, The Standish Group reported that 31% of software projects never deliver anything, only 16.2% are on time and within budget, overruns were up to 222%, and the total cost to U.S. organizations in 1995 for overruns and cancelled projects was estimated to be $132 billion (*Chaos*, 1995). In 1996, the Organizational Aspects Special Interest Group (OASIG) of the U.K. reported the experiences of over 14,000 organizations. The report, supported by the Economic and Social Research Council and the U.K. Department of Trade and Industry, stated, in part, the following:
- 80–90% of IT investments do not meet their performance objectives; the reasons for this are rarely purely technical in origin.
- Most organizations are not good at evaluating the performance and impact of their investments in IT (OASIG, 1996).

In response to this situation, the IS industry has, over the years, introduced a number of methodologies and techniques. These include, but are not limited to the following:
- Structured systems analysis and design
- More emphasis on the user's needs (requirements engineering/analysis)

- Automated support for the software development process (computer aided software engineering, information engineering)
- Emphasis on user involvement (joint application development) (Day, 2000)

However, the references cited earlier indicate that the success rate of IS implementation has not improved even with these innovations. Many writers maintain that one reason for this is that most of the methods used within the IS community focus on the technical aspects of analysing and designing a system. They require a strict definition of information and business rules. These writers maintain that many of the problems with IS implementation are associated with the softer sociotechnical issues (Curtis, Kellner, & Over, 1992; Curtis, Krasner, & Iscoe, 1988; Day, 2000; Gruhn & Wolf, 1995; Kueng & Kawalek, 1997; McGrath, 1997b; OASIG, 1996). One of these writers (Day, 2000) goes further and argues that the environment in which an IS is developed can affect its successful development and implementation. To develop his argument, he quotes Churchman (1979): "... no problem can be solved simply on its own basis. Every problem has an 'environment', to which it is inextricably united." Day then maintains that a simple, structured, fixed, and predetermined IS cannot hope to replicate the complex, changing, and environment-modifying situation of a business organization. That is, an information system is affected by the environment in which it is developed. This article argues that not only is an information system affected during development, but its performance can be affected by that environment once it has been implemented.

The focus of IS developers is to reduce organizational information and business rules to fit the characteristics of an IS—simple, structured, and fixed. The methods and tools that are used emphasize this "hard" aspect of data and business rules (Gasson & Holland, 1996). This aspect suits the tasks and responsibilities that are typically allocated to IS developers. However, we have observed that rarely is anyone given the responsibility of determining the effect of the wider business on the development of an IS, or its effect on the IS once it has been implemented. This problem is anything but simple, structured, or fixed. It normally falls into a category of problem described by Vennix (1996) as "messy." Often, there is only a vague idea that something is wrong. Rarely can the "problem" be precisely identified, and different stakeholders hold different views on what constitutes the problem.

In an IS development situation, business managers and IS developers may be vaguely aware that if a process is being changed by implementing or modifying an IS, then it is probably going to impact the wider organizational business community (including external stakeholders) and be impacted by that community. But, how this may occur and the likely results are unknown. The emphasis is on completing the IS on time and on budget, and normally, little thought is given to these other aspects. These other aspects include motivation and measurement, human resources, policies and politics, and facilities (Sharp & McDermott, 2001). In any event, the methods and tools used by a software development team are normally unsuitable for analysing this type of organizational problem. Additionally, people generally have difficulty understanding these messy situations and have developed a number of techniques to simplify the problem.

Vennix (1996) has noted that messy problems are characterised by complexity, uncertainty, interrelated subproblems, recursive dependencies, and multiple interpretations. To complicate matters further, the following factors exacerbate the process of resolving these types of problems:

Selective perception: Generally, we use selective perception where we see only what we want, or expect, to see. This often leads to self-fulfilling prophecies. In an IS situation this often manifests itself by all problems being seen as purely technical—organizational problems are not even recognised. In many instances, our interpretation of a situation is influenced by our background, education, functional position within an organization, and our strongly held beliefs. For example, a poorly performing supply process could be seen as a management, engineering, financial, marketing, human resources, or inventory problem, depending on the viewer's functional position. In each case, different "fixes" could be recommended to remedy the situation.

Creating our own social reality: Here, the perception becomes the reality. For example, if someone believes that one of their coworkers does not like them, they will tend to show that in their dealings with that person. Quite probably, the second party will respond in kind, and a somewhat frosty relationship will almost certainly be the result. This, of course, is closely related to the self-fulfilling prophecy phenomenon discussed above.

Reinforcement: Reinforcement is inherent in many systems and is discussed in more detail in the following section. For example, if a person believes that others in their organization are playing power/political games, they may tend to react to many situations in a political way. In turn, this will quite probably elicit a political response, thus reinforcing the original perception.

Oversimplification: Most people also have a tendency to oversimplify problems in an effort to understand them. This includes reducing a problem so that it can be represented by a single cause/effect relationship. It also includes reducing the number of variables to be considered to a minimum, typically as little as four (de Geus, 1997; Lee, Barua & Whinstone, 1997; Vennix, 1996).

We tend NOT to learn from experience: To compound the error of simplification, we tend not to learn from experience. We tend to fit an experience/result to previously held beliefs—a form of selective perception. For example, an employee attributes success to his/her abilities, but blames failure on external circumstances (Vennix, 1996).

Most people have difficulty connecting cause and effect, where these are separated by time and/or space, and this problem is exacerbated further when the system is dynamic (changes over time) or contains feedback loops (Dangerfield & Roberts, 1995; Moxnes, 1998; Sterman, 1989, 1994; Vennix, 1996). Separated cause and effect occurs regularly within most social systems, which are also often dynamic and contain many feedback loops. This, combined with the techniques we use to simplify a problem still further, makes understanding the complex relationships that occur within a business particularly problematic. We need a technique, other than those traditionally used within IS development, to understand the relationships that occur between an IS and its environment—(the organization into which it is placed). Causal-loop diagrams (CLDs), a technique used within the system dynamics field (itself a subset of systems thinking), is one such technique, and we now present the essentials of this approach.

Causal-Loop Diagrams

The following discussion is collated from work by Richardson (1986), Richardson & Pugh (1981), Sterman (2000) and Vennix (1996). Sterman's book, in particular, is a good source of information on CLDs. It contains a chapter devoted entirely to the subject, and there are many business case studies throughout the book, where the author has developed accompanying causal-loop diagrams.

A causal-loop diagram consists of variables that are connected by arrows denoting the causal influence among variables. The connections inevitably create loops, hence the name "causal-loop diagrams." The diagrams are easy to construct, but the discussions that ensue during construction are often extremely illuminating (the reasons for diagram construction).

CLDs should *never* be constructed by one person—they are only effective if the problem is discussed by stakeholders. This, then, helps to minimise the situation in which people adopt a stance defined partly by the functional area in which they work. Anything should be considered. It can then be discussed, and a decision can be made to include or exclude it from the diagram. Often, a throwaway comment will start a whole new area of investigation that is vital to understanding the problem.

An example CLD is shown in Figure 1 (all CLDs were developed in this paper using VensimPLE from Ventana Corporation, www.ventana.com).

The variables, such as *Birth Rate, Population, Death Rate*, are connected by negative causal links (the arrows). Each causal link is assigned a polarity (the "+" or "-" sign next to the arrowhead).

The polarity on the causal link between *Birth Rate* and *Population* indicates that if the cause increases (*Birth Rate*), then the effect (*Population*) increases

Figure 1: CLD example—the impact of birth and death rates on population size

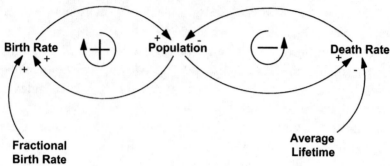

above what it would otherwise have been (all other variables remaining constant). The reverse is also true. If the cause decreases, the effect will also decrease below what it would otherwise have been. This is known as a positive or reinforcing causal link.

In a negative causal link, such as that between *Death Rate* and *Population*, any increase in the cause will mean a decrease in the effect below what it would otherwise have been.

Note that the variable that feeds into *Population* has been named *Birth Rate* and not *Births*. This is important, as it makes it obvious that it is a rate of flow into a stock or accumulation. If the variable had been named *Births*, a serious mistake in interpreting the diagram could be made. The implicit assumption in this instance is that if *Population* decreases, then *Births* also decrease, leading to a further decrease in *Population*. This is not the case. A decrease in *Population* leads to a decrease in the number of births, but the population is still increasing, although at a lesser rate. Care should be taken to identify rates of flow of matter into a stock and to name these appropriately.

Each loop also has a polarity. This is shown by a large circular arrow within the loop. Convention is that these travel in the same direction as the causal link arrows.

Determining loop polarity can be done two ways. Pick any variable, assume it changes in a given direction. Then trace around the loop determining in which direction each variable moves. If, when you arrive back at your starting point, the original variable then wants to move in the same direction as you originally intended, you have a positive feedback loop. If the original variable wants to move in the opposite direction, it is a negative feedback loop.

An easier way, that can lead to errors, is to count the number of negative causal links within the loop. If the sum is a negative number, it is a negative feedback loop. If the sum is positive, it is a positive feedback loop.

Positive feedback loops are often known as reinforcing loops, vicious cycles, or virtuous cycles. Once they start moving in a given direction, they keep reinforcing their action, forming the classical snowball effect. Examples include money left in a bank attracting interest, or individual drug users each introducing two new users to the habit.

Negative feedback loops always try to negate, or cancel, the action you originally took. They are endemic in social and organizational situations but are rarely recognised. An example is a business cutting staff numbers to reduce costs and increase profits, which it does. However, the tendency is, when profits increase, to employ more staff, negating the initial action of cutting staff. This is a very small section of a much more complicated situation. A long-term effect is that when staff numbers are cut, service levels eventually drop, customers leave, and profits decline, requiring another cut in staff numbers to restore profits. A diagram of this situation is shown in Figure 2.

Figure 2 introduces three more conventions of CLDs.

- Loops should be named. This makes it easier to discuss the situation with people who were not involved in model building.
- There are often time delays between a cause and the resulting effect. These are indicated by two short parallel lines drawn across the causal link or by a named "delay" box within the causal link.
- There is always some goal, or desired state, of a negative loop that triggers the initial action. In Figure 2, this is *Rqd Profit*. The normal behaviour of a negative loop is then an attempt to cancel the action of this trigger. The goal of the loop should be made explicit.

Causal loop diagrams are excellent for the following:
- Quickly capturing your hypotheses about the causes of dynamics

Figure 2: A further CLD example—some factors that impact organizational profits

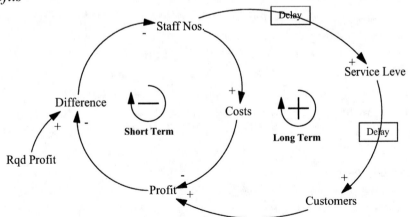

- Eliciting and capturing the mental models of individuals or teams
- Communicating the important feedbacks you believe are responsible for a problem (Sterman, 2000)

The technique, however, has a number of limitations (Richardson, 1986). The major one is that you cannot use CLDs to determine the effect of a change in a variable on system behaviour. Repeated experiments have shown that the human brain is generally not capable of linking cause and effect when these are separated by time and/or distance (Moxnes, 1998; Sterman, 1989). Determining system behaviour requires the use of a simulation model run on a computer. This is often done using the stock and flow simulation models used within system dynamics. This technique is, however, beyond the scope of this chapter. An introduction to system dynamics analysis is given in Sterman (2000).

It was mentioned earlier that CLDs should never be constructed in isolation. This is for a number of reasons: if a model is constructed by one person, that person will bring with him/her all the mental models and limitations of understanding a complex problem previously discussed; second, a major objective of most CLD modeling initiatives is to provide stakeholders with insights to the behaviour of the system under investigation. Unless they participate this is unlikely to occur.

There has been considerable research in recent years on how to conduct group model building sessions to maximise their usefulness (Akkermans & Vennix, 1996; Andersen, Richardson, & Vennix, 1997; Richardson & Andersen, 1995; Vennix, 1996, 1999). Andersen and Richardson (Andersen & Richardson, 1997) review much of this literature, which comes from the systems thinking, soft systems methodology, and system dynamics disciplines, and provide a number of suggestions to enhance group model building developed from that literature and their own extensive experience. Some of their recommendations include the following:

- Plan for the group model building session. Determine purpose, goal, and scope for the session. This is usually determined by the sponsor within the organization, with input from the facilitator of the modeling session.
- Clarify the audience of the model—who is ultimately going to use the insights from the modeling session and implement recommendations—and identify those people who will be involved in model building.
- Determine who is going to take the roles of facilitator, process coach, recorder and gatekeeper. The latter is usually the sponsor within the organization.
- Schedule the day. Be aware of differences in vocabulary. Often, people from different functional areas will use a similar term to describe two entirely different entities or vice versa. These must be identified and agreement reached.
- Avoid talking heads. The corollary of this is to ensure that everyone is involved.
- Reflect after each major piece of the model has been constructed.

- Elicit the problem statement. As mentioned earlier, this is often difficult with messy problems; however, it is vital. Because of the interrelatedness of many things within messy problems, the scope, if not properly defined, has a tendency to creep to include everything within, and without, the organization. The problem definition and scope must be settled to focus discussion. The current authors have had experience, once, where this did not occur. At least one of us has taken a most fervent oath that this will never, ever, happen again. It is not a pleasant experience. Andersen and Richardson (1997) provide guides for eliciting the problem statement developed from the systems thinking, system dynamics, and soft systems methodology literature.

- Determine feedback loops. Clients often have difficulty thinking in loops—we are taught to "think straight" from an early age. The easiest way of doing this is to select an important variable and then ask what affects this. An issue that often arises is that participants from various functional areas within the organization will often want to start with a variable within their area as they see this as being the most important. It does not really matter which variable is used, eventually, the feedback loops will include the favourite variables of all stakeholders.

Group model building has been used successfully for some years within the general system thinking community. Some of the benefits include the gaining of insights by participants for the behaviour of the system under review, the identification of variables that can be used to lever system performance, an increase in commitment to implementation of recommendations and an increase in the openness of communication. It has been observed that during group model building sessions, participants tend to focus on the problem rather than individual political agendas (Akkermans & Vennix, 1996), although perceived career risk will modify participant behaviour.

The use of a series of CLD group model building sessions within a large Australian organization is now described, starting with a description of the case study.

THE CASE STUDY

Gigante is a large Australian telecommunications organization that is experiencing rapid change in products, processes, and organizational structure. It has branches in every state and territory of Australia with a workforce in the tens of thousands. It has faced increasing competition since 1991, and a decision was made at that time to base its competitive strategy on market differentiation in an attempt to maintain market share (Porter, 1980). The differentiation strategy has led, in part, to rapid change in products and processes. The market in which Gigante operates is also experiencing rapid technological change that, in turn, accelerates the rate of its introduction of new products and services.

Structurally, it is divided into largely autonomous groups, reflecting the nature of customers and some of its functional areas. At the commencement of the research project (1997), Gigante had seven functional units that included two customer groups that reflected Gigante's customer type, a marketing group together with a technology group. There were also a number of administrative groups.

A product manager within the marketing group has overall responsibility for the introduction of a new product and its revenue stream, even though these products are actually developed by the technology group. Most customer contact is via customer service representatives (CSRs) located within customer service centres (CSCs) run by the two customer groups. Being largely autonomous, these groups have structured themselves to suit their individual situations. In addition, although the products they deliver are often the same, the process of providing these may be different in the two groups, thus leading to a lack of consistency in their operations and processes.

Each product within the organization's catalogue has its own code, and as any change to an existing product is regarded as a new product, the number of codes is quite large—in excess of 40,000 at the commencement of the research project. To exacerbate the situation, the same product often has different codes in each of the company's provisioning, billing, and network systems.

The process investigated is illustrated in Figure 3. A customer requests a product from a CSR who then enters the customer details into a provisioning system and a separate billing system. The technology group then supplies the product, the billing system is updated to reflect the connection of service, and the customer can commence using the product/service and is billed for that use. Errors occur at a

Figure 3: Gigante's provisioning and billing processes

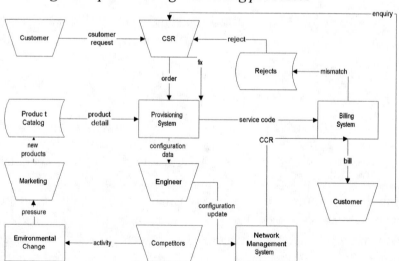

number of locations, primarily when product codes are entered into the various systems. When there is a mismatch of codes in the systems, the customer records drop to an error bucket. The value of the unbilled revenue contained in this bucket varies but is considerable.

In most instances, error causes are relatively straightforward and easily corrected by CSRs. Note, however, that it is not the CSR who made the original entry who has to correct the error. Whenever CSRs have spare time, they are supposed to correct any errors that are within the error bucket. In the system that was in place at the time of the research, it was not possible to determine where, or by whom, errors were being made.

Like many organizations, Gigante has, for some time, been pursuing a policy of cost reduction. This has led to a reduction in staff numbers and an increase in managers' span of control. In pursuit of this policy, it has also hired base grade personnel as CSRs. These people, who normally are the only contact Gigante has with its customers, are among the lowest-paid of all Gigante employees. Due to the reduction of middle management numbers, CSRs have very few promotional prospects and most see the position as temporary employment, as moving on to other positions within Gigante or resigning.

Gigante has made a number of attempts in the past to improve its provisioning process and to reduce the number of errors that were occurring. Initially, it attempted to "fix the information system," which involved updating the automated sections of the provisioning and billing systems (McGrath, 1997a; McGrath, Dampney, & More, 1998).

In early 1993, Gigante commissioned an external consultant to examine the problems it was having in its provisioning system. At the request of Gigante the consultants concentrated primarily on the social aspects of the system. The report, by Booz, Allen, & Hamilton,[1] made a number of observations:

- 7% of Gigante's customers had contacted it about their most recent bill. As CSRs are responsible for these enquiries, this immediately impacts their workload.
- The only key performance indicator that Gigante consistently monitored was the number of customer calls that CSRs take per day. Emphasis was on quantity or work performed rather than quality.
- Approximately 80,000 service orders were being processed per day. Of these, 12,000 were dropping to the error bucket, and of these, 1500 would error more than twice.

In one CSC studied, 37% of staff, with a mean tenure of four years, left in the preceding 12 months. The remaining senior staff were then relatively unproductive, as they were spending much of their time training new hires. On occasion, staff turnover exceeded 200% per annum.

Workload was growing and was expected to increase further.

The consultants then made a number of recommendations that included the introduction of a formal training scheme for new staff. Lack of training was seen as a root cause of the error rate. Also, Gigante should address the staff turnover rate within CSCs. As a result of the report, Gigante introduced a formal training scheme for new CSRs. However, in an attempt to control costs, it did not modify its hiring policy and continued to hire base-grade personnel.

Gigante then abandoned this formal training scheme, as it did not appear to make a significant difference to the error rate, and staff numbers had fallen to a point where staff could not be removed from CSCs for training purposes. All training is now "on-the-job."

This was the position at the time of the research reported here. The current writers were sponsored by a senior manager within Gigante and contracted under a research project jointly funded by Gigante and the Australian Research Council to investigate ways of reducing the error rate within CSCs. We were working within a small section of Gigante with members of the sponsor's team. These members are among very few staff from Gigante who work with the provisioning system from end-to-end. Their task is to identify problems with the provisioning and billing processes and to recommended remedial action. This action is reactive, occurring after a serious error has been detected, and is normally associated with the automated sections of the system. The concern of the sponsor was that many of the recalcitrant errors were not due to malfunctions of the information system but to other, organizational, issues.

The decision was made to take a systemic view of the problem, as it was believed that a number of conflicting issues were at play. An early task was to gain an understanding of the problem and the interactions of various issues. This was achieved by conducting a number of group model building sessions using the CLD method described earlier.

Before the model building sessions were conducted, the authors had to familiarise themselves with the problem area. This was done, partially, by the construction of a data-flow diagram of the process under investigation. Although this is a very large process generating millions of records per day, sufficient understanding was gained by decomposing the data-flow diagrams to level 2.

After this familiarisation, the authors then determined the approximate scope of the problem to be investigated with the sponsor. At the same time, the members of the modeling group were determined, and invitations were sent to them. They were also made familiar with the problem area and what it was hoped to achieve.

One of the current writers was the designated facilitator for the three modeling sessions held. Each session lasted approximately one hour (the only available time within Gigante). Other members of the group consisted of the sponsor of the research and three members of his team together with a senior manager from a CSC and the other writer.

About 15 minutes was spent in the first session explaining CLDs. All members of the group were able to understand the modeling concept within this period of time. The remainder of the session was then spent discussing the general problem and establishing its boundaries. A very tentative CLD was constructed as the discussion proceeded. A number of issues arose that we were not able to resolve at the time, and various group members were asked to investigate these prior to the next meeting.

At the second meeting, the initial model was reviewed, and the additional information was added. Construction of the model then continued.

An issue that arose here, and in other modelling projects undertaken by the authors, is that of a suitable level of granularity, or aggregation, of detail. Most of the people involved in the model construction had had some analysis experience, and their tendency was to focus on detail rather than the larger picture. This tendency of analysts has been reported elsewhere (Sharp & McDermott, 2001). It took a while for the group to arrive at a suitable level of detail.

The model shown in Figure 4 was arrived at after the third modeling session.

The model depicted in Figure 4 indicates that there are two external variables that affect the workflow within a CSC—customer requests and new products. If the rate of customer requests for services increase, as they do whenever a new product is introduced or during the availability of "specials," the amount of work to do also increases. The traditional reaction within a CSC to this situation is to

Figure 4: Causal-loop diagram of work within a customer service centre within Gigante

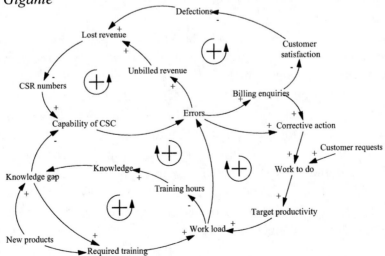

increase target productivity—attempt to get CSRs to work faster. This, in turn, increases their workload. Another aspect of this is to increase the number of errors introduced into the information system, which then increases the amount of corrective action required by CSRs. This, in turn increases the work to do, creating a positive feedback loop, in this case, a vicious cycle.

To gain competitive advantage, Gigante has adopted a product differentiation strategy, introducing new products on a regular basis. Each time a new product is introduced, CSRs need training, required training, to enable them to deal with its provisioning. At the same time, their knowledge gap (the gap between perfect knowledge of how to provide all products versus their actual knowledge) increases, again increasing their required training. Any training of CSRs leads to less time available to deal with customers, so increasing workload. The increase in workload then means less time available for further training, meaning that their overall knowledge can drop, so increasing their knowledge gap. Simply, the introduction of new products requires more training that is problematic due to the high workload. This, partly, has resulted in the removal of formal training within CSCs.

The remaining loops can be traced through in a similar fashion. Any increase in knowledge gap will lead, eventually, to an increase in the error rate, which, in turn, leads to an increase in workload as well as a decrease in customer satisfaction and defections. This leads to a drop in profits and the resultant strategy, to date, of shedding more staff.

A variable not shown in the model at Figure 4, but extensively discussed, was staff turnover. Gigante's participants in the model construction were able, for the first time, to understand why the increase in formal training as recommended by Booz Allen & Hamilton in 1993 had not been effective. The high staff turnover meant that as soon as staff were trained, they were leaving (either resigning or moving to other areas within Gigante). It was impossible to improve the overall capability of a CSC.

Model construction also gave two other important insights. First, there is a link between the rate at which new products are introduced and the error rate of data entry into the information system. The removal of formal training and total reliance on on-the-job training means that it is difficult for staff to learn about new products. If products are introduced too quickly, staff are unable to learn their peculiarities in sufficient time, and so the data entry error rate increases.

Second, participants were able to see that increasing target productivity was actually counterproductive. This just led to an increase in the error rate and an even higher workload for CSRs. A better policy would probably be to make more staff available during peak periods. It is also interesting to note that although Gigante has an espoused policy of superior customer service, the only measure of CSR performance is the length of time spent with each customer. CSRs are very conscious of this. In one CSC observed by the authors, there was a large counter indicating the number of calls waiting to be answered. CSRs watched this carefully. We have anecdotal evidence to suggest that telephone calls are "lost" as the allotted time for a call approaches, or the caller is forwarded to another employee. The sponsor of the project also indicated that incorrect combinations of data that the system would still accept were passed around within, and between, CSCs very quickly. This allowed CSRs to "complete" an entry very quickly and so remain within their allotted period of time per customer call. Obviously, the error rate increased, but CSRs are not measured on the quality of their work.

CONCLUSION

The foregoing indicates that, as suggested by Sharp & McDermott (2001), IT and workflow are not the only enablers of a business process that must be taken into consideration when designing an information system. It seems pointless spending much time and effort maximising the performance of an IS, when organizational issues can have such a dramatic impact on the performance of the overall process (Campbell, 2000). Unfortunately, these organizational issues often fall into the category of problems classified as "messy." One way of addressing these messy problems, by using causal-loop diagrams within a group model building environment, has been presented. If we are to increase the performance of an information system or the process of which it is a part, we must start taking a systemic view of the overall situation. Maximising the performance of a part of the system is unlikely to optimise the overall performance.

ENDNOTE

1   Details of this internal report are not given in the bibliography, as it is not generally available.

REFERENCES

Akkermans, H. & Vennix, J. A. M. (1996). *Client's opinions on group model-building: An exploratory study*. Retrieved July 16, 1997, from the World Wide Web: http://www.origin.ext/facts/company/homepage/eiscc/doc/isdc96.htm.

Andersen, D. & Richardson, G. P. (1997). Scrips for group model building.

System Dynamics Review, 13(2), 107–129.

Andersen, D., Richardson, G. P., & Vennix, J. A. M. (1997). Group model building: Adding more science to the craft. *System Dynamics Review, 13*(2), 187–201.

Campbell, B. R. (2000). Systems dynamics in information systems analysis: An evaluation case study. In Bustard, D., Kawalek, P., & Norris, M. (Eds.), *Systems modeling for business process improvement*, 33–46. London: Artech House.

Chaos. (1995). The Standish Group. Retrieved in 1999 from the World Wide Web: http://www.standishgroup.com/chaos.html.

Curtis, B., Kellner, M. I., & Over, J. (1992). Process modelling. *Communications of the ACM, 35*(9), 75–90.

Curtis, B., Krasner, H., & Iscoe, N. (1988). A field study of the software design process for large systems. *Communications of the ACM, 31*(11), 1268–1287.

Dangerfield, B. & Roberts, C. (1995). Projecting dynamic behaviour in the absence of a model: An experiment. *System Dynamics Review, 11*(2), 157–172.

Day, J. (2000). Software development as organizational conversation: Analogy as a systems intervention. *Systems Research and Behavioral Science, 17*, 349–358.

de Geus, A. P. (1997). *The living company*. Longview Publishing Limited.

DeMarco, T. (1982). *Controlling software projects: Management, measurement and estimation*. Englewood Cliffs, NJ: Yourdon Press/Prentice Hall.

Gasson, S. & Holland, N. (1996). The nature and processes of IT-related change. In Orlikowski, W., Walsham, G., Jones, M. R., & DeGross, J. I. (Eds.), *Information technology and changes in organizational work*, 213–234. London: Chapman and Hall.

Gruhn, V. & Wolf, S. (1995). Software process improvement by business process orientation. *Software Process—Improvement and Practice* (Pilot Issue).

Kueng, P. & Kawalek, P. (1997). Process models: A help or a burden? Paper presented at the *Association for Information Systems 1997 Americas Conference*, August, Indianapolis.

Lee, B., Barua, A., & Whinstone, A. B. (1997). Discovery and representation of causal relationships in MIS research: A methodological framework. *MIS Quarterly*, 109–133.

McGrath, G. M. (1997a). An implementation of a data-centered information systems strategy: A power/political perspective. *Failure & Lessons Learned in Information Technology Management, 1*, 3–17.

McGrath, G. M. (1997b). A process modelling framework: Capturing key aspects of organizational behaviour. Paper presented at the *Australian Software Engineering Conference*, Sept. 29–Oct. 2, Sydney, Australia.

McGrath, G. M., Dampney, C. N. G., & More, E. (1998). A structured approach to conflict prediction in information systems strategy implementation. *International Journal of Intelligent Systems in Accounting, Finance & Management, 7*, 107–124.

Moxnes, E. (1998). Not only the tragedy of the commons: Misperceptions of bioeconomics. *Management Science, 44*(9), 1234–1248.

OASIG. (1996). *The performance of Information Technology and the role of human and organizational factors*. Organizational Aspects Special Interest Group. Retrieved in 1997 from the World Wide Web: http://www.shef.ac.uk/~iwp/resprogs/itperf.html.

Porter, M. E. (1980). *Competitive strategy: Techniques for analysing industries and competitors*. New York: Free Press.

Richardson, G. P. (1986). Problems with causal loop diagrams. *System Dynamics Review, 2*, 158–170.

Richardson, G. P. & Andersen, D. (1995). Teamwork in group model building. *System Dynamics Review, 11*(2), 113–137.

Richardson, G. P. & Pugh, A. L. (1981). *Introduction to System Dynamics Modeling*. Oregon: Productivity Press.

Sharp, A. & McDermott, P. (2001). *Workflow modeling: tools for process improvement and application development*. London: Artech House.

Sterman, J. D. (1989). Modeling managerial behavior: Misperceptions of feedback in a dynamic decision making experiment. *Management Science, 35*(3), 321–339.

Sterman, J. D. (1994). Learning in and about complex systems. *System Dynamics Review, 10*(2/3), 291–330.

Sterman, J. D. (2000). *Business dynamics: Systems thinking and modeling for a complex world*. New York: Irwin McGraw-Hill.

Vennix, J. A. M. (1996). *Group model building: Facilitating team learning using system dynamics*. Chichester: John Wiley & Sons.

Vennix, J. A. M. (1999). Group model-building: Tackling messy problems. *System Dynamics Review, 15*(4), 379–401.

Section VI

Tendencies and Perspectives

Chapter XI

Implementation of Collaborative Technologies as a Learning Process

Tatyana Bondarouk and Klaas Sikkel
University of Twente, The Netherlands

ABSTRACT

Nowadays, more and more information and communication technologies (ICT) gain the characteristics of groupware as they strive to support different aspects of collaborative work. These types of ICT become progressively intertwined in the infrastructures of companies and therefore their implementation deserves as much attention as their design and development. However the literature keeps on providing examples of failures of groupware projects. In this paper we propose a novel theoretical perspective to understand implementation of such technologies based on learning theories. A technology implementation process is regarded as a learning process. The model describes two levels of the implementation process: the user level (individuals and groups) and the organisational level. At the group level it is based on five steps of collaborative learning within a group of users. At the organisational level it is related to the learning climate. By means of the longitudinal case study we have operationalized the constructs from the model towards concrete user-group and managerial activities that advance implementation of groupware. The discussion leads us to conjecture that a better organisational learning climate could promote successful implementation of groupware through group learning. Ultimately the insights derived from the model should lead to the tangible ways to foster the learning climate.

INTRODUCTION

Implementation of technology in an organization can be regarded as a learning process and, in particular, implementation of groupware technology, as a collaborative learning process. In this chapter, we propose a model of learning-oriented implementation of groupware technologies. We believe that the model is useful in several ways. The model provides novel insights, highlighting issues relevant to the human aspects of implementation processes. Moreover, we envisage that it is possible to improve such processes, based on the understanding provided by our model.

With collaborative technologies, we mean computer-based systems that give support for collaborative work. Systems specifically designed to do so are commonly called *groupware*. But with the rise of Internet technologies on the one hand and integrated office environments on the other hand, the distinction between groupware and other information and communication technology gets blurred. Relevant for our perspective is not whether a system to be implemented classifies as a groupware system, but whether the technology is to be instrumental in supporting collaborative work.

The perspective presented here is a novel one; therefore, it is worthwhile to motivate our view before we present the theoretical framework. Why would we want to consider a collaborative technology implementation process as a collaborative on-the-job learning process?

- User groups adapt a novel way of working when a new technology is introduced. Not all groups do this in the same manner, and this adoption process, called *appropriation* (DeSanctis & Poole, 1994; Ruel, 2001) depends on the group processes. The terms in which one describes the appropriation process—sharing understanding, mutual adjustment—are closely related to learning theory.
- Changes in technology do not only allow more effective ways of doing the same work, but, in addition, lead to changes in various aspects of professional competency such as knowledge, skills, and attitudes. That, in turn, could influence on-going use of technology. Hence, in theory, there is an on-going evolutionary process of professional and technological development.
- While using collaborative technology in practical situations, user groups gradually discover the affordances provided by the system and come up with new, unforeseen ways of working. We believe that lots could be gained from collaborative technology if users exploit their group learning potential to a large extent.
- In several accounts of case studies, the implementation process did not take place in an optimal way, and the cause of this has been attributed to a lack of reflective restructuring among the users (Tucker et al., 2001; Hettinga et al., 2001).

These arguments suggest that an appropriate collaborative learning climate in an organization could lead to better implementation of groupware. Having insights in the relevant aspects, we are able to recognize obstacles to the proper learning process, and we could improve the process by eliminating, or at least diminishing these obstacles.

On a general level, an approach based on learning fits well to a systemic view. As indicated by numerous case studies (e.g., Bikson & Eveland, 1996; Orlikowski, 1996), implementation of collaborative technologies does not follow a straight path that can be laid out in advance. Implementation of technology leads to perturbations in systems dependent on it, and the process is to be adapted as the implementation unfolds. Central in our approach is the group as a systemic entity. While the organizational climate and the individual users do influence the acceptance of groupware, ultimately the success of the system depends on how it is appropriated by collaborating groups. We do not follow a specific systems approach, hard (Maani & Cavana, 2000) or soft (Checkland & Scholes, 1990), but in our view, our model has a lot in common with the general line of thought of systems theory.

The purposes of this chapter, are sum, is, firstly, to present our ideas about the influence of group learning on on-going use of collaborative technologies, and secondly, to propose a model, in which implementation is regarded as a learning process that takes place at different levels, reaching from the individual user to the entire organization. Our vision is presented in a descriptive model, which can be considered as a "cognitive map" rather than a causal model. We believe that the model is useful because it provides novel insights, highlighting issues relevant to an evolutionary implementation process of collaborative technologies.

The chapter is structured as follows. We start with an elaboration of the theoretical background. Next, we present a model of collaborative on-the-job learning in general terms, and we provide an operationalization for the model from a particular case study. Finally, we present our model of groupware implementation, in which collaborative learning is embedded in an organizational context, and we discuss the variables influencing the learning process.

THE LEARNING-ORIENTED APPROACH TO GROUPWARE IMPLEMENTATION: THEORETICAL FRAMEWORK OF THE STUDY

To compose the framework of the learning approach, we combine important and specific characteristics extracted from three distinct areas of research. Implementation of technology is considered from an organizational and management science perspective. Computer-Supported Cooperative Work is a distinct interdisciplinary research area that provides understanding of the design and use of collaborative technologies.

Collaborative learning, finally, draws upon educational sciences. To introduce our theoretical basis, we briefly describe each of these three domains.

Implementation of Technology

Anybody writing about implementation of technology should address the question how the author defines *implementation*. Gottschalk (1999, p.80) notes that "the term implementation is given a variety of meanings in the literature"—and we would add that in lots of IT studies, implementation is mentioned as an implicitly clear word (Joshi, 1991; Orlikowski & Robey, 1991; Lederer & Salmela, 1996; Griffith, 1996; Mark & Wulf, 1999; Pipek & Wulf, 1999).

To shed some light on understanding of technology implementation, we follow the proposition of Gottschalk (1999) and consider the critical point as a stage of implementation completion. In Table 1, the reviewed studies on implementation are classified in accordance to the authors' opinions on the phases of implementation completion. This table is based on the research of Gottschalk (1999), but we have added some new entries.

Table 1: Stages of implementation completion (adapted from Gottschalk, 1999)

Implementation is completed when	Study
A new system (or some changes in the system) is technically installed.	Lucas, 1981
	Nutt, 1986
The system is accepted by users.	Baronas & Louis, 1988
	Alavi & Joachimsthaler, 1992
	Lou & Scamell, 1996
The system is adapted.	Leonard-Barton & Deschamps, 198
	Orlikowski, 1992; 1993
	DeSanctis & Poole, 1994
	Volkoff & Ivey, 1999
Satisfaction with the system is achieved.	Griffith, 1996
	Klein & Sorra, 1996
Intended objectives are met.	Lederer & Salmela, 1996
There is a need for removing the system or for a major change of it.	Sanderson, 1992
	Pipek & Wulf, 1999

Obvious is that implementation is a process that takes certain time until complete. And, the completion stage can be crucial issue in understanding the implementation process, but it needs to be accurately determined.

We found descriptions of implementation in organizational studies about implementation of innovation. Important is that implementation is considered not in terms of what is being introduced, but in terms of changes in behavior of targeted employees—how they appropriate an innovation (Baronas & Louis, 1988; Klein & Sorra, 1996).

We propose to root implementation completion of groupware in the stage when the employees start to use the system quite stable in order to perform a certain task. Routine use of technology is limited by the nature of the task, if the task is changed, it may have the consequence that use of technology will be different.

We regard implementation of groupware as *adoption of a system during the transition period between the initiative to get a new system and the stable use of it within a task* (Bondarouk & Sikkel, 2001a). The transition period includes certain actions based on the users' experience. Evolution of the implementation process ranges from non-use, or even avoidance of the system, through bored and passive exercising, to enthusiastic, skilled, and consistent use. Typically the adoption process will stabilize after some time.

"Stable use" of a system assumes the range in the adoption process when the targeted employees use the system within a certain task skillfully, actively, and task-consistently. From the learning perspective, targeted employees use technology in a stable way when they are able to learn on their own from the system how to operate in order improve their task performance further.

Collaborative Technologies

Computer-Supported Cooperative Work (CSCW) emerged as an identifi-able field of study in the second half of the 1980s (Greif, 1988). Studying the role of computers in group work is an interdisciplinary effort. In order to construct systems that effectively support teamwork, knowledge is needed on how teams do work together. Studies in CSCW range from construction and experimenting with groupware system prototypes, via implementation studies in various organizations, to ethnografic studies on team work in specific settings.

Characteristic for the way of thinking in the CSCW research community is that the real nature of work is hard to capture and eludes a completely formal description. Informal work practices differ from formal work procedures. Work is situated (Suchman, 1987), what people do in order to cope with a given task depends on the situation at hand. This holds for individual work, but even more for teamwork, the essence of teamwork being that people collaborate in addressing a task. This makes CSCW as a research field essentially different from Human-Computer Interaction. The focus of study is not merely how users interact with groupware in order to address a task, but how a group of users collectively uses technology to achieve something. Bannon and Schmidt (1989) define CSCW as "an endeavor to understand the nature and characteristic of cooperative work with the objective of designing adequate computer technologies."

The main characteristic of *collaborative work* (or cooperative work; the terms are used as synonyms) is mutual dependence of the involved persons. This means that one relies positively on the quality and timeliness of the work of one's collaborators, and vice versa, resulting in positive (though not necessarily harmonious) interdependence (Schmidt & Bannon, 1992).

Systems to support collaborative work are commonly called *groupware.* Baecker (1993) sees groupware as any "multi-user software supporting computer-assisted coordinating activities." Ellis, Gibbs, and Rein (1991), define groupware as "computer-based systems that support groups of people engaged in a common task or goal and that provide an interface to a shared environment." Specifically excluded are multiuser systems like time-sharing systems and databases, in which resources are shared for various reasons, but the user interface carefully hides the fact that multiple users interact with the system simultaneously.

Groupware systems traditionally are classified along the dimension's time (synchronous vs. asynchronous collaboration) and space (local vs. distributed). Most types of groupware are intended to support teamwork in geographically distributed groups. Synchronous distributed collaboration is supported, for example, by desk-top conferencing, in which documents and applications can be shared in addition to a video connection. An example of an environment for asynchronous distributed collaboration is a "shared workspace," which may contain work objects, messages, and other information (Bentley et al., 1997). Electronic meeting systems, on the other hand, are a class of groupware systems to support local collaboration. Such systems facilitate brainstorming and decision making in a meeting room, in which every place is equipped with a workstation.

Until around 1995, the construction of collaborative technologies was a major technical effort. The availability of Lotus Notes and internet/intranet technologies have brought a qualitative change in the construction of groupware. Such general platforms can be extended with groupware add-ons, which take less effort to construct and – more importantly – reconstruct based on experiences in real use.

In the 21st century, in our view, with a variety of technologies around, implementation of these technologies deserves at least as much attention as the development of new technologies. The prime aspect of interest in CSCW implementation studies is how technology is used to support collaborative work and how the implementation process can be improved to increase the effectiveness of this support. Whether the technology that is used is a groupware system or another product is relatively unimportant, as long as the technology is instrumental in the teamwork.

Collaborative Learning

The concept of collaborative learning promotes our view on the social issues in adopting of groupware. We define learning as changing knowledge and behavior, and focus not on learning in general, but learning 'in the work place' (Watkins & Marsick, 1996), or on-the-job learning (Onstenk, 1995).

The findings from a number of studies (Watkins, 1991; Onstenk, 1995; Dixon, 1994; Crossan et al., 1999) have validated that the fundamental characteristic of learning in the workplace is work socialization. It includes acquisition of the spirit of a company, norms and values of the occupation. It plays a significant role not only during first entering a company, but also during the following periods in the organization as a whole. Work socialization implies that individual learning depends upon the collaborative learning. And the converse is also true: individuals influence collaborative learning.

Socialization does not consist of the "arithmetical sums" of individual learning contributions, but appears to be a more complex and integrated phenomenon. If employees work collaboratively and engage in a common task with the use of technology, on-the-job learning gets the features of group learning.

Group understanding of technology seems to be something different than individual understanding of it. Collectively operating a system, reflecting on it, and making sense of the system is a different and more complicated process than the individual process of acquiring an understanding of the situation.

Orlikowski and Gash (1994) have introduced the term technological frames to identify that subset of the employees' cognitive structures that concern the assumptions, expectations, and knowledge they use to understand technology in organisations (p.178). Collaborative understanding of technology is related to the concept of shared technological frames (Orlikowski & Gash, 1994). Common meaning of the system is developed in a *dialogue,* when users share their mental models about technology. Particular opinions about why and how the system was introduced, about its basic and specific functionality, about the most effective ways of using it, – these are the issues that are shared in one collaborative unit or group of users.

We view group learning as behavior that consists of actions carried out by team members through which a team obtains and processes data that improves cooperation (adapted from Druskat & Kayes, 2000). In other words, team learning is team interactional processes, like seeking feedback, asking for help, talking about errors, experimenting, discussing of failure, looking for information from outside, critiquing, comparing, evaluating, developing a collective vision, etc. (Edmondson, 1999; Schippers et al., 2001; Stahl, 2002).

We describe four, in our view, basic components of team learning:

- *Positive interdependence*. It is supposed that we are linked with others in a way so that we cannot succeed unless they do. There are mutual benefits of the work: our colleagues' performance benefits us, and our work profits them as well.

- *Individual accountability or individual responsibility*. Employees learn together so they can subsequently perform higher as individuals. At the same time, individual accountability tends to eliminate "free riders" and "work-horses" (Nolinske & Millis, 1999).

- *Person-to-person promotive interaction*. Employees promote each other's success by helping, advising, assisting, encouraging and supporting. Certain activities and interpersonal dynamics occur only in the case of stimulating discussions, oral explanations, formal and informal communication.

- *Group maintenance* (Nolinske & Millis, 1999) is oriented on building a group capability to reflect on working together, i.e., to maintain and develop co-operative efforts.

Collaborative learning provides a suitable theoretical foundation for such a further understanding. It fits with the insights developed so far from implementation studies of collaborative technologies and seems readily applicable. For example, consider the observation of Robinson (1991) that collaboration always involves different types of communication, with a social level distinct from the formal level. The perspective of collaborative on-the-job learning not only confirms this, but, moreover, gives insight in different aspects of interaction at the social level. The relevant concepts in implementation of collaborative technology and collaborative learning are related, and the latter can be used as an extension of the former.

In sum, the value of a learning approach in this context is that it provides us with an extension (as opposed to an alternative paradigm) to the theoretical foundation of implementation of collaborative technologies and, moreover, one which promises to give guidelines for improving implementation processes.

A MODEL OF COLLABORATIVE LEARNING AS BASIS FOR GROUPWARE IMPLEMENTATION

The model for groupware implementation that we propose is process-based and aims at understanding the behavioral mechanism of on-going use of groupware as collaborative on-the-job learning.

In order to build our understanding and develop a model, we have transferred the experiential individual learning cycle of "acting-reflecting-thinking-deciding" (Kolb, 1984) to the collective one. On the interpersonal level, the mechanism of team learning is described with the following wheel: "collective actions – team reflection – sharing understanding – knowledge sharing – mutual adjusting" (Figure

Figure 1: Collaborative learning cycle based on Kolb's (1984) experiential learning cycle

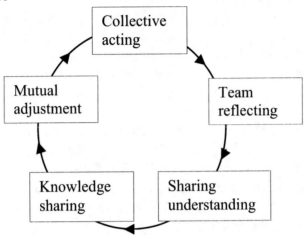

1). The team learning cycle consists of five steps (as opposed to the four steps of individual learning), for reasons that we will elaborate below.

A group learning cycle begins with collective experiences and actions, when a group of people is given a certain task to perform. According to Schippers et al. (2001), action refers to the goal-directed behaviors relevant to achieving the desired changes in team objectives, strategies.

This stage turns to the group reflection, the extent to which group members communicate about the group's objectives and strategies (e.g., decision making), and update them to the current circumstances (Schippers et al., 2001).

The most crucial difference between individual and cooperative learning lies in the knowledge domain. When we are to transfer individual learning to cooperative one, the act of knowing becomes more complicated. People ought to share their knowledge. In a strict sense, knowledge can be hardly shared. Knowledge is not something that can be passed around (Hendriks, 1999). We agree that to share someone's knowledge, there is a need of its reconstruction. Knowledge sharing as the process itself can be divided into, at least, two subphases: sharing understanding, or knowledge externalization and then, sharing knowledge itself, or knowledge internalization (Hendriks, 1999).

Sharing understanding implies mutual informal acceptance and respectfulness of diverse ideas and suggestions. It can appear in many forms, including presentations, lectures, oral explanations of ideas, or "codifying it in any intelligent knowledge system" (Hendriks, 1999). This sub-process is not necessarily conscious. For example, employees can learn by watching someone's performance, even if they are unaware of the specific knowledge needed for the task performance.

After that, the wheel cycles to knowledge sharing. Knowledge sharing involves using insights to help people see their own situation better (Kim, 1993). Internalization also takes on a great variety of forms: learning by doing, reading books, etc. It is oriented to those people who look for acquisition of knowledge.

The last step in the cooperative learning is mutual adjustment. This supposes joint regulations, planning, arrangement, and deciding. After planning is completed, its implementing starts that provokes a new wheel beginning with collective acting. A new learning cycle will be based on the previous group experience and knowledge. Planning can also take place during the action, or executing a task, when plans are developed and shaped by seeking feedback, group reflecting processes, that strengthens importance of group reflexivity.

It should be underlined that the division of the learning cycle in five consecutive steps is a theoretical construct. In reality, one does not observe these steps to be executed in the prescribed order. A team typically engages in activities that relate to different learning steps at the same time–and there is nothing wrong with that. But, in order to describe and understand the learning process in a team, it is helpful to split it into the five elementary steps.

Collaborative learning is a dynamic process that balances between two dimensions: exploration and exploitation in an organizational context. We label this as the tension between *feed forward* (assimilating new learning) and *feed back* (exploiting what has already been learned). Through feed forward processes, new knowledge and actions are developed; while feed back processes affect people on what has been known (Crossan et al., 1999).

If learning is a mechanism of on-going practice, it will run evolutionary when employees are engaged in a common task over new technology. Exercising with the new system provokes externalization of knowledge about it, then sharing of knowledge and collective regulation of activities for the future. The use of groupware is supported by the learning mechanism (Figure 2).

This process of learning through working using groupware technology takes place not only at the beginning, but while the system is being used.

Operationalization of the Model

The five elementary steps in the team learning model are abstract concepts. In order to apply them in a given situation, the terms have to be operationalized, i.e., translated to terms and activities making sense to the persons doing the work. The operationalization may vary according to the circumstances.

In order to validate the model, an explanatory case study was conducted in a local hospital in the Netherlands, where a new system was introduced six months before our research started. The system implied group work to administrate personnel information. With a qualitative approach, we collected and analyzed data in order to understand

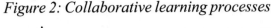

Figure 2: Collaborative learning processes

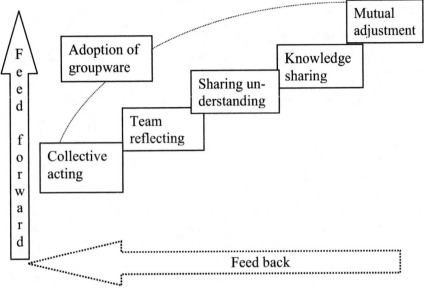

group learning processes and improve the model. A detailed data collection was conducted through semistructured interviews, observations in the field, and documents analysis.

Thirty-two interviews were employed lasting from 45 minutes to 2 hours, in total of 46 hours. Most of the interviews were individual, and also three group interviews were used because of the office environment. Some of the interviews took two meetings, as there was a need in additional clarification and information. We asked employees to describe the way a new system was introduced and group activities toward the system implementation. Postscripts of all 32 interviews were again discussed with interviewees. Analysis of data collected allowed operationalize the cooperative learning cycle regarding groupware implementation (Bondarouk & Sikkel, 2001b), see Table 2.

A SYSTEMATIC LEARNING APPROACH TO GROUPWARE IMPLEMENTATION

After having introduced the collaborative learning model in the previous section, we will now place it in the context of groupware implementation.

The proposition is to provide a learning atmosphere systematically and study its impact in two directions: *horizontal* (contextual constructs, adoption of groupware, indicators of stable use) and *vertical* (organizational learning climate,

Table 2: Operationalization of collaborative learning in groupware implementation

Collaborative learning processes	Activities
Collective acting	- Replication of instructions in usual job tasks - Searching for new techniques in a system - Testing new procedures
Team reflecting	- Discovering and interpreting a problem - Comparing with another experience - Critiquing ongoing use
Sharing understanding	- Demonstrating ongoing use - Asking for clarification - Discussing errors
Sharing knowledge	- Knowledge about intention of the system - Recognition of functional adequacy of a system - Comprehension of operating with the system
Mutual adjustment	- Developing of collective vision on a problem and a way to solve it. - Arrangements further learning activities - Evaluating intermediate results

Figure 3: The systematic learning approach for groupware implementation

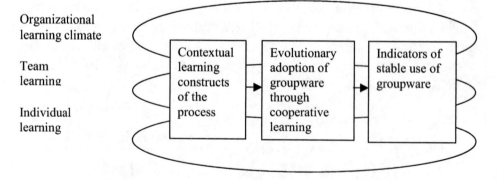

team learning, individual learning), see Figure 3.

A body of literature shows that four contextual constructs are important and influence the process of groupware implementation (Okamuro et al., 1994; Bikson,

Table 3: Learning contextual constructs for implementationo f groupware

Contextual variables	Indicators
Organizational learning climate	(a) Ensuring employee skills in use of groupware (b) Encouraging use of technology (c) Promoting effective communication
Team learning potential	(a) Interpersonal understanding (b) Interdependency (c) Psychological safety (d) Pro-activity in implementation problem solving
Individual learning towards groupware implementation	(a) Understanding of functional and technica features of technology (b) Knowledge and skills in software use (c) Attitudes about content and technical functionality of groupware (d) Involvement in the operating of groupwa
Technological prerequisites	(a) The role of technology in a company (b) Specification of software architecture for organizational context (c) Users' requirements (d) Enabling fruitful collaboration (e) Reliability and flexibility of technology

1996; Campion et al., 1996; Kinney & Panko, 1996; Klein & Sorra, 1996; Orlikowski, 1996; Mankin et al., 1997; Mark & Wulf, 1999; Nolinske & Millis, 1999; Pipek & Wulf, 1999; Druskat & Kayes, 2000). Each dimension consists of several items (Table 3).

Organizational Learning Climate

The discussion of this dimension is based on the management studies about organizational climate (Klein & Sorra, 1996; Schneider, 1990). Schneider (1990) defines climate as employees' "perceptions of the events, practices, and procedures and the kinds of behaviors that are rewarded, supported, and expected in a setting" (p. 384). Klein and Sorra (1996) detail this definition toward climate for the implementation of innovation and view it as "employees" shared summary perceptions of the extent to which their use of a specific innovation is rewarded, supported and expected within their organization" (p.1060).

In our view, *learning climate for technology implementation* is referred to the organizational environment in which skilled, active, and consistent use of technology is supported and encouraged. We have transferred the indicators given by Klein and Sorra (1996) to the interest of this study. If a company is about to implement a new technology, a strong *learning climate* within a company (department) may foster technology adaptation by (a) ensuring employee skills in use of groupware; (b) encouraging use of technology and disincentives for its avoidance; and (c) supporting effective user-user communication.

Group Learning Potential

We define the group learning potential as a group's ability to change its behavior through acquiring and sharing knowledge and examining what is helping team performance to continually improve it.

Interpersonal understanding (Druskat & Kayes, 2000) means that team-mates understand each other's concerns, preferences, tendencies, and strengths. Similar variables can be found in the literature: personal relationships (Kinney & Panko, 1996), awareness of teammates characteristics (Cannon-Bowers et al., 1995).

Close to this dimension would be interdependence (Sundstrom et al., 1990; Kagan, 1993; Campion et al., 1996; Nolinske & Millis, 1999). It is supposed that we are linked with others in a way so that we cannot succeed unless they do. There are mutual benefits of the work: our colleagues' performance benefits us, and our work profits them as well.

Psychological safety is defined as "shared belief about the consequences of interpersonal risk-taking" (Edmondson, 1999, p. 375). The construct implies that the group will not embarrass, reject, or punish someone for speaking up. Psycho-logical safety implies willingness of all parties for open discussions, but it differs from group cohesiveness.

Individual Learning Characteristics

Individual learning characteristics are (a) understanding of technologi-cal features, (b) knowledge and skills in software use, (c) attitudes about content and technical functionality of groupware, and (d) active involvement in the operating of groupware.

We state that an understanding of users' interpretations of a technology is critical to realize their interactions with it. To interact with technology, people have to make sense of it; and in the sense-making process, they develop their under-standing of the nature of technology.

Technological Prerequisites

Technology-related dimensions, or technological prerequisites: (a) the role of technology in a company; (b) specification of software architecture for an organizational context, (c) users' requirements, (d) enabling of collaboration, and (e) reliability and flexibility of technology. It should be noted that the main research interest concerning technological prerequisites is not on the technical features, but on the extent to which those technical characteristics are transferred into the needs of individuals and teams.

FUTURE WORK

In this chapter, we have proposed a model for implementation of collaborative technologies, which is regarded as a learning process. In fact, there are learning processes at different levels, ranging from the individual to the organizational level. Specific for groupware implementation, and pivotal in the model, is learning at the team level that supports stable use of collaborative technologies.

In a collaborative learning process, five elementary steps can be distinguished—collective acting, team reflecting, sharing understanding, sharing knowledge, and mutual adjustment—as elaborated above. We have operationalized these in the context of our case study research.

We believe that the model is useful, because it provides novel insights, highlighting issues relevant to implementation processes of collaborative technologies. We conjecture that a better learning climate in an organization could lead to a more successful implementation. Ultimately, the insights derived from this perspective should lead to ways to foster the learning climate. For the near future, we intend to consolidate the model by applying it to several case studies.

REFERENCES

Alavi, M. & Joachimsthaler, E. A. (1992). Revisiting DSS implementation research: A meta-analysis of the literature and suggestions for researchers. *MIS Quarterly, 16*, 95–113.

Baecker, R. M. (Ed.). (1993). *Readings in groupware and computer-suppored cooperative work: Assisting human-human collaboration.* San Mateo, CA: Morgan Kaufman.

Bannon, L. & Schmidt, K. (1989). CSCW: Four characters in search of a context. In Bowers, J. M. & Benford, S. D. (Eds.), *Proceedings First European Conference on Computer Supported Coooperative Work*, 3–16. Amsterdam: North Holland.

Baronas, A.-M. K. & Louis, M. R. (1988). Restoring a sense of control during implementation: How user involvement leads to system acceptance. *MIS Quarterly, 12*, 111–123.

Bentley, R., Appelt, W., Busbach, U., Hinrichts, E., Kerr, D., Sikkel., K., Trevor, J., & Woetzel, G. (1997). Basic support for cooperative work on the World Wide Web. *International Journal on Human-Computer Studies, 46*, 827–846.

Bikson, T. K. & Eveland, J. D. (1996). Groupware implementation: Reinvention in the sociotechnical frame. In Ackerman, M. (Ed.), *Proceedings of the ACM 1996 Conference on Computer-Supported Cooperative Work,* 428–437. New York, NY: ACM Press.

Bondarouk, T. & Sikkel, K. (2001a). A learning perspective on groupware implementation. In Khosrowpour, M. (Ed.), *Managing information technology in a global economy. Proceedings of the International IRMA Conference,* 701–703. Hershey, PA: Idea Group Publishing.

Bondarouk, T. & Sikkel, K. (2001b). Cooperative learning in groupware implementation. In Sikkel, K., Hettinga, M., Bondarouk, T., Schuurman, & J. G. (Eds.), *Learning groups—The role of learning processes in evolutionary implementation of groupware.* Report TI/SS/2001/064, Telematica Instituut, the Netherlands, December.

Campion, M. A., Papper, E. M. & Medsker, G. J. (1996). Relations between work team characteristics and effectiveness: A replication and extention. *Personnel Psychology, 49*, 429–452.

Cannon-Bowers, J. A., Tannenbaum, S. I., Salas, E. & Volpe, C. E. (1995). Defining competencies and establishing team training requirements. In Guzzo, R. A. and Salas, E. (Ed.), *Team effectiveness and decision making in organisations,* 333–380. San Francisco, CA: Jossey-Bass

Checkland, P. & Scholes, J. (1990). *Soft systems methodology in action.* Chichester, UK: John Wiley & Sons Ltd.

Crossan, M. M., Lane, H. W. & White, R. E. (1999). An organizational learning framework: from intuition to institution. *Academy of Management Review, 24,* 522–537.

DeSanctis, G. & Poole, M. (1994). Capturing the complexity in advanced technology use: Adaptive structuration theory. *Organization Science, 5,* 121–147.

Dixon, N. (1994). *The organizational learning cycle.* London: McGraw-Hill.

Druskat, V. U. & Kayes, D. C. (2000). Learning versus performance in short-term project teams. *Small Group Research, 31,* 328–353.

Edmondson, A. (1999). Psychological safety and learning behavior in work teams. *Administrative Science Quarterly, 44,* 350–383.

Ellis, C. A., Gibbs, S. J. & Rein, G. L. (1991). Groupware: Some issues and experiences. *Communications of the ACM, 34*(1), 38–58.

Gottschalk, P. (1999). Implementation predictors of strategic information systems plans. *Information & Management, 36*, 77–91.

Greif, I (Ed.). (1988). *Computer-supported cooperative work: A book of readings*. San Mateo, CA: Morgan Kaufman Publishers.

Griffith, T. L. (1996). Cognitive elements in the implementation of new technology: Can less information provide more benefits? *MIS Quarterly, 20*, 99–110.

Hendriks, P. (1999). Why share knowledge? The influence of ICT on the motivation for knowledge sharing. *Knowledge and Process Management, 6*, 91–100.

Hettinga, M. (2000). *Appropriation of teleconsultation*.

Hettinga, M., Schippers, M. & Schuurman, J. G. (2001). Invisible forces in favor of the status quo: Stimulating reflective restructuring. In Sikkel, K., Hettinga, M., Bondarouk, T. and Schuurman, J. G. (Eds.), *Learning groups—Report of a Workshop at the 7th European Conference on Computer Supported Cooperative Work*, Telematica Instituut, Enschede, The Netherlands.

Joshi, K. (1991). A model of users' perspective on change: The case of information systems technology implementation. *MIS Quarterly, 15*, 229–242.

Kagan, S. (1993). *Co-operative learning*. San Clemente, CA: Kagan.

Kim, D. H. (1993). The link between individual and organizational learning. *Sloan Management Review, 35*, 37–50.

Kinney, S. T. & Panko, R. R. (1996). Project teams: Profiles and member perceptions. *Proceedings of the 29th Hawaii International Conference on System Sciences*.

Klein, K. J. & Sorra, J. S. (1996). The challenge of innovation implementation. *Academy of Management Review, 21*, 1055–1080.

Kolb, D. A. (1984). *Experiential learning. Experience as the source of learning and development*. Englewood Cliffs, NJ: Prentice-Hall.

Lederer, A. L. & Salmela, H. (1996). Towards a theory of strategic information systems planning. *Journal of Strategic Information Systems, 5*, 237–253.

Lou, H. & Scamell, R. W. (1996). Acceptance of groupware: The relationships among use, satisfaction, and outcomes. *Journal of Organizational Computing and Electronic Commerce, 6*, 173–190.

Lucas, H. C. (1981). *Implementation—The key to successful information systems*. New York: Columbia University Press.

Maani, K. E. & Cavana, R. Y. (2000). *Systems thinking and modelling—Understanding change and complexity*. Englewood Cliffs, NJ: Prentice Hall.

Mankin, D., Cohen, S. G. & Bikson, T. K. (1997). Teams and technology: Tensions in participatory design. *Organizational Dynamics, 26*, 63–76.

Mark, G. & Wulf, V. (1999). Changing interpersonal communication through groupware use. *Behaviour & Information Technology, 18*, 385–395.

Nolinske, T. & Millis, B. (1999). Co-operative learning as an approach to pedagogy. *The American Journal of Occupational Therapy, 53*, 31–40.

Nunamaker, J. F., Dennis, A. R., Valacich, J. S., Vogel, D. R. & George, J. F. (1991). Electronic meeting systems to support group work. *Communications of the ACM, 34*(7), 40–61.

Nutt, P. C. (1986). Tactics of implementation. *Academy of Management Journal, 29,* 230–261.

Okamura, K., Orlikowski, W. J., Fujimoto, M. & Yates, J. (1994). Helping CSCW applications succeed: The role of mediators in the context of use. In Futura, R. & Neuwirth, C. (Eds.), *Proceedings of the Conference on Computer Supported Cooperative Work (CSCW '94)*, 55–65. New York: ACM Press.

Onstenk, J. H. A. M. (1995). Human resources development and on-the-job learning. In Mulder, M., Nijhof, W. J. & Brinkerhoff, R. O. (Eds.), *Corporate training for effective performance*. Boston, MA: Kluwer Academic Publishers.

Orlikowski, W. (1992). Learning from notes: Organizational issues in groupware implementation. *Proceedings of the Conference on Computer-Supported Cooperative Work (CSCW '92)*, 362–369. New York: ACM Press.

Orlikowski, W. (1993). CASE tools as organizational change: Investigating incremental and radical changes in systems development. *MIS Quarterly, 17*, 309-339.

Orlikowski, W. (1996). Evolving with notes: Organizational change around groupware technology. In Ciborra, C. U. (Ed.), *Groupware and teamwork*, 23–59. Chichester, UK: John Wiley & Sons Ltd.

Orlikowski, W. J. & Gash, C. (1994). Technological frames: Making sense of information technology in organisations. *ACM Transactions on Information Systems, 12*, 174–207.

Orlikowski, W. & Robey, D. (1991). Information technology and the structuring of organisations. *Information Systems Research, 2*, 143–169.

Pipek, V. & Wulf, V. (1999). A groupware's life. In Bødker, S., Kyng, M. & Schmidt, K. (Eds.), *Proceedings of the Sixth European Conference on Computer-Supported Cooperative Work*, 199–218. Dordrecht, The Netherlands: Kluwer Academic Publishers.

Robey, D., Boudreau, M.-C. & Rose, G. M. (2000). Information technology and organizational learning: A review and assessment of research. *Accounting Management and Information Technologies*, *10*, 125–155.

Robinson, M. (1991). Double-level languages and co-operative working. *Artificial Intelligence and Society*, *5*, 34–60.

Ruel, H. J. M. (2001). *The non-technical side of office technology; managing the clarity of the spirit and the appropriation of office technology. PhD thesis*. Enschede, the Netherlands: Twente University Press.

Sanderson, D. (1992). The CSCW implementation process: An interpretative model and case study of the implementation of a videoconference system. *Proceedings of the Conference on Computer Supported Cooperative Work (CSCW'1992)*, 370–377. New York, NY: ACM Press.

Schippers, M. C., Den Hartog, D. N. & Koopman, P. L. (2001). *Reflexivity in teams: The relation with trust, group potency, team leadership, and performance in work teams. Paper presented at the Academy of Management*, 3–8 August, Washington DC.

Schmidt, K. & Bannon, L. (1992). Taking CSCW seriously—Supporting articulation work. *Computer Supported Collaborative Work*, *1*, 7–40.

Schneider, B. (1990). The climate for service: An application of the climate construct. In Schneider, B. (Ed.), *Organisational climate and culture*, 383–412. San Francisco, CA: Jossey-Bass.

Stahl, G. (2002). Contributions to a theoretical framework for CSCL. Manuscript submitted for publication.

Suchman, L. (1987). *Plans and situated actions. The problem of human-machine communication.* Cambridge, U.K.: Cambridge University Press.

Sundstrom, E., Meuse, K.P. De & Futrel, D. (1990). Work teams. *American Psychologist*, *45*, 120–133.

Tucker, A. L., Edmondson, A. C. & Spear, S. (2001). *When problem solving prevents organizational learning.* Harvard Business School working paper 01–073.

Volkoff, O. & Ivey (1999). Using the structurational model of technology to analyse an ERP implementation. *Proceedings of the Fifth Americas Conference on Information Systems,* 235–237. Milwaukee, WI, August.

Watkins, K. & Marsick, V. (Eds.) (1996). *Creating the learning organization.* Alexandria, VA: ASTD.

Chapter XII

A Framework for Building Learning Organizations

Sushil K. Sharma
Ball State University, USA

Jatinder N. D. Gupta
The University of Alabama in Huntsville, USA

ABSTRACT

The concept of the learning organization that strives continually to develop its people and processes will be an accepted philosophy of all competitive organizations in the future. Organizations are increasingly being challenged to leverage learning, as it has been widely articulated that knowledge creation and continuous learning at the individual, team, and organizational levels may be the only source of sustainable competitive advantage. Continuous learning is essential for surviving, let alone prospering, in dynamic and competitive environments. Because of this increased emphasis on learning, there has been a tremendous interest in the concept of learning organizations and the capabilities required to build learning organizations. Organizations of the future will not be able to expand into new markets and win market share unless they have a framework (technologies, people, processes, and methodologies) to use their past knowledge to gain a competitive advantage. Organizations of the 21st century have to use the latest information technology and methodologies that can enable them to be cost effective, faster, flexible, and more competitive. Despite the growing interest in learning organizations, there are knowledge gaps in understanding about how to exploit technologies to create a suitable framework for learning organization. Our chapter attempts to suggest a framework for building learning organizations and shows the use of systemic approach to implement our proposed framework to create learning organizations.

INTRODUCTION

As we move into the 21st century, the need for rapid access to relevant knowledge has never been greater. The business world is becoming increasingly competitive, and the demand for innovative products and services is very high. The Internet revolution has requires organizations to change. Today, organizations have to be much more flexible and open than they used to be 5 years ago and need entirely different strategies for competitive advantage. Organizations are becoming more knowledge-intensive in order to learn from past experiences and from others to reshape themselves and to change in order to survive and prosper. Organizations need to utilize knowledge across processes and functions to become knowledge-driven organizations or learning organizations. A learning organization is an organization that has an enhanced capacity to learn, adapt, and change (Levine, 2001). Matrix and network structures and the design of organizations are some of the developments in this direction that have reduced the barriers between work groups. The distinguishing features of a learning organization are shown in Figure 1.

At all levels, the explosive growth of information technology, the Internet, and the rapid rise of the so-called "New Economy," based on knowledge-intensive industries, has led to growing recognition of the importance of knowledge as a critical resource for competitive advantage. Although many definitions exist, learning organizations are generally described as those that continuously acquire, process, and disseminate knowledge about markets, products, technologies, and business processes. This knowledge is often based on experience, experimentation, and information provided by customers, suppliers, competitors, and other sources. Learning at individual and organizational levels involves the transformation of data (uninterrupted information) into knowledge (interpreted information). This chapter presents the concept of learning organizations—learning, memory, and organizational learning—and how they can be supported by today's information technologies. We first describe the concept of learning organizations and then discuss knowledge management, which is becoming a necessary resource and asset for learning organizations. This is followed by a discussion of the suggested framework for building learning organizations and the use of systemic approach for its implementation.

Figure 1: Distinguishing features of learning organizations

Human capital (people power)
Structural capital (databases, patents, intellectual property, and related items

E-VOLVING ORGANIZATIONS

The new economy with its three pillars: e-business, knowledge management, and partnership (as shown in Figure 2) is transforming organizations into e-organizations. E-business is changing trading processes, realigning internal business processes, and introducing many businesses to new channels to reach end users or customers. For example, moving to e-procurement can serve to cut sourcing costs and free valuable purchasing specialists for more strategic sourcing tasks, such as vendor negotiation, relationship management and more thoughtful analysis of current purchasing activities (Moore, 2000).

The organizations of the 21st century must attract the most valuable knowledge workers and involve their suppliers and customers in a strategic alliance for business growth. Because total quality management (TQM), business process reengineering (BPR), and other schemes to improve productivity may not be a source of competitive advantage in the future but a minimum entry standard to compete in the global market (Thorne & Smith, 2000). Evolving organizations of the future would have the following factors of their core competencies (Thorne & Smith, 2000).

Responsiveness

Responsiveness is key in e-commerce and e-business and is the prime ingredient of e-volving organizations to compete in hypercompetitive markets. Speed, speed and more speed is central to a knowledge-based economy. Organizations have to make investments in technology to transact business at higher speeds (Moore, 2000).

Figure 2: Pillars of the new economy

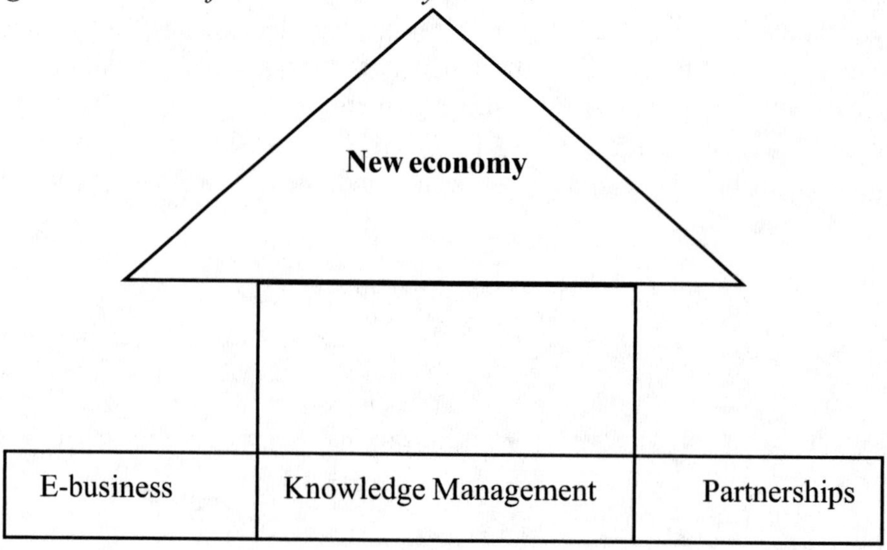

Global Markets

Economic, technological, and ecological forces intensify demands for global integration and uniformity. The advancements in information and communication technologies have forced the organizations to market their products and services in global markets. The Internet revolution has allowed customers to shop at any time from anywhere. The Internet has not only changed our lifestyles but has also transformed businesses radically. It is the backbone for the new digital economy that is changing business models around the globe. The Internet has introduced easily usable and low-cost commerce by streamlining interactions, products, and payments from customer to companies and companies to companies. Through the combination of interactivity, networking, multimedia, and data processing, Internet commerce offers a wide variety of e-commerce opportunities. The commerce includes trading of physical goods and of intangibles such as information. This encompasses all the trading steps: on-line marketing, ordering, payment, and support for delivery. It provides electronic support for collaboration between companies, including online collaborative design and engineering.

The Internet has also empowered customers by providing access to a vast amount of information, as well as knowledge about a variety of products and services. This has led to the globalization of markets. As the technology-driven economy helps to remove trade barriers across nations, markets can be challenged by competitors from anywhere on the globe. On one side, this global presence through a geographically diversified online market will enable organizations to take advantage of economies of scale and global brand recognition in their search for sustainable competitive advantage, but on the other side, it poses a threat of intense competition (Thorne & Smith, 2000). Recognition of one global market and electronic interfaces that eliminate international boundaries creates increasing pressures for employers and employees. E-culture stresses worldwide learning, customer segments in many countries, and 24/7 service (Moore, 2000).

Internet-Based Businesses and Efficient Supply Chains

Evolving organizations have to offer electronic commerce for connectivity and communication between companies in order to benefit from on-line marketing, ordering, payment, and support for delivery. The Internet is cheap, interactive, ubiquitous, global, is one-to-one, and provides a 24-hour business. Business processes like procurement, supply chain management, and customer relationship management depicted in Figure 3 prominently influence organizations to streamline business processes. Each of these processes can be made more effective and efficient through the use of Internet and e-commerce concepts.

Supply chain management is the coordination of material, information, and financial flows between and among all the participating enterprises. Traditional supply chains are based on fragmented information storage and transfer between companies. Modern supply chains using Internet-based technology enable continuous and rapid information sharing between various enterprises. With such an Internet-based system, decision makers along various enterprises in the supply chain can share a common base of readily available sales and inventory information (Gupta & Sharma, 2001). The integration of the supplier into the organizational structure adds value to the organization's customers. As price competition ceases to be a global force, reducing costs is not enough. The suppliers need to add value as well. Customers and suppliers will work together and form interorganizational teams that will facilitate improved communication between organizations and increase the rate of learning. Benefits will be gained from the effects of sharing mutual experience and knowledge, which will result in the whole chain becoming better, aligned with the final customer requirements and objectives (Thorne & Smith, 2000).

Customer Relationship Management

Customer resource management is aimed at acquiring new business customers, enhancing the profitability of existing customers, and retaining profitable customers for life. Companies are profiling their most valuable customers and using adept marketing and product development strategies to target those customers. Evolving organizations are concentrating on customer relationships, as customers are becoming strategic assets for success. Most companies have already started interacting with customers on-line and have started offering many self-service transactions to their customers. Organizations of the future will compete based on customers as strategic assets, which will focus organizations on adopting customer relationship management systems.

Figure 3: Three important business processes of organizations

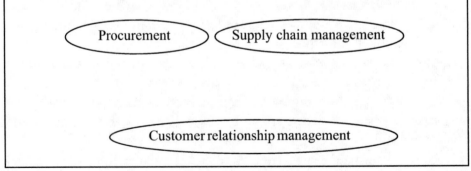

E-Procurement

Many Internet-based on-line marketplaces are currently available for maximizing the efficiency of business-to-business on-line procurement process. By acquiring millions of products from thousands of suppliers, on-line marketplaces are helping the procurement processes. This, in turn, can result in about 35% cost savings in the procurement of raw materials. Companies, by outsourcing their purchase functions, are improving their efficiencies and cost reductions. At the same time, companies have wider choices, global reach, one-stop shopping, more efficient price discovery, and better pricing than traditional procurement.

Virtual Organizational Structure

The workforce for many organizations will be decentralized and even home-based via interactive networks. In recent years, the general trend has been toward the decentralization of organizations. The decision-making process is being moved downward through the organization, from managers to subordinates. Not only has decision making been detached from managers, some employees have been physically removed from the workplace through decentralization. Telecommuting is the ultimate extension of decentralization, as the individual is placed in an environment physically removed from the organization. The merging of information technology and telecommunications has seen a revolution in our society that will continue and allow for communication from any number of locations. Teleworking, therefore, could be viewed as a natural progression, as organizations grow to the point where they must grant more autonomy to their employees. The pragmatic benefits of telecommuting are related to employee productivity, expansion of the workforce and ultimately the ability to conduct business anytime and anywhere in the form of a "Virtual Corporation."

Telecommuting extends geographic recruiting boundaries and makes the company more attractive by offering new and flexible work structures. It provides employees alternatives to lengthy and costly commuting and more flexibility in choosing their city of residence. Telecommuting enables satellite offices to be in nonpremium areas. Absenteeism related to travel and geographic barriers, as well as emergency childcare situations are eliminated. Overall, telecommuting benefits employees mentally and emotionally and has the potential for reduction of long-term disability costs. The successful organizations have to make a shift from a control-based to a trust-based system through dedicated, trustworthy, and loyal employees (Thorne & Smith, 2000).

Technological Innovation

Organizations need to embrace technology innovations as their priority to create dynamic and flexible business processes in order to meet the requirements of dynamic global markets. Organizations must use sophisticated technological innovations to improve work processes and accommodate horizontal workflows by providing cross-functional information flows and performance feedback. The technology of the future will enable organizations to be cheaper, faster, flexible and more competitive (Thorne & Smith, 2000). Technological innovations will help organizations in many ways by removing redundant processes and creating knowledge management-oriented systems, etc. Innovation and continuous improvement are based on the company's ability to be creative and to learn (Martensen & Dahlgaard, 1999). Technology helps to integrate with partners. In the new economy, no single firm can do it all. Firms develop strategic alliances and partnerships to take advantage of core competencies and also to exploit economies of scale.

Intellectual Capitalism

Information and communication technologies are playing a pivotal role in the emergence of intellectual capitalism. Globally, organizations and their human resource departments are struggling to attract talented employees. Organizations that are successful in that endeavor then become concerned with retaining the knowledge and experience of those sought-after workers. Intellectual capitalism can be defined as employees, their knowledge of products and services, and their creativity and innovation that act as a crucial source of knowledge assets. In broad terms, intellectual capitalism can be interpreted as resulting from a confluence of a capitalist economy and a knowledge or information economy in which intellectual capital in some sense is dominant (Granstrand, 2000).

Companies must find ways to encourage creativity and to nurture and utilize each employee's unique knowledge and capabilities. World-class organizations will increasingly treat their employees as their most important assets. Despite the pervasive influence of technological innovation, the most successful enterprises will be the ones with the quickest reactions, innovative management, and the best people (Thorne & Smith, 2000). A new strength of the knowledge and creativity of the workforce has to be taken into consideration to create the competitive advantage in the next century.

Team-Based Organizational Structure

Leadership of the organizations will be transformed from an individual to a team structure. Advancements in technology have already made it possible to have virtual teams. Team-based organizational structures will provide quick and better solutions than function-oriented structures. Participative management through teams will increasingly replace the hierarchical structures of today. Individuals, along with their team members, with specific knowledge and competencies will combine to make decisions to achieve relevant organizational goals. Organizations that are able to align the collective productive and creative energies of their people through teams will be able to maintain and expand their competitive advantage (Thorne & Smith, 2000).

Customers Not as Targets but as Partners

Organizations are becoming more customer-centric rather than product-centric. To meet the expectations of customers, it is becoming desirable that organizations involve customers as partners for product design, innovations, and services. Organizations need to create a new organizational culture whereby customers will be treated as partners in the business. They have to extend their resources to customers for their involvement in innovation and creativity. Organizations can then offer the customer higher stakes in the business and may, in turn, retain and create more loyal customers.

Due to intense competition in global markets, organizations will require a good database of consumer preferences to analyze their likes and dislikes. Organizations can have a real competitive advantage if they have systems to determine and influence market behavior by aligning organizational activities with emerging trends in global consumer preferences (Thorne & Smith, 2000).

Becoming customer-centric is easier said than done. Having knowledge about customers is critical to the success of an enterprise. Today, due to global connectivity, competitors can easily access information about others' products and services. Deriving value from customer knowledge can be a competitive advantage and contributor to success. Having knowledge about customers can give an organization a "first mover advantage." This is so because an organization can use this knowledge to design and offer new or improved products and services that may better serve customer wants and needs. Simultaneously, organizations can reduce inventory requirements and unused manufacturing or service capacities once it knows patterns of customer demand (Lesser et al., 2000).

Managing customer knowledge requires a range of knowledge creation activities including acquiring, capturing, and storing data about customers, suppliers, and competitors. Once the knowledge is captured, organizations need to have an integrated delivery mechanism through which it can diffuse knowledge across organizational units. Employees can then incorporate it into day-to-day business processes to realize its full value. (Lesser et al., 2000).

Focus on Specialization

Organizations will need to be tightly focused and highly specialized. The emphasis will be on distinguishing core capabilities, supporting core processes, and all other activities will be outsourced. Organizations will need to focus on its core values in order to make work meaningful and attract, motivate and retain outstanding people. Organizational purpose will be more than just increasing profit or market share; it will reflect an ongoing commitment to adding value to employees, customers, and the wider community (Thorne & Smith, 2000).

LEARNING ORGANIZATIONS

The concept of learning organizations is catching attention, and organizations have begun to think about building learning organizations. Learning is the company's ability to adapt to a rapidly changing environment. Continuous learning is essential for surviving—let alone prospering—in dynamic and competitive environments (Popper & Lipshitz, 2000). Through learning capabilities, organizations can exploit those opportunities rapidly, which other competitors are not able to foresee. Organizations need to create a knowledge of products, markets, processes, etc., in the form of learning for sustainable competitive advantage (Ellerman, 1999). This is only possible if organizations have knowledge creation and continuous learning at the individual, team, and organizational levels (Ellinger et al., 1999).

Learning takes place at two levels—individual and organizational. Hedberg (1981) suggests that organizations do not have brains, but they have cognitive systems and memories (Popper & Lipshitz, 2000). As individuals develop their personalities, personal habits, and beliefs over time, organizations develop their views and ideologies (Hedberg, 1981). Learning at individual and organizational levels involves the transformation of data (uninterpreted information) into knowledge (interpreted information). Individual learning and organizational learning are similar, except that organizational learning involves an additional phase, dissemination, i.e., the transmission of information and knowledge among different persons and organizational units (Popper & Lipshitz, 2000).

Learning Organizations—Definition

In 1990, Peter M. Senge introduced the concept of the "learning organization" to the business world in his landmark book *The Fifth Discipline: The Art and Practice of the Learning Organization*. Learning organizations are generally described as those that continuously acquire, process, and disseminate knowledge about markets, products, technologies, and business processes (Slater & Narver, 1994). This knowledge is often based on experience, experimentation, and information provided by customers, suppliers, competitors, and other sources (Ellinger et al., 1999). A learning organization is a complex interrelationship of systems composed of people, technology, practices, and tools designed so that new information is embraced (Simon, 1999). Learning organizations are organizations that embed institutionalized learning mechanisms into a learning culture (Popper & Lipshitz, 2000).

Organizations are shifting their structures from a command-and-control orientation to a more lean and matrix kind to facilitate and empower employees for their learning. Today, organizations have to attract and motivate the best people; reward, recognize, train, educate, and improve them (Ellinger et al., 1999) so that the highly skilled and more independent workers can exploit technologies to create knowledge in learning organizations (Thorne & Smith, 2000). Learning organizations see learning as a system involving vision and strategy, culture and values, leadership, structure, systems, and processes (Stratigos, 2001).

KNOWLEDGE MANAGEMENT

Instantaneous communications have created the opportunities for people around the world to come together in global forums and virtual teams to create and share knowledge. As we move into the 21st century, the need for rapid access to relevant knowledge has never been greater (Srikantaiah, 2000). The business world is increasingly competitive, and the demand for innovative products and services is even greater. In this century of creativity and ideas, the most valuable resources available to any organization are human skills, expertise, and relationships. Knowledge management (KM) is about capitalizing on these precious assets (Duffy, 2001). Most companies do not capitalize on the wealth of expertise in the form of knowledge scattered across their levels (Hansen et al., 2001).

Knowledge management is quickly gaining recognition as a key determinant of value in the marketplace, organizational success, and competitive edge. Today, companies compete not only on the basis of product, service, and operational superiority, but also through the enhanced management of their corporate memory and intellectual assets. They are beginning to realize their edge lies in how they manage the efficient flow and transfer of knowledge across the organization (Silver, 2000). The recently published report *Knowledge Management Software Market Forecast and Analysis, 2000/2004* estimated that the total KM software market would reach $5.4 billion by 2004 (Duffy, 2001).

A review of business literature indicates there are many definitions of knowledge management posited by various researchers and practitioners. A few of them are:

Gartner group describes; "Knowledge management is a discipline that promotes an integrated approach to identifying, managing, and sharing all of an enterprise's information needs. These information assets may include databases, documents, policies, and procedures as well as previously unarticulated expertise and experience resident in individual workers" (Lee Sr., 2000).

"Knowledge management is an intelligent process by which raw data is gathered and transformed into information elements. These information elements are assembled and organized into context-relevant structures that represent knowledge" (Onge, 2001).

"KM as a formal process that engages an organization's people, processes, and technology in a solution that captures knowledge and delivers it to the right people at the right time" (Duffy, 2001).

Arthur Andersen defines KM as "the discipline of enabling individuals in an organization to collectively acquire, share, and leverage knowledge to achieve business objectives" (Duffy, 2001).

"As its name suggests, knowledge management is concerned with systematic, effective management and utilization of an organization's knowledge resources. It encompasses the creation, storage, arrangement, retrieval, and distribution of an organization's knowledge" (Anonymous, 2000).

"Knowledge is a fluid mix of framed values, contextual information, and expert insight that provides a framework for evaluating and incorporating new experiences and information. It originates and is applied in the minds of "knowers." In organizations, it often becomes embedded not only in documents or repositories, but also in organizational routines, processes, practices, and norms." (Prusak & Davenport, 1998; Phillips & Vollmer, 2000).

The common factor in all of the definitions is the recognition of the enormous value that human resources contribute to the knowledge of an organization. Regarding knowledge creation, organizations have information about products, services, processes stored in various systems such as databases, file servers, Web pages, e-mails, and enterprise resource planning (ERP). If all of this information is stored centrally and is available and accessible to all of the employees in the form of knowledge, it will not only reduce the time searching for data to make better business decisions throughout the enterprise, but also provide decision makers with more time for innovation and creativity (Hammond, 2001). Organizations need to create enterprise information portals of knowledge that store a wide variety of structured and unstructured data sources in the form of knowledge, and this knowledge will be accessible to all employees through easy Web-based interfaces. Information centers, market intelligence, and learning are converging to form knowledge management functions (Stratigos, 2001).

What is Knowledge?

Data is defined as a series of observations, measurements, or facts in the form of numbers, words, sounds, and/or images. When this data is processed, and organized into a context, it becomes information (Roberts, 2000). Data is simply an observation of states, which may have little context associated with it. (Lee Sr., 2000). Information is defined as data that has been arranged into a meaningful pattern (Roberts, 2000). Data that has been endowed with relevance and purpose is information (Lee Sr., 2000).

Knowledge is defined as the application and productive use of information. Knowledge is more than information, because it involves an awareness or understanding gained through experience, familiarity or learning (Roberts, 2000). Information embedded and synthesized in the brain is knowledge. Knowledge by its nature is highly personal and extremely difficult to transfer (Lee Sr., 2000).

Knowledge can be codified or embodied in a tangible form in software systems. This is known as explicit knowledge. Another type of knowledge, which is known as tacit knowledge, is noncodified knowledge that is acquired via the informal take-up of learning behaviors and procedures. It is often referred to as know-how (Roberts, 2000).

Knowledge can be gained by analyzing documents, database records by observing business processes or operations, by performing specific tasks individually, by participating in collaborative activities, or by a combination of these and other methods (Anonymous, 2000). Knowledge can be created inside an organization, or it is acquired from external sources. KMs major objective is to connect people with people and stimulate collaboration (Duffy, 2000). Knowledge management relies on the melding of three elements: process, technology, and culture (Phillips & Vollmer, 2000). A successful knowledge management implementation requires cultivators of change at all levels of the organization (Phillips & Vollmer, 2000).

Knowledge Management Tools and Technologies

Information and communication technologies are helping the organizations for creation and exploitation of knowledge that is seen as a predominant part in the creation of new economy (Roberts, 2000). New technologies also provide opportunities for transferability of knowledge across time and space. Figure 4 describes the architecture of KM tools and technologies. There are five layers of KM infrastructure. Each is described below (Sharma & Gupta 2001).

Communication Systems Layer

The communication systems layer represents all the communication systems involved such as local area network (LAN) or intranet, extranet, and Web or

Internet. Organizations need to have their communication systems in place before they can manage knowledge.

Enterprise Data Source Layer

The enterprise data source layer provides the base or platform upon which KM solutions are built. It consists of repositories for unstructured data (i.e., document and content management) and structured data (i.e., databases, e-mail) and groupware, etc. (Duffy, 2001). Companies use databases and ERP systems for structured data and varieties of document management systems for unstructured data.

Knowledge Repository Layer

The knowledge repository layer mainly consists of repositories for unstructured data (i.e., document and content management), structured data (i.e., data warehousing, generation, and management), and groupware for supporting the collaboration needed for knowledge (Duffy, 2001). This layer has the content management component of KM that would take care of requirements of KM initiatives through a process that involves capture, storage, access, selection, and document publication of text retrieval, and document management. Data is stored in databases or in tables as database fields. These database tables and fields are mapped into the intuitive query tools that endusers will eventually see on their desktops. This knowledge repository is a virtual entity that transforms data and information into knowledge. At the lowest level, the knowledge warehouse consists of raw data relevant to customer orders, receipts, inventory, procurement processes, supplier performance status, and a host of other data streams. One level up is where information is converted into knowledge such as customer profiles and resource capacity versus order demand (Onge, 2001).

Middleware Layer

The middleware layer integrates the applications of knowledge repository and enterprise information portals.

End User Application Layer

The end user application layer represents the user interface into the applications and knowledge. Because the Web is used as a medium for interface, it uses web-based interactive tools to access knowledge from knowledge management systems. Here, KM solutions are built in the form of enterprise information portals (EIPs). EIPs will provide integrated access to heterogeneous types of data. EIP provide access to structured and unstructured data, through easy Web-based query interface. Enterprise information portals (EIP) integrate access to information and applications to enhance the decision support and productivity of the user for the user. EIP functionality ranges from access to structured data, to classifying and searching unstructured data, to supporting collaborative processes. Portals provide a single point of entry for all the disparate sources of knowledge and information both within and outside an organization, usually through the Internet or a company intranet. Portals need to be fully integrated with legacy systems to support collaboration and teams working across diverse communities. Portals help companies interact with their customers, business partners, suppliers, and employees through on-line tools (Silver, 2000).

Internet as Tool for KM

There are a variety of information retrieval and organization tools that help to pull information from texts in heterogeneous formats—such as PDF files, e-mails, and Web pages, and convert them to a single homogeneous form (Adams, 2001). The Internet provides an opportunity to share, access, and use information resources with all those who matter to enhance business efficiency. Through a Web-based interface, the Internet also helps to manage the asset of knowledge to employee and customer satisfaction.

Figure 4: Knowledge management tools and technologies

Layer	Tools and Technologies
End user application layer	Enterprise information portal (EIP) and Web-based access system
Middleware layer	XML technology and various routing and retrieval algorithms
Knowledge repository layer	Data warehouse, data marts, document management systems, groupware applications
Enterprise data source layer	Databases, ERP, groupware, document management systems, e-mail, etc.
Communication systems layer	Systems: LAN, intranet, extranet, and internet

The Concept of an Intelligent Enterprise

Intelligent enterprises are those where knowledge management and other business intelligence (BI) solutions provide the in-depth analytical capabilities needed to turn raw data into actionable knowledge for an enterprise. In an intelligent enterprise, various information systems are integrated with knowledge gathering and analyzing tools for data analysis, and dynamic end-user querying of a variety of enterprise data sources (Hammond, 2001). These solutions offer enterprises the ability to improve customer services and partner relationships and to create marketable knowledge products from their own internal data.

Intelligent enterprises make all employees more informed and better equipped to reduce unwarranted costs of production and delivery and ultimately enhance revenue. Intelligent enterprises have customers, suppliers and other partners embedded into a single integrated system. Customers can view their own purchasing habits, and suppliers can see the demand pattern that may help them decide to offer volume discounts, etc. This information can help all customers, suppliers, and enterprises to analyze data and provide them competitive advantage. The intelligence of a company is not only available to internal users but can even be leveraged by selling it to other consumers who may be interested (Clegg, 1999).

Architecturally, intelligent enterprises have three layers. The first layer is where all the data is collected and stored in a variety of information systems. The second layer provides tools for organizing, cleansing, and analyzing data with the help of many analysis tools. The third layer is a translation layer. The translation layer between enterprise data sources and the end-user application simplifies user interaction with the enterprise data. The translation layer helps end users execute or develop their own self-service queries or data products of enterprise. Web-based interface systems with thin client architecture means no software installation on the client end and possibly no additional server hardware. Web interface of intelligent enterprise securely distribute information derived from this data to all interested customers such as suppliers or partners that could use the data to better target their own marketing programs or make enhancements in their operations. Organizations can more efficiently leverage their information resources and, in turn, make better use of an organization's human resources.

Creating intelligent enterprises will not be a easy exercises as an enterprise may have to overcome tremendous hurdles in bringing disparate enterprise data sources into a cohesive data warehouse or knowledge management system.

A FRAMEWORK FOR BUILDING LEARNING ORGANIZATIONS

Learning organizations require a framework that encourages knowledge-creation, storage, and collaborative systems that enable knowledge capture and access. We propose an integrated approach to build learning organizations. Our suggested framework is consistent with and requires the systemic approach for its implementation.

In the systemic approach, technology creates discontinuities in complex systems and interaction of those systems. One of the salient characteristics of systemic behavior is the accelerating nature of change. Orlikowski and Barley (2001) argue that because of important epistemological differences between the fields of information technology and organization studies, much can be gained from greater interaction between them. They further suggest that the transformations currently occurring in the nature of work and organizing cannot be understood without considering the technological changes and the institutional contexts that are reshaping economic and organizational activity (Orlikowski & Barley, 2001). Orlikowski and Hofman (1997) further suggest that organizations need an improvisational change model about managing the introduction and ongoing use of information technologies to support the more flexible, complex, and integrated structures and processes demanded in organizations. Adopting a new and comprehensive systemic approach to analysis and solution of complex problems can indeed make great progress. For knowledge management (KM), continuous improvement must be made in the knowledge, processes, skills, and tools necessary to be ever more effective and efficient. Based on a thorough understanding of the new global paradigm and models of risk behavior, we can apply proven tools for systemic intervention or redirection.

Using the systemic approach, a learning organization framework requires technology to support the capturing and sharing of people's knowledge, promoting collaboration, and providing unhindered access to an extensive range of information. Technology must support all activities involved in the knowledge life cycle (e.g., capture, organization, retrieval, distribution, and maintenance). (Duffy, 2000). KM infrastructure would be an appropriate technological infrastructure to support a learning organization framework. KM infrastructure (tools and technologies) provides the platform upon which learning can be built. KM infrastructure includes repositories for unstructured data (i.e., document and content management), structured data (i.e., data warehousing, generation, and management), and groupware that supports the collaboration needed for knowledge sharing. It also includes tools like e-mail for other forms of interpersonal communication required for the efficient, time, and location-independent exchange of information (Duffy,

2001). Our framework suggests that learning organizations should have a knowledge transfer network in place. This network should consist of a communications infrastructure for facilitating effective communication. Additionally, an organizational memory, an establishment of KM infrastructure, a human asset infrastructure to encourage participation and willingness of people, and an infrastructure for collaboration should be in place (Srikantaiah, 2000). These components of the proposed framework are shown in Figure 5 and described in detail further.

Knowledge Transfer Network—A Communications Infrastructure for Facilitating Effective Communication

The prime component of learning organizations will be an effective communication infrastructure to diffuse knowledge effectively. Unless there is a strong communication infrastructure in place, employees are not able to communicate and thus cannot transfer knowledge. This is especially true when people are located in many organizations at different geographic locations. Companies can use Internet and intranets for creating the knowledge transfer network. People can use the discussion rooms, and bulletin boards for meetings as well as for display of information. Many experts (knowledge workers) are often quiet by nature and reserved about sharing their ideas. Some may have inhibitions to share in-group. Therefore, bulletin boards may provide an opportunity for those individuals to post their messages and information that could be vital for knowledge creation. Organizations should create the ability to intelligently use the knowledge already inherent within it as well as the new intellectual capital created daily, and they should use technology to ensure efficient knowledge transfer (Lee Sr., 2000).

Figure 5: A framework for building learning organizations

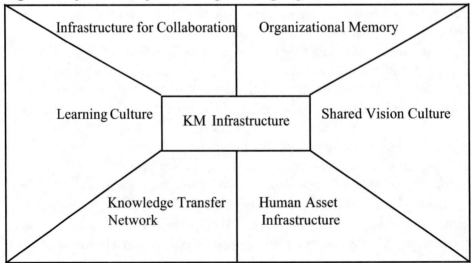

Retention of Organizational Memory

Organizational memory keeps a record of knowledge resources. Organizational memory systems in terms of records and record-keeping systems are valuable knowledge resources. Recorded information, whether in human-readable or electronic form, is an important embodiment of an organization's knowledge and intellectual capital (Roberts, 2000). It is essential to have a strong organizational memory system so that access of information or knowledge could be provided to everyone at any time (Croasdell, 2001).

Establishment of KM Infrastructure

The KM infrastructure, in terms of tools and technologies (hardware as well as software), should be established so that knowledge can be created from any new events or activity on a continual basis. This is the most important component of a learning organization. New knowledge can only be created for exchange if KM infrastructure is established effectively. KM infrastructure will have a repository of knowledge, distribution systems to distribute the knowledge to the members of organization, and a facilitator system for creation of new knowledge. A knowledge-based infrastructure will foster the creation of knowledge and provide an integrated system to share and diffuse the knowledge in the organization (Srikantaiah, 2000).

Human Asset Infrastructure—Participation and Willingness of People

Learning organizations will need high participation and willingness of their members to develop and create knowledge. As mentioned earlier, human intelligence plays an important role in understanding the behavior and pattern of products and processes. These patterns in the form of the knowledge component are added to existing knowledge for further diffusion in the organization. Learning organizations also need high involvement of people for assimilating the knowledge on a continual basis. Human asset infrastructure helps to identify and utilize the special skills of people who can create business value. There has to be a strong commitment of people to continuous experimentation and the ability to learn from the past. Organizations will also have to create an atmosphere where people feel comfortable to exchange ideas and knowledge with others (Srikantaiah, 2000). Organizations should value their people as their vital human asset infrastructure.

Infrastructure for Collaboration

Learning organizations not only draw upon the strengths of internal people but also may involve outside experts as consultants or strategic partners for creation of knowledge. The key to competitive advantage and improving customer satisfaction lies in the ability of organizations to form learning alliances; these being strategic partnerships based on a business environment that encourages mutual (and reflective) learning between partners (Holt et al., 2000). Organizations can utilize their strategy framework to identify partners and collaborators for enhancing the value chain. It would be mandatory to tap the expertise or knowledge of outsourced solutions into an organizational knowledge repository. A learning organization environment dictates decentralization of information resources (Srikantaiah, 2000).

Systemic Approach for Learning Organizations

Figure 6 shows the systemic relationship of technology for the creation of knowledge management systems for building learning organizations. Information technology (IT) acquisition and implementation along with people's expertise is primarily and essentially aimed at developing work templates and models, manualization, process documentation, and encoding into electronic formats of information for knowledge work, customer satisfaction, and business performance. So, IT acquisition and implementation become the processes to create work with which templates and models, process documentation, and encode into electronic formats as product. KM initiatives may evolve new paradigms. New paradigms may need new technologies, and new technology may need new information technology (IT), acquisition, and implementation (Bacon and Fitzgerald, 2001).

Using technology, organizations can codify the knowledge that is generated by the processes and the people involved. Codification can involve creation of new concepts. Teams doing design, R&D, or innovation often find themselves inventing new terminologies to capture the sense of an emerging new idea and provide a

Figure 6: The relationship between IT and knowledge management for building learning organizations

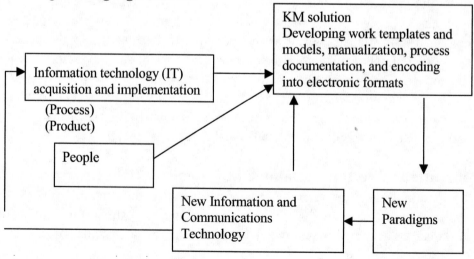

vehicle for group communication and imaginative thinking. New terms like "ubiquitous computing," "intelligent house," "reflective employee," and "learning organization" help communicate concepts that were tacit among those who first found them useful. The conversion from tacit to explicit knowledge provides a new framework for appreciating familiar procedures such as developing work templates and models, processing documentation, and encoding into electronic formats. Codification becomes an important step in knowledge management. Codification can take the form of work templates. Work templates are useful, workable documents or models with embedded experience and skill. They are knowledge artifacts worth preserving for future reuse. Reusing them creates value by saving time, money, and expertise. Process documentation is another form. It is a detailed description of how a process was undertaken. More than keeping a record, its purpose may be to document who, how, and why certain decisions were reached, to track expenses and incomes, or to evaluate the performance of every participant. It is useful for evaluative review of what went wrong and what went well, and why. If a team is a high-performance team, the process documentation seeks to codify their best practices for transfer and reuse by other teams. Process documentation becomes a learning device. The systemic approach involves linking KM initiatives with existing systems and core activities of the organization.

While a systemic approach is expected to be comprehensive, it also needs to be simple and flexible. Learning organizations are possible only when KM systems are integrated fully with customer, vendor, and employee programs. Organizations may assimilate codification via establishing collaborations with inside and outside experts. Organizations may institutionalize collaborative relationships and also may design systems for continuous capture and control of knowledge. Organizations may alter existing systems to accommodate new ideas or knowledge. Systemic approaches to incorporate KM may lead to change of structures and processes as well as to more diverse people in the organization. Resulting realignments often entail mutual learning and adjustment. Organizations use different methods to incorporate a systemic approach to learning from employees and the processes.

CONCLUSIONS

The concept of a learning organization that strives continually to develop its people and processes will be an accepted philosophy of all competitive organizations in the future. Learning is defined as acquiring new knowledge and enhancing existing knowledge. Organizations have to focus outwardly and involve their suppliers and customers in a strategic alliance for business growth. Learning organizations have to continually expand their capacity to be creative and innovative. The only way to sustain competitive advantage is to ensure that your organization is learning faster than the competition. Organizations are realizing that their human capital (people power) and structural capital (databases, patents, intellectual property, and related items) are the distinguishing elements of their organizations.

Only two key contributors can create learning organizations: people and technology. It is the combination of these two factors with new business processes and business models that will underpin success in the next decade. The power of learning from customers, employees, and suppliers will provide an enormous advantage to learning organizations for competitive advantage. The variety of technologies, particularly KM, will help to create learning organizations. Learning organizations integrate a myriad of technologies with the power of human intelligence. Therefore, the systemic approach to building learning organizations through the use of knowledge management tools and techniques is quite useful.

Creating learning organizations will not be an easy task, as it has to leverage the most valuable resource—employees. The importance of learning organizations and the role they will play in organizational success cannot help but increase. A proper framework is essential in order to support the transformation of data into knowledge in learning organizations. The proposed framework identifies the components that are needed to convert them into learning organizations and suggests the use of the systemic approach for its implementation. Further, research can be undertaken to identify the appropriate methodologies that can help organizations to convert them into learning organizations.

REFERENCES

Adams, K. C. (2001). The Web as a database: New extraction technologies and content management. *Online, 25*(2), 27–32.

Anonymous. (2000). Knowledge management: An overview. *Information Management Journal, 34*(4), 4.

Bacon, C. J. & Fitzgerald, B. (2001). A systemic framework for the field of information systems. *Database for Advances in Information Systems, 32*(2), 46–67.

Clegg, S. (1999). Globalizing the intelligent organization: Learning organizations, smart workers, (not so) clever countries and the sociological imagination. *Management Learning, 30*(3), 259–280.

Croasdell, D. C. (2001). IT's role in organizational memory and learning. *Information Systems Management, 18*(1), 8–11.

Davenport, T. & Prusak, L. (1998). *Working knowledge.* Cambridge, MA: Harvard Business School Press.

Duffy, J. (2000). The KM technology infrastructure. *Information Management Journal, 34*(2), 62–66.

Duffy, J. (2001). The tools and technologies needed for knowledge management. *Information Management Journal, 35*(1), 64–67.

Ellerman, D. P. (1999). Global institutions: Transforming international development agencies into learning organizations. *The Academy of Management Executive, 13*(1), 25–35.

Ellinger, A. D., Watkins, K. E., & Bostrom, R. P. (1999). Managers as facilitators of learning in learning organizations. *Human Resource Development Quarterly, 10*(2), 105–125.

Granstrand, O. (2000). The shift towards intellectual capitalism—The role of infocom technologies. *Research Policy, 29*(9), 1061–1080.

Gupta, J. N. D. & Sharma, S. K. (2001). Role of application service providers in the Internet based business. *Working Paper*, Department of Management, Ball State University, Muncie, IN 47306. *Journal of Applied Systems Studies.*

Hammond, C. (2001). The intelligent enterprise. *InfoWorld, 23*(6), 45–46.

Hansen, M. T. & Oetinger, B. V. (2001). Introducing T-shaped managers: Knowledge management's next generation. *Harvard Business Review, 79*(3), 106–116.

Holt, G. D., Love, P. E. D., & Li, H. (2000). The learning organization: Toward a paradigm for mutually beneficial strategic construction alliances. *International Journal of Project Management, 18*(6), 415–421.

Lee Sr., J. (2000). Knowledge management: The intellectual revolution. *IIE Solutions, 32*(10), 34–37.

Lesser, E., Mundel, D., & Wiecha, C. (2000). Managing customer knowledge. *The Journal of Business Strategy, 21*(6), 35–37.

Levine, L. (2001). Integrating knowledge and processes in a learning organization. *Information Systems Management, 18*(1), 21–33.

Mahe, S. & Rieu, C. (1998). A pull approach to knowledge management. *Proceedings of the 2nd International Conference on Practical Aspects of Knowledge Management*, Basel, Switzerland, October 29–30.

Martensen, A. & Dahlgaard, J. J. (1999). Integrating business excellence and innovation management: Developing vision, blueprint and strategy for innovation in creative and learning organizations. *Total Quality Management, 10*(4/5), 627–635.

Moore, K. (2000). The e-volving organization. *Ivey Business Journal, 65*(2), 25–28.

Onge, A. S. (2001). Knowledge management and warehousing. *Modern Materials Handling, 56*(3), 33.

Orlikowski, W. J & Barley S. R. (2001). Technology and institutions: What can research on information technology and research on organizations learn from each other? *MIS Quarterly, 25*(2), 145–165.

Orlikowski, W. J. & Hofman, J. D. (1997). An improvisational model for change management: The case of groupware technologies. *Sloan Management Review,* 38, 11–21.

Phillips, T. & Vollmer, M. (2000). Knowledge management in the current marketplace. *Oil & Gas Journal,* 4–5.

Popper, M. & Lipshitz, R. (2000). Organizational learning: Mechanisms, culture, and feasibility. *Management Learning, 31*(2), 181–196.

Roberts, J. (2000). From know-how to show-how? Questioning the role of information and communication technologies in knowledge transfer. *Technology Analysis & Strategic Management, 12*(4), 429–443.

Sharma, S. K. & Gupta, J. N. D. (2001). Information technology assessment for knowledge management. *Working Paper,* Department of Management, Ball State University, Muncie, IN 47306.

Silver, C. A. (2000). Where technology and knowledge meet. *The Journal of Business Strategy, 21*(6), 28–33.

Simon, N. J. (1999). The learning organization. *Competitive Intelligence Magazine, 2*(2), 40–42.

Srikantaiah, T. K. (2000). Knowledge management for information professional. *ASIS Monograph Series,* Information Today, Inc.

Stratigos, A. (2001). Knowledge management meets future information users. *Online, 25*(1), 65-67.

Thorne, K. & Smith, M. (2000). Competitive advantage in world class organizations. *Management Accounting, 78*(3), 22–26.

About the Authors

Jeimy J. Cano received his B.S. and M.Sc. in systems and computer science from Universidad de los Andes, Bogotá, Colombia, in 1996 and 1997, respectively. In 2000, he received his Ph.D. in Business Administration from Newport University, California, USA. He is International Tutor at Newport University, Colombia Branch. Since 1995, he has been a part-time professor at Engineering Faculty in Computer and System Science Department and Law Faculty at Universidad de los Andes. He also belongs to international research groups like Cryptology and Information Security Iberoamerican Network—in Spanish CriptoRED—and Computer Law International Community—in Spanish Alfa-REDI. In the last years, he has published for national and international conferences and magazines. Likewise, he has been involved in consulting activities and contributed to the diffusion of Systems Science in Colombia. His current research interest is mainly in systems science applied to MIS, management cybernetics, and computer and information security.

***

Ala Abu-Samaha, B.SC., M.Sc., Ph.D. The author has developed research interests in many areas of the Information Systems discipline, mainly in two major areas: Information Systems Development Methodologies and Information Systems/Technology Evaluation. The author has many publications in both of these areas. The author holds a Ph.D. in Information Systems from the Information Systems Research Centre (ISRC) at the Information Systems Institute, University of Salford in the UK. The author obtained his master's in the same area of interest from the department of Mathematics and Computer Science, University of Salford. The master's thesis was dedicated to developing an evaluation approach to assess the success/failure of Information Systems/Technology from a systemic multiperspective oriented view. The Ph.D. thesis was dedicated to address the issue of emerging telecommunication-based systems in terms of development and evaluation.

Tatyana Bondarouk has an M.Sc. and Ph.D. in Educational Sciences from the University of Saint-Petersburg (Russia). She was involved in implementation of ICT in educational settings. Since 1999, she has been working at the University of Twente on another Ph.D. project in the field of Business Administration. Her research interests include organisational issues of information communication technology implementation, lifelong learning, and research methodology.

Bruce R. Campbell gained his M.Sc. (Hons) from Macquarie University, Sydney, Australia, in 2000. He is currently employed as a lecturer at the University of Technology, Sydney. He had over 20 years of experience in industry prior to commencing his studies and entering academia. This experience led to his interest in the sociotechnical aspects of IT, in particular, process modeling and IT management, with an emphasis on a systemic approach to these issues. His current research interests include these issues together with business and IS alignment. He is particularly interested in the relationship between the IT manager and his/her peer managers within medium-sized businesses and the effect of that relationship on IS/business alignment. He has presented papers at numerous international conferences and has had chapters published within a number of IS based books.

Francisco Cervantes received his B.S. in Mechanical Electrical Engineering in 1978 from the National Autonomous University of Mexico (UNAM), a M.Sc. in Electrical Engineering in 1982 from the same university, and his Ph.D. in Computer and Information Sciences from the University of Massachusetts at Amherst in 1985. He is currently a full professor at the Department of Computer Engineering, and the Director of the Masters in Information Technology and Administration at the Mexico Autonomous Institute of Technology (ITAM). His research interests are the analysis of the dynamic and computational properties shown by neuronal systems underlying sensori-motor coordination behaviors in living animals; and the synthesis of neural and schema-theoretic models to build automata that solve practical problems in robotics, nonlinear control, and pattern recognition.

José Rodrigo Córdoba has a B.Sc. in Computer Science and Systems Engineering from the University of Los Andes in Bogotá, Colombia, and an M.A. and Ph.D. in Management Systems from the University of Hull, U.K. He has also worked as a project manager on information technology planning processes for financial groups in Colombia. His research is focused on the use of critical systems thinking for information technology policy planning and implementation. He is also interested in the synergy between different types of methods for information systems planning in developing countries.

Philip J. Dobson graduated with a Masters degree in Information Systems from Curtin University in 1992, his thesis examining a number of decision conferences held at the school. Since graduating, he has been working full time at Edith Cowan University in Perth, Western Australia. He has a particular interest in the philosophy of the IS field and is in the final stages of submitting his Ph.D. thesis, which documents the radical changes underway at a governmental IT department. The thesis examines the usefulness of critical realism as underlabourer for the research process.

Niek du Plooy worked as a physicist at various research institutes. In 1966, he decided on a career change and was trained as a programmer and a systems analyst in a large corporation. Seven years later, he joined the University of South Africa as a lecturer. At that university, he was appointed Professor in 1982 and Head of the Department of Computer Science and Information Systems. In 1990, he joined the University of Pretoria's newly established Department of Informatics. He is now retired. He holds an M.Sc. in Physics and an MBA and a Doctorate in Information Systems.

Ovsei Gelman received his B.S., M.Sc., and Ph.D. in Physics and Mathematics from the University of Tbilisi, Georgia, in 1955 and 1962, respectively, where he worked in the Geological and Cybernetic Institutes. Since 1976 he has lived in Mexico, and he is a full research professor in the Engineering Institute and is actually engaged as an Academic Secretary of the Center of Instruments of the National Autonomous University of Mexico (UNAM). He also is a faculty member of the Graduate Engineering School at UNAM. In the last 30 years, he has published a vast quantity of papers for national and international congress, journals and books, having been involved in consulting activities and contributing strongly to the diffusion of the Systems Science in Mexico. His current research interests are mainly in Applied Cybernetics, Systems Science and Engineering, Risk Management, Interdisciplinary Disasters Research, and Decision-Making Support Systems.

Jatinder N. D. Gupta is currently Eminent Scholar of Management, Professor of Management Information Systems, and Chairperson of the Department of Accounting and Information Systems in the College of Administrative Science at the University of Alabama in Huntsville, Alabama. Most recently, he was Professor of Management, Information and Communication Sciences, and Industry and Technology at the Ball State University, Muncie, Indiana. He holds a Ph.D. in Industrial Engineering (with specialization in Production Management and Information Systems) from Texas Tech University. Coauthor of a textbook in Operations Research, Dr. Gupta serves on the editorial boards of several national and international journals. Recipient of the Outstanding Faculty and Outstanding Researcher awards from Ball State University, he has published numerous papers in such journals as *Journal of Management Information Systems*, *International Journal of Information Management*, *INFORMS Journal of Computing*, *Annals of Operations Research*, and *Mathematics of Operations Research*. More recently, he served as a coeditor of a special issue on *Neural Networks in Business* of *Computers and Operations Research* and a book entitled, *Neural Networks in Business: Techniques and Applications*. His current research interests include information and decision technologies, scheduling, planning and control, organizational learning and effectiveness, systems education, and knowledge management. Dr. Gupta is a member of several academic and professional societies including the Production and Operations Management Society (POMS), the Decision Sciences Institute (DSI), and the Information Resources Management Association (IRMA).

Antonio Leal, Ph.D., is Professor of Business Administration in the Department of Business Administration and Marketing at the University of Seville (Spain). Dr. Leal is the author of five books on management. He has published several articles and authored numerous international conference proceedings. He has been Visiting Professor at different European and Latin American Universities. His research interests include management support systems, knowledge management, total quality management, benchmarking, organisational culture, and change management.

Hernán López-Garay received his Electrical Engineering degree at the University of Los Andes, in Bogotá, Colombia; his M.Sc. in Systems Engineering at Case Institute of Technology, Cleveland; his M.A. in Systems at Lancaster University, England; and a Ph.D. in Systems Theory and Planning from The Wharton School, University of Pennsylvania. He is a senior researcher and member of the board of directors of the Center for Interpretive Systemology, University of Los Andes, in Mérida, where, since 1974, he has been discharging various teaching, research, and administrative roles. He has published in the systems field over 50 articles in national and international journals, contributed to several books, and has been visiting professor in various European universities. He has contributed to the creation of a new stream of systems thinking known as *Interpretive Systemology* and is currently investigating the justice system in Latin America with this approach.

G. Michael McGrath is a Professor of Information Systems at Victoria University in Australia. He gained his Ph.D. in computing science from Macquarie University, Sydney, in 1993. He was Deputy Director of the CSIRO-Macquarie University Joint Research Centre for Advanced Systems Engineering (JRCASE), where he headed a research strand focusing on sociotechnical aspects of systems and software engineering. He has over 20 years experience in the IT industry—mostly at Australia's largest PTC, Telstra, where he worked in a variety of technical and management positions. These included Senior Project Manager, responsible for the development of Telstra's multimillion dollar supply systems applications, and an executive-level position, as Manager Information Architecture within the organisation's Corporate Strategy Directorate. His current research interests include strategic information systems planning (SISP), business data and process modeling, knowledge base systems, software requirements elicitation, simulations of organisational decision-making processes, and electronic commerce applications. He is the author of over 60 journal and conference publications and, in particular, is a regular supporter of and contributor to information systems conferences worldwide (where, in recent years, he has presented papers at the International, Americas, Australasian, and European Conferences on Information Systems). Other recent publications have appeared in the *Journals of Management Development, Communication Management, Decision Support Systems* and *Intelligent Systems in Accounting, Finance and Management*, as well as the *Australian Computer Journal*.

Marcelo Mejía received his B.S. in Biomedical Engineering in 1982 from the Metropolitan Autonomous University (UAM). He also has M.Sc. studies in Computer Sciences from the UAM and the National Autonomous University of Mexico (UNAM), and M.Sc. in Informatics Networkings from the Superior School of Electricity in France. In 1989, he received his degree of Doctor in Informatics, from the University of Rennes I at France. Currently, he is full professor and the head of the Computer Department in the Mexico Autonomous Institute of Technology (ITAM) and a member of the Doctoral Advising Committee at the National Autonomous University of Mexico (UNAM). His current research interests are computer networking design and software engineering.

Gerald Midgley is Director of the Centre for Systems Studies, a research institute in the Business School at the University of Hull (U.K.). He has had over 150 papers published in international journals, edited books, and practitioner magazines, and has developed his thinking about systems methodology through engagement in a wide variety of applied projects. He is the author of *Systemic Intervention: Philosophy, Methodology, and Practice* (Kluwer/Plenum, 2000); co-author of *Operational Research and Environmental Management: A New Agenda* (Operational Research Society, 2001); and editor of *Systems Thinking* (Sage, forthcoming).

Manuel Mora has been an associate professor in the Autonomous University of Aguascalientes (UAA) since 1995 and currently is a doctoral candidate in

Engineering in the National Autonomous University of Mexico (UNAM). He received his B.S. in Computer Systems Engineering in 1984 and his M.Sc. in Computer Sciences with Artificial Intelligence as major area in 1989, both from the Monterrey Tech (ITESM). His current research interests are the design and implementation of Integrated Decision-Making Support Systems and Theoretical Foundations of Information Systems, using in both research streams the Systems Approach as the theoretical frame.

José L. Roldán obtained a Ph.D. in 2000 from the University of Seville on a dissertation titled: "Executive Information Systems: Emergence, Implementation and Organisational Impact." He has published three books and several articles on management aspects. He has authored diverse proceedings and conference papers. He has been Visiting Professor at the Technical University of Brno (Czech Republic) and at the Central American University of San Salvador (El Salvador). His current research interests focus on executive information systems, knowledge management, and structural equation modeling.

Sushil K. Sharma is currently Assistant Professor of Management at the Ball State University, Muncie, Indiana. He received his Ph.D. in Information Systems from Pune University, India, and taught at the Indian Institute of Management, Lucknow, for 11 years before joining Ball State University. Prior to joining Ball State, Dr. Sharma held the position of Visiting Research Associate Professor at the Department of Management Science, University of Waterloo, Canada. Dr. Sharma's primary teaching interests are e-commerce, computer communication networks, database management systems, management information systems, and information systems analysis and design. He has extensive experience in providing consulting services to several government and private organizations including World Bank funded projects in the areas of information systems, e-commerce, and knowledge management. Dr. Sharma is the author of two books and has numerous articles in national and international journals. His current research interests include database management systems, networking environments, electronic commerce (e-commerce), knowledge management, and corporate information systems.

Klaas Sikkel has an M.Sc. in Software Engineering and a Ph.D. in Theoretical Computer Science. Since 1994, he has been involved in the design and implementation of groupware systems. At GMD, the German National Research Institute for Computer Science, he was one of the founders of the project "Basic Support for Cooperative Work," one of the first to deliver Web-based groupware services. Currently, he is assistant professor at the Information Systems group at the University of Twente. His interests include requirements analysis, evolutionary use of groupware, and the use of ICT in higher education.

Roberto Vinaja is Assistant Professor of Computer Information Systems at the University of Texas Pan American and has a Ph.D. from the University of Texas at Arlington. He has published in the *Handbook of IS Management*, presented at international/national conferences, and developed software for EDS, Mattel Toys and AETNA.

Alfredro Weitzenfeld is a professor in the Computer Engineering Department at the Autonomous Technological Institute of Mexico (ITAM). He received his B.S. in Electrical Engineering from Israel's Institute of Technology (TECHNION). He has an M.Sc. in Computer Engineering and a Ph.D. in Computer Science, both from the University of Southern California, where he was a Research Assistant Professor. He is the co-founder and director of the CANNES Laboratory for Brain Simulation at ITAM. He is a member of the Mexican National Research System (SNI) as well as a member of the Doctoral Advising Committee at the National Autonomous University of Mexico (UNAM).

Index

The International Journal of IT Standards and Standardization Research(JITSR)

NEW!   **NEW!**

The International Source for Advances in IT Standards and Standardization Research

ISSN:	1539-3062
eISSN:	1539-3054
Subscription:	Annual fee per volume (2 issues):
	Individual US $85
	Institutional US $145
Editor:	Kai Jakobs
	Technical University
	of Aachen, Germany

Mission

The primary mission of *The International Journal of IT Standards & Standardization Research* is to publish research findings to advance knowledge and research in all aspects of IT standards and standardization in modern organizations. Furthermore, *The International Journal of IT Standards & Standardization Research* will be considered as an authoritative source and information outlet for the diverse community of IT standards researchers. JITSR is targeted towards researchers, scholars, policymakers, IT managers, and IT standards associations and organizations.

Coverage

JITSR will include contibutions from disciplines in computer science, information systems, management, business, social sciences, economics, engineering, political science, and communications. Potential topics include: Technological innovation and standardization; Standards for information infrastructures; standardization and economic development; open source and standardization; intellectual property rights; economics of standardization; emerging roles of standards organizations and consortia; conformity assessment; standards strategies; standarization and regulation; standardization in the public sphere; standardization in public policy; tools and services related to standardiztion; and other relevant issues related to standards and standardization.

For subscription information, contact:

Idea Group Publishing
701 E Chocolate Ave., Ste 200
Hershey PA 17033-1240, USA
cust@idea-group.com

For paper submission information:

Dr. Kai Jakobs
Technical University of Aachen, Germany
Kai.Jakobs@i4mail.informatik.rwth-aachen.de